AF361452

Old Nations, New Voters

Old Nations, New Voters

*Nationalism, Transnationalism, and Democracy
in the Era of Global Migration*

David C. Earnest

Published by
State University of New York Press, Albany

For information, contact State University of New York Press, Albany, NY
www.sunypress.edu

Production by Marilyn P. Semerad
Marketing by Anne M. Valentine

Library of Congress Cataloging-in-Publication Data

Earnest, David C.
    Old nations, new voters : nationalism, transnationalism, and democracy in the era of global migration / David C. Earnest.
        p. cm.
    Includes bibliographical references and index.
    ISBN 978–0–7914–7613–0 (hardcover : alk. paper)
    1. Immigrants—Suffrage. 2. Immigrants—Political activity. 3. Transnationalism. 4. Emigration and Immigration. I. Title.

JV6255.E27 2008
320.54—dc22

                                                                    2007052316

10 9 8 7 6 5 4 3 2 1

To Carla and Zachary

Contents

Illustrations

Acknowledgments

Iam deeply indebted to many colleagues and friends who contributed to this project over the years. At Old Dominion University, Joshua Behr, Kurt Taylor Gaubatz, and Jesse Richman took time out of their busy schedules to discuss methodological issues with me. Simon Serfaty met with me on several occasions and provided thoughtful commentary on my ideas. In addition to her efforts to relieve my teaching and service responsibilities so that I had time to write, Regina Karp translated German-language news items for me. Hua Liu was an invaluable source of technical expertise for the preparation of the maps this manuscript presents. Timothy Breslin, Jose Caballe, Jack Covarrubias, and Khutso Madubanya provided invaluable research assistance. Earlier in the project, the faculty of the Department of Political Science at The George Washington University shaped my poorly-formed ideas into a viable research agenda. Martha Finnemore supported and encouraged my desire to probe the minutiae of citizenship politics and helped me frame my curiosity in a theoretically productive framework. James N. Rosenau and Susan K. Sell both provided regular and thoughtful commentary on my work as well as considerable encouragement during my moments of doubt. Erik Voeten guided me through several minefields of methodology and patiently checked (and rechecked) my formal notation. Bruce Dickson was a constructive critic of this project from its inception. Several other faculty members and students at The George Washington University deserve special thanks for their feedback. Jay Smith called my attention to the work of Beth Simmons, while Deborah Avant, Ingrid Creppell, Chris Deering, William (Bud) Kiamie, Forrest Maltzman, and Lee Sigelman all gave me constructive commentary.

Colleagues from around the country and world have also provided invaluable feedback on various portions of the manuscript. Sybil D. Rhodes and Sheri L. Rogers, both of Western Michigan University, and Mark F. N. Franke from Huron University College read and criticized a conference paper that became chapter 6. Dirk Jacobs of the Université Libre de Bruxelles patiently and collegially corrected my misapprehensions about the citizenship politics of the Netherlands and Belgium. On several occasions, Ron Hayduk shared with me his extensive knowledge of noncitizen voting practices. His groundbreaking scholarship in *Democracy for All* and his passion for the topic of noncitizen voting has set a high intellectual standard that I can only hope to meet.

I also thank Mark J. Miller of the University of Delaware, who presided over a panel at the Northeast Political Science Association annual conference in November 2003 to which I presented some preliminary findings. The panel's other participants—Thomas Berger, Matthew Fouse, Lisa Wilson, and Hasan Yonten—were knowledgeable and harsh critics who made me rethink and clarify several important points. The faculty and students of the Department of Political Science at Syracuse University and of the United States Air War College provided me with opportunities to talk about this research, for which I am grateful. Hans Peter Schmitz of Syracuse University engaged me in a debate about human rights norms that profoundly shaped my thinking about the political rights of resident aliens. T. Alexander Aleinikoff of Georgetown University School of Law gave numerous constructive suggestions. Kathleen Coll of Harvard University corrected my misapprehensions about school board voting practices in Chicago.

In addition to the academic community, I am indebted to numerous individuals in the Washington policy community who patiently explained the finer points of citizenship politics in their respective countries. I thank Massimo Drei, Matt Francis, Maria Hilker, Kirsti Kaasinen, Martin Kraemer, Arne Lauritsen, Christoph Meran, Cathy Monaghan, Catarina Rodrigues, Mario Liori Sanchez, Anna Schwan, Gareth Smith, and Ian Smith for responding to my written inquiries. Claes Thorson and Ragne Beiming of the Embassy of Sweden took time out of their busy schedules to meet with me in person, as did Carlos Orga of the Embassy of Switzerland. Andreas Carlgren, Director General of the Swedish Integration Board, and Tomas Uddin, also of the Board, surely had more important obligations during their visit to the United States but nevertheless provided me with an invaluable opportunity to learn from their vast knowledge and experiences. Brita Cronquist patiently worked with me to assure I would meet Mr. Carlgren, Mr. Uddin, Mr. Thorson, and Mr. Beiming.

Several scholars at the Center for Strategic and International Studies in Washington, D.C., also provided invaluable assistance. In particular, Linda Jamison helped me revitalize professional relationships that I have neglected over the years. Eri Hirano, Tsuneo "Nabe" Watanabe, and Akihiko Mayura introduced me to colleagues in the Japanese Embassy in Washington.

Sally Montague of The George Washington University provided me with translations of German documents on several occasions. George Corliss and Adriane Bullard deserve two thank yous—one for providing me with a workspace and computer on the day after Christmas 2003, and another for politely declining to mention that I should have been home with my family. Olive Corliss, Mike Earnest, and Vicki Earnest all provided childcare on too many occasions to count, so that I could spend more time doing the research for this project.

I appreciate the assistance and patience of the editors and staff at the State University of New York Press. In particular, I thank Michael Rinella, Marilyn P. Semerad, Anne M. Valentine, and freelance copyeditor, Amy Paradysz.

Finally, I thank my wife, Carla Earnest, for all the support she has provided. She not only has listened patiently to my thoughts but also has assuaged my frustrations and shored up my spirits when my confidence flagged. She deserves much more than the modest dedication I have asked her to share with our beautiful son Zachary.

I am responsible for any errors in this study.

1

The Democratic Dilemma of Migration

> ...It is in the nation's best interest to encourage people who live here permanently to become citizens and throw in their lot with the interests of the United States. Extending the most important benefits of citizenship to those who still hold their first allegiance to another country seems counterproductive.
>
> —"A Citizen's Right," *New York Times*, April 19, 2004

As this quote from a *New York Times* editorial page suggests, the current era of global migration often raises difficult questions about the obligations and rights of both citizens and immigrants. These questions reflect both moral and practical dilemmas for democratic societies and their governments. For those states from which large numbers of citizens emigrate—sometimes referred to as "sending states"—their overseas migrant population may have considerable economic and political influence. Through its remittances, the émigré community is an important source of foreign exchange for many sending states. Émigrés also wield political power through channels as diverse as absentee voting, donations to political parties, or even informal networks of family and friends. Yet, despite their growing economic and political importance, these émigrés traditionally have had few political rights in their states of origin, and even fewer in their states of residence. These "host" states also face a dilemma when faced with a large and growing population of migrants. Democratic societies traditionally have asked their migrant populations to shoulder many of the civic responsibilities they impose upon the citizenry. In most democracies, migrants pay taxes, and in some, they serve in the military and are eligible for conscription. The United States even counts aliens in national censuses for purposes of apportionment and representation in Congress. In exchange for these civic responsibilities, states gradually have given migrants some civil and economic rights. However, far fewer of these democracies have offered to these migrants the opportunity to participate in the political life of the societies in which they reside. In both host and sending states, migrants are important members of the polity yet historically they have lacked the political rights that citizens enjoy. Until the last few decades, migrants were perhaps the one remaining societal group against whom democratic states willingly—and as the *Times* quote suggests, some might say legitimately—discriminated in the allocation of the right to vote.

Yet in the latter half of the twentieth century and early in the twenty-first, democratic states gradually have expanded the opportunities for migrants to participate in democratic politics. Sending states have expanded the use of the absentee ballot, and some have created legislative districts to represent solely those citizens who reside overseas. In the 1996 presidential elections in Armenia, for example, eligible Armenian voters who resided overseas may have outnumbered those voters who resided in Armenia proper.[1] Political parties have expanded their presence abroad, from then-candidate Vicente Fox stumping in the United States for the votes of Mexican migrants, to Dominican political parties establishing offices in New York City. Sending states and host states alike increasingly tolerate "plural nationality," or the practice of a person maintaining citizenship in more than one state. In 1997 Mexico changed its citizenship laws to draw a distinction between Mexican "nationality" and "citizenship." Mexican émigrés overseas can now naturalize in their host states without losing their Mexican nationality and its attendant rights, most importantly the right to own land. Mexican expatriates now can reactivate their citizenship upon their return to Mexico. Democratic states also have broadened the rights of the migrants they host, so much so that Hammar for one argues that there are few substantive, but many symbolic, distinctions between the rights of citizens and aliens.[2] These innovative institutions and practices for the political incorporation of migrants suggest that states have disembedded the rights of citizenship from their territorial basis.

One of the more important examples of this unbundling of citizenship, place, and rights is the practice of enfranchising resident aliens in their countries of residence. In the last forty-five years, more than thirty democracies have adopted laws that entitle resident aliens to vote in at least local elections, and some even allow aliens to vote in parliamentary elections. Aliens who reside in the Swiss cantons of

Neuchâtel and Jura can vote in cantonal elections; citizens of Commonwealth states who reside in the United Kingdom can vote for candidates for Parliament; any alien who has resided for three years in Norway can vote in provincial elections; and in New Zealand, any alien who has resided for a year can vote for a member of parliament. The practice appears to have broad appeal today. The municipal government of Vienna, Austria, attempted in 2004 to enfranchise resident aliens, though national courts overturned the legislation. After the November 2005 riots in the suburbs of Paris, both Mayor Bertrand Delanoë and then Interior Minister and now President Nicolas Sarkozy expressed support for allowing immigrants in France to vote in local elections. The title of a recent book on the subject suggests the normative appeal of enfranchising resident aliens: *Democracy for All*.[3]

This provision of voting rights for resident aliens raises some interesting questions about the relationship between the institutions of citizenship and sovereignty. The state's practices for the incorporation of resident aliens reside at the nexus of a theoretical debate in international relations scholarship. This dialogue focuses on the sources of the state's policies for the constitution of its political community. Do states construct their polities in response to purely domestic politics and pressures? Are states responding instead to emerging international norms of human rights, the burgeoning influence of transnational organizations, or to what researchers call "global civil society"? Do incorporation practices like voting rights for resident aliens represent an erosion of the traditional links between the state, the polity, and the "nation"? That is, have states constructed their polities along "postnational" instead of "national" lines? If so, why? How have these practices changed over time?

These questions highlight a paradox that underscores this study: one can begin to understand the changing nature of citizenship and sovereignty by looking, ironically, at the ways democratic states treat their aliens. There are several good reasons to believe that an exploration of the rights of resident aliens will shed light on the changing nature of state sovereignty. In a juridical sense, citizenship policy is inextricable from the state's policies and practices toward those who are not citizens. As Salzmann notes, a primary goal of the modern, centralized state is to "individuate, enumerate, and categorize subjects as well as to mobilize their resources and bodies."[4] Sovereignty is thus a construction not only of the territorial boundaries of the state but also of a delimited community of individuals who are the subjects of the state's authority. Similarly, Bauböck argues that citizenship policies include not only the rights and obligations the state affords to members of a polity but the more fundamental questions of which individuals belong to the polity and the nature and shape of the polity itself.[5] By construction, then, citizenship policies seek to exclude individuals as "not citizens" from the polity as much as they include them as citizens. Historically, at least since the French Revolution, sovereign states typically have delimited their political communities to the body known as the "citizenry" or the "nation," rather than the medieval construction of "subjects." Just as the French Revolution gave rise to new institutions for the enumeration and individuation of political participants, however, some scholars argue the current era of expanding rights and obligations for those individuals who are not citizens is a harbinger of changes in the form and functions of the nation-state. The state is becoming more inclusive, these scholars argue, by creating institutional alternatives to citizenship. In this sense, an examination of the political rights of migrants is an exploration of the broader meaning of state sovereignty during an era of growing transnational flows of people, ideas, and values.

Another reason to suspect the rights of noncitizens hold clues to the changing nature of sovereignty arises from what this study and others call the "transnationalist" thesis.[6] A number of citizenship scholars argue that today the rights and obligations of citizens and noncitizens increasingly are blurred, to the point that one cannot easily disentangle the legal statuses of "citizen" and "alien," or between "national" and "foreigner." While states may define each largely in terms of the other in order to demarcate a juridical boundary between the two categories, the growth of civil, economic, and political rights for resident aliens erases the substantive differences between the two groups. For this reason, Sassen argues:

> Immigration can be seen as a strategic research site for the examination of the relation—the distance, the tension—between the idea of sovereignty as control over who enters, and the constraints states encounter in making actual policy about the matter. Immigration is thus a sort of wrench one can throw into theories about sovereignty.[7]

The proliferation of new institutions for the incorporation of migrants—from plural nationality to absentee voting, overseas legislative districts, and this book's subject, voting rights for resident aliens—suggests there are numerous theoretical wrenches to throw. The hypothesized erosion of the distinctions between the substantive rights of the citizen and those of the alien is a puzzle that motivated this study.

The changing relationships between "citizens" and "aliens"—or, alternatively, the changing ways in which democratic states draw a boundary between the two categories—suggests another important reason to look at aliens as an approach to questions about citizenship. Has the emergence of political rights for resident aliens caused a reconfiguration of the state, or is it a consequence of such a reconstituted state? The following analysis will provide a glimpse of an answer. By looking at both the domestic and international sources of the state's citizenship policies, this study seeks to offer insight into the question of whether these new rights in some way have changed the institution of sovereignty, or whether such a reconfiguration presaged the emergence of these new rights. The distinction between domestic and international sources of the state's policies may offer a tentative answer. If the state expanded the rights of resident aliens in response to domestic factors, one might surmise that rather than these rights reconfiguring sovereignty, the state itself remains the locus of institutional contestation over the rights and responsibilities of citizenship—or as Shanahan argues, "globalization has undermined neither nations nor citizenship; it has fortified them both."[8] If international factors explain state citizenship policies, however, one may infer that, expressed in the extreme, states no longer define their citizenry in any terms except that of totems and symbolism. The political rights of resident aliens may not necessarily *cause* changes in state sovereignty; rather, like changes in the content and meaning of sovereignty, they may be a *consequence* of a variety of transnational and global processes.

Many discussions of the evolution of the political rights of the state's subjects begin with T. H. Marshall's influential thesis.[9] Marshall argued that states extend rights to citizens in a specific historical sequence that follows the institutional development of the nation-state. Citizens first gained civil and legal protections when states developed independent judiciaries. These developments enabled citizens to assert their initial claims for political participation. Only when citizens were enfranchised were they then able to gain social protections from the state. Yet as numerous other researchers have pointed out, to some degree the rights of immigrants have reversed the evolutionary sequence Marshall identified.[10] Historically immigrants have acquired social protections first, followed by civil rights and, only to a limited degree, political rights. In this sense the rights of aliens are not related to the institutional development of the state, as Marshall asserted was the case with citizens' rights. Traditionally immigrants who wished to partake in the politics of their host states could do so only through naturalization. These observations beg several important questions. Why have migrants come to enjoy political rights only recently? Why has the institution for the incorporation of migrants historically been naturalization? Why have states recently adopted institutional alternatives to naturalization?

Underlying these questions is a historical assumption that deserves consideration: that states have tied political rights to citizenship. As the next chapter discusses, this historical assumption is not entirely accurate. Judging by history, the relationship between the institutions of citizenship and political participation is a confounding one with numerous exceptions. As both Aylsworth and Raskin note, even the United States historically has not required citizenship as a condition for political participation.[11] Aylsworth notes that resident aliens voted in every presidential election up until the mid-1920s. Interestingly, however, the enfranchisement of resident aliens in the United States in part served a discriminatory rather than inclusive role: it sought to legitimate property and race qualifications for voting by demonstrating to citizens—including African Americans and women—that citizenship alone did not entitle a person to the right to vote. As Raskin notes:

> Alien voting occupied a logical place in a self-defined immigrant republic of propertied white men: It reflected both openness to new-comers and the idea that the defining principle for political member-ship was not American citizenship but the exclusionary categories of race, gender, property, and wealth.[12]

The Netherlands provides another interesting historical example. Prak notes that following the invasion of the revolutionary French armies in the 1790s, with their Napoleonic template for a bureaucratized and centralized state, the Netherlands sought to construct a "Dutch" citizenry from the polities of the seven disparate Dutch provinces.[13] To do so, the draft constitution of 1796 and that eventually adopted in 1798 defined a "Dutch citizen" as anyone entitled to vote in one of the seven provinces. Two elements of Prak's analysis deserve emphasis. The first is that prior to 1796 cities themselves determined citizenship practices; many allowed non-natives to purchase citizenship with its attendant rights, including the right to vote. In the merchant state, numerous non-native residents consequently became citizens of the Netherlands since they previously had purchased the rights of citizenship in their province of residence. Second, in 1798 the centralized Dutch state constructed the polity based on the right to vote. In this way the institution of the franchise predated, and was the foundation for, the institution of national citizenship. This reverses our traditional thinking about voting rights: rather than citizenship leading to voting rights, the right to vote led to Dutch citizenship. Clearly, as the cases of the United States and the Netherlands demonstrate, it is ahistorical to assume that citizenship necessarily leads to political rights. It is neither necessary nor sufficient for the political incorporation of an individual.

Many people nevertheless seem surprised that resident aliens may enjoy such rights and object to proposals to enfranchise resident aliens. "If you divorce citizenship and voting," one critic of such voting rights asserts, "citizenship stops having any meaning at all."[14] Likewise, in 1990 the German Constitutional Court struck down local laws that enfranchised some resident aliens in Schleswig-Holstein and Hamburg, ruling "Elections in which foreigners can vote cannot convey democratic legitimacy."[15] Joppke's analysis of the court's decision concludes that "alien suffrage would take away the last major privilege of citizenship: the right to vote, and devalue the later by leaving only duties, not rights as its distinguishing mark."[16] A recent initiative to enfranchise New York City's population of resident aliens met with the opinion from *The New York Times* that forms this chapter's epigraph. As Germany's debate and the position of the *Times's* editorial board indicates, the alien franchise speaks to the very meaning of citizenship and nationhood—the foundational institutions of modern democracy.[17] Though these criticisms seem to regret the loss of the "meaning" of citizenship or to question the legitimacy of such voting rights, they perhaps unwittingly touch on the concerns that motivate this study. What meaning does "citizenship" now have? Moreover, what do changes in the meaning of citizenship, and by extension the political community, say about the relationship of democratic societies to their states?

This book addresses these broad questions, looking at the voting rights of resident aliens in twenty-five democratic states. Chapter 2 provides an empirical overview of the practices of more than thirty democratic states that allow resident aliens to vote at least in local elections, plus several others that have either considered but rejected or have rescinded such rights. This empirical overview shows that the practice of enfranchising resident aliens has spread over the last four decades. Chapter 3 derives hypotheses that may explain variations in the voting rights of resident aliens in the study's population of twenty-five democracies. While some social scientists have written specifically about voting rights for resident aliens (though none to my knowledge have conducted a large-sample comparison across cases), many have addressed broader questions about the social, economic and political integration of migrants into democratic societies. From this review of the literature, one may identify two broad theses that seek to explain how democratic societies incorporate their resident aliens. The nationalist thesis explains these variations as a product of traditional politics within the state, and asserts that such practices reinforce the historical relationship between the polity and the state. The transnationalist thesis argues, by contrast, that international and transnational factors explain variations in the incorporation of migrant communities in democratic states. Transnationalists cite the growth of practices such as plural nationality as evidence of a separation of the polity from traditional, nation-based conceptions of the political community, whether these conceptions are based on ethnicity, language, or religion. They expect a convergence of democratic practice around a common set of inclusive, nondiscriminatory principles and norms, if not a common institutional design.

In chapter 4, the study derives measures for the nationalist and transnationalist theses as well as for variables that may confound an analysis of the relationship between nationalism, transnationalism, and voting rights for resident aliens. This chapter identifies a population of twenty-five democracies for the study, selected on the basis of several criteria of democracy, and proposes to test nationalist and transnationalist hypotheses over a time span of four decades. This chapter also develops two time-series cross-sectional models for testing the nationalist and transnationalist hypotheses. Chapter 5 analyzes the findings of these models and their implications for the nationalist-transnationalist debate. A common criticism of such statistical analyses is that they tend to overlook the unique, historical and particularistic attributes of democracies. The case studies in chapter 6 redress this imbalance by tracing the popular debates in the Netherlands, Germany, and Belgium over the enfranchisement of resident aliens. This qualitative narrative illustrates how the processes highlighted in the statistical analysis played out in unique ways in each democracy. Finally, the book concludes with a discussion of the implications of the analysis of voting rights for resident aliens for our understanding of state sovereignty in a world of increasing transnational flows and growing interdependence.

One final note about the terminology that this study uses: As is evident from this introduction, the dilemma of democratic states has an analog for researchers—what does one call an alien who has rights, one who seeks them, and one who has none? In practice, the exercise in categorizing the population of the state's subjects—even those who are citizens let alone those who lack citizenship—is somewhat difficult. Jean-Jacques Rousseau captured some of this difficulty in *The Social Contract*:

> The public person thus formed by the union of all the others formerly assumed the name City and now assumes that of Republic or body politic, which its members call State when it is passive, Sovereign when it is active, Power when comparing it to similar bodies. As for the associates, they collectively assume the name people and individually call themselves Citizens as participants in the sovereign authority, and Subjects as subjected to the laws of the State. But these terms are often confused and mistaken for one another; it is enough to be able to distinguish them where they are used in their precise sense.[18]

How would Rousseau write this in today's era of mass migration? "Citizens" and the "people" hardly capture the entirety of the political community since many "subjects" of the law and its obligations include aliens who have little or no rights to participate in the making of policy. Among these aliens, furthermore, are distinctions with conceptual ramifications: resident aliens versus migrant workers, and documented (or "legal") versus undocumented ("illegal") aliens are two such distinctions. "Noncitizens" may be an inclusive and logically dichotomous term, but as this study shows only a subset of noncitizens—those who satisfy a residency criterion—typically receives the franchise. For this reason, from here forward this study focuses on the rights of resident aliens only—those who have resided for a period of time in their host states and have proper documentation.

It is interesting to note that the phrase "resident alien" may not have much portability across the nation-states in this study, or even across languages. The residency criteria states employ vary considerably, such that some resident aliens in New Zealand, for example, might not qualify for the same political rights if they resided in Sweden for the same period of time. As the next chapter shows, furthermore, the criterion of residency may serve discriminatory as well as inclusive goals. Even the vernacular that states use to identify their citizens reflects the ambiguity of the dichotomy between citizen and alien. Shanahan notes that the 1981 British Nationality Act divided citizenship into the constructs of British citizen, British overseas citizen, British protected persons, and British subjects.[19] As already noted, Mexican law draws a distinction between Mexican "nationals" and Mexican "citizens"—all Mexican citizens are nationals, but not all Mexican nationals are citizens. German citizenship law recognizes "status Germans" or Germans without German citizenship: "ethnic German refugees and their families, to whom the Basic Law grants a status intermediate between citizen and aliens."[20] The problem is confounded, furthermore, by differences in each state's policies for naturalization. Until recently, children of resident aliens in Germany took the foreign nationality of their parents; in the United States by contrast all children born there can become citizens. Therefore, Germany counts as "aliens" a population that the United States counts as "citizens," with obvious problems for comparison across the cases. This proliferation of terms and laws to identify, describe, or enumerate aliens, and to distinguish them from citizens, mirrors the growth of institutions for the incorporation of migrants but confounds any analysis of the state's policies toward aliens. Yet the fact that a diverse body of states, with disparate legal systems and terminologies for aliens, has chosen nevertheless to enfranchise people who are not citizens only underscores the puzzle that motivates this project. Why has a common practice emerged from states with such disparate cultures, policies of incorporation, and even vernaculars for enumerating their foreign populations?

This study chooses the term "resident aliens" to refer to the population of migrants in a host state that is subject to civic responsibilities under the law and that may qualify for social, economic, and political rights. While not all states may recognize a legal category of "resident aliens," the term connotes a sense of settlement: aliens reside within and belong to a community if not a polity. The adjective "resident" seeks to separate settling residents from their "temporary" counterparts, though even this distinction defies simple categorization—Hugo notes that the circular migration of temporary migrants back and forth between states has grown to unprecedented levels.[21] For this reason, this study eschews the term "permanent resident aliens," since the criterion of permanency seems as inexact as other qualifications. A final reason to focus on residency as a criterion is a practical one. Most states require a period of residency before migrants may qualify for social, economic, and political benefits from the state. Though "resident aliens" is an inexact category, it captures most of the individuals that states recognize as subjects of its authorities and to whom democratic states have obligations to provide social, economic, and political opportunities.

It is also important to note this study focuses only on one type of political participation: the casting of a vote in an election for local, regional, or national public office. Resident aliens undoubtedly continue to participate in the politics of their sending states, through absentee ballots, return migration, and personal networks. In some democracies resident aliens have, furthermore, a range of other forms of political participation that Dahrendorf labeled "secondary political rights."[22] These include the rights of resident aliens in some European states to vote for candidates for offices in works' councils, unions, and even churches.[23] Resident aliens may also participate in the election or appointment of individuals to local, regional, or national advisory councils that specifically represent the interests of aliens to public officials.[24] While these are important forms of political incorporation that are theoretically interesting on their own merits, this study does not consider such secondary rights for two reasons. First, the participation of resident aliens in elections for works' councils, unions, or churches interposes a layer of governance between resident aliens and the political life of their host states. Since citizens do not face a comparable intervening political institution, these voting practices are by construction highly discriminatory and consequently will shed no light on the question of whether or not the historical linkage between the nation and the state is eroding. This objection anticipates a second reason to ignore such practices. A number of researchers argue that the interposition of works' council or union officials actually insulates the state from the claims of resident aliens rather than making it more receptive to them. If this argument is correct, secondary political rights demobilize resident aliens rather than integrate them into the political life of their host states. For these reasons, I examine only the rights of resident aliens to vote in elections for offices in municipal, regional, or national governments.

This study seeks to add to our understanding of why democracies choose to offer political rights to their resident aliens. In doing so, it strives to contribute to the broader debate in international relations and comparative politics about the impact of transnational migratory, commercial, and normative processes on the state's exercise of its sovereignty. Using a longitudinal cross-sectional research design, this study offers two important additions to the existing literature on citizenship politics. First, most citizenship literature relies on a single or a small number of case studies. While these case studies often illuminate potentially important factors in citizenship policies, their small sample sizes call for the larger statistical test of significance this study provides. If systemic and transnational processes explain why democracies have given their aliens the right to vote, it behooves researchers to test these factors across a broad sample of democratic states. Evidence of a large number of democracies converging around a common practice or institution would be powerful support for those scholars who cite the importance of transnational factors. Second, the pattern in which voting rights for resident aliens have emerged suggests the possibility that norms for voting rights for resident aliens have emerged regionally. This study explicitly probes the geographic patterns of the emergence of voting rights for resident aliens as an approach to broader questions about the evolution of normative processes among states.

The exact number of resident aliens worldwide who are entitled to vote in their states of domicile is unknown, but it almost certainly is a relatively small proportion of the electorates of the world's democracies.[25] Yet this small size belies the potential theoretical import of innovative citizenship practices such as voting rights for resident aliens. As migration continues to grow, international, non-governmental, and even local authorities—not to mention resident aliens themselves—increasingly contest the meaning of citizenship and the state's practices for political incorporation. Perhaps because of this increasing contentiousness of citizenship politics, social scientists paradoxically have cited these conflicts as evidence both of the state's robustness and of its permeation by transnational forces. This theoretical debate indicates the need for this study's test of the competing hypotheses of the nationalist and transnationalist schools of thought. The book's findings not only clarify the relative importance of domestic and international variables in citizenship politics but also inform broader debates within political science about the changing institutions of sovereignty and democracy in a world of growing global flows of goods, people, and ideas.

2

The Voting Rights of Resident Aliens:
An Empirical Overview

> ...The citizenship qualification carries the aura of inevitability that once attached to the property, race and gender [voter] qualifications.
> —Jamin B. Raskin, "Legal Aliens, Local Citizens: the Historical, Constitutional, and Theoretical Meanings of Alien Suffrage"

As Raskin suggests, to many observers it seems only natural that citizenship is a prima facie qualification for the right to vote. Yet, like previously "natural" qualifications for voting such as race, gender, or wealth, states and citizens of democracies across the globe have questioned both the practicality and the morality of limiting the franchise to those who are citizens. In an era of large-scale migration, all democracies today host populations of aliens that reside within their borders for years—if not decades or lifetimes—and pay taxes, face compulsory obligations like drafts, and often share more political interests with their local neighbors than they do with the citizens in their home countries.[1] It is little surprise, then, that in the last five decades governments and citizens have come to embrace voting rights for aliens.

What is surprising, however, is the extent of alien suffrage today. One recent survey found forty-five democracies in which resident aliens have at least some voting rights or whose constitutions explicitly permit their legislatures the discretion to enfranchise resident aliens.[2] Though rights in these states differ widely in their scale (that is, the right to vote in local versus national elections) and in their scope (the right belongs to specific alien nationalities versus a general right for all resident aliens) this variability raises important questions about the sources of these rights. Why do some states limit rights to aliens of specific nationalities, while others extend the rights to all resident aliens? Why can resident aliens vote in national elections in some states, and only in local elections in others? Why can resident aliens within a given nation-state vote in some municipalities, but those in other municipalities have no voting rights? There are several states, furthermore, which have considered various forms of alien suffrage but have rejected them. These states—plus two others that "rolled back" or rescinded the rights—offer important opportunities for comparison. Why did the Netherlands easily enact alien suffrage with nearly universal support, for example, but Belgium took three decades to do so? Why did Australia roll back the rights it once offered to British nationals, but New Zealand expanded its voting rights for resident aliens to become the most permissive state in the world?

Taken together, the forty-five democracies that have alien franchise rights, have rescinded such rights, or have considered but specifically rejected such rights represent one in four of the world's democracies. As Bauböck notes, "the practice of extending voting rights to non-citizens can no longer be regarded as an irregularity at odds with the international community's conception of citizenship."[3] This is an important democratic practice that deserves broader investigation. This chapter proceeds to develop a typology of voting rights based on three criteria—whether local or national governments grant resident aliens the right to vote, the discriminatory or nondiscriminatory nature of the right, and the type of election in which resident aliens may vote. The chapter concludes with a discussion of the implications of this typology for an investigation of the reasons why states have adopted voting rights for resident aliens.

It is important to note that while this chapter attempts to be comprehensive, the cases it identifies may not include every example of a state that enfranchises resident aliens.[4] There are a number of reasons to suspect it is not exhaustive. For one, as this chapter shows, some states allow municipalities and subnational jurisdictions to determine their own qualifications for the franchise. This is typical of federal states such as the United States and Switzerland. As a consequence, there may well be a number of cities, towns, or provinces in which resident aliens can vote but may not participate in national elections. Vienna, Austria, recently tried to enfranchise its entire population of resident aliens for local elections, for example, but the measure failed to survive the scrutiny of the courts, which found national law limits the franchise to citizens of European Union member states.[5] These cases may be obscure and easy to overlook.[6] Because the political rights of resident aliens may vary within states as well as between them, may vary over time, and may even vary on the basis of issues (such as the practice in New York City of allowing resident aliens to vote in school board elections) one can reasonably surmise that a number of cases may be omitted from this chapter.[7] Another reason to suspect this chapter is not exhaustive is that the practice of enfranchising resident aliens remains controversial. The German Federal Constitutional Court argued that such rights undermined democratic legitimacy when it struck down the voting rights that Schleswig-Holstein and Hamburg allotted to their resident aliens.[8] Negative observations by their nature are difficult to observe; the controversy surrounding the enfranchisement of resident aliens may make them more so.

A final reason to suspect this chapter may overlook important examples is, at least in recent years, political scientists largely have ignored "technical" issues like voter qualification requirements. Most political science data on electoral systems today—such as the Comparative Study of Electoral Systems dataset—collect data only on electoral institutions such as legislative, executive and judicial structures; electoral rules for the counting and casting of votes; and apportionment. It seems as if political scientists treat voter eligibility as an axiomatic, technical or legal issue that is largely apolitical. If so, this is an ironic assumption since legal scholars have argued that the reasons for and barriers to alien enfranchisement, at least in the United States, are political rather than legal.[9] The issue of voting rights for resident aliens reminds us that, just as in the era of suffragettes and the civil rights movement, the establishment of voter eligibility requirements remains a highly contested political process that is centrally constitutive to politics since it defines the body politic. Alien suffrage is an important example of an expansion of the franchise for another reason, furthermore: resident aliens are perhaps the first social group to receive voting rights in the absence of large-scale social unrest or war. Unlike the women's suffrage and civil rights movements, resident aliens have received the franchise without an attendant social upheaval, for reasons that are not readily apparent. Voter eligibility requirements remain highly political, yet at least for resident aliens it appears the nature of this contestation may have changed.

Despite these reasons for possible oversights, the available evidence shows that the practice of enfranchising resident aliens is prevalent among democracies. As the time line in Figure 2.1 and the

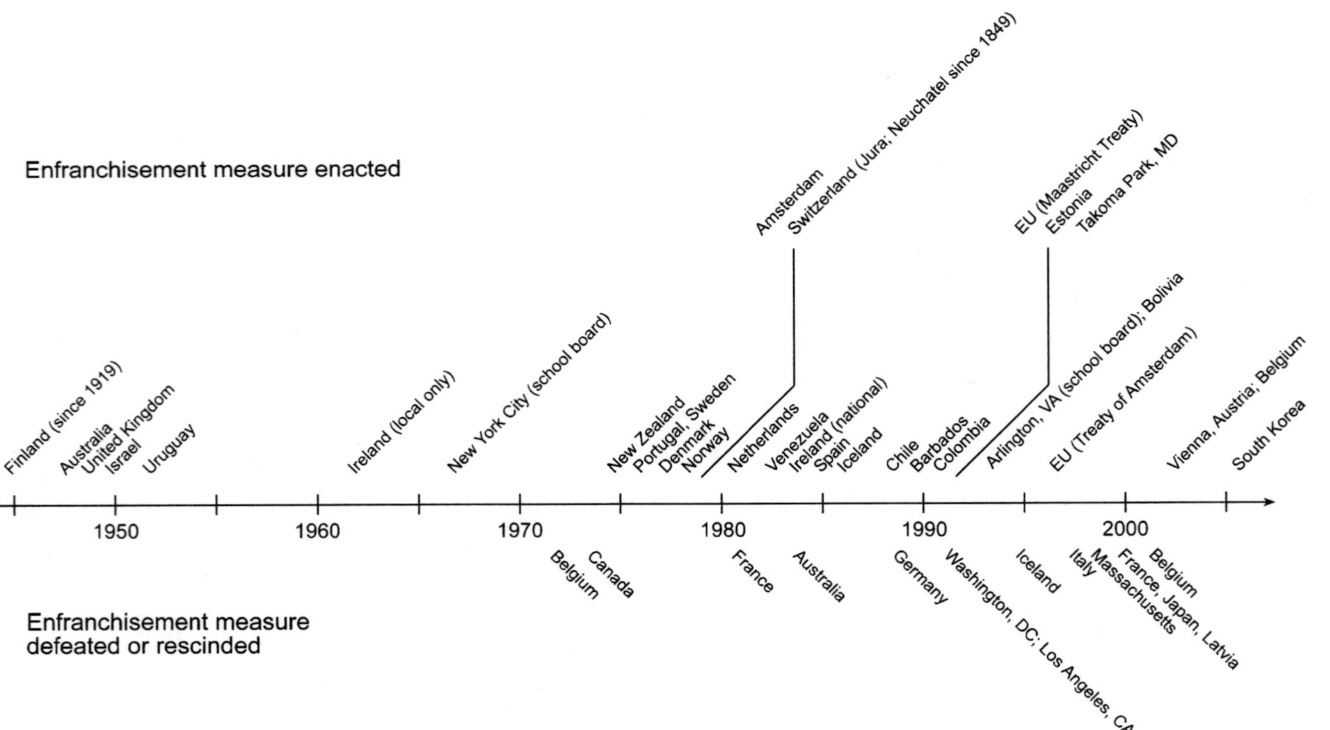

Figure 2.1. Postwar time line of resident-alien voting rights

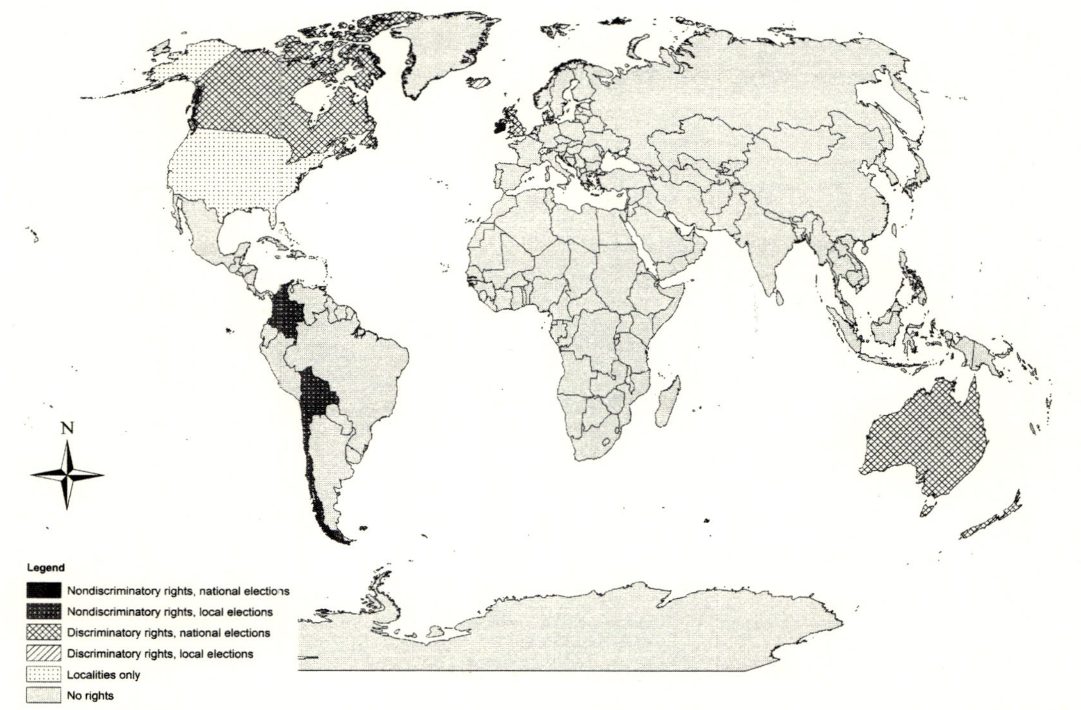

Figure 2.2. World map showing democracies that enfranchised resident aliens in 1970, categorized by the scale and scope of the rights

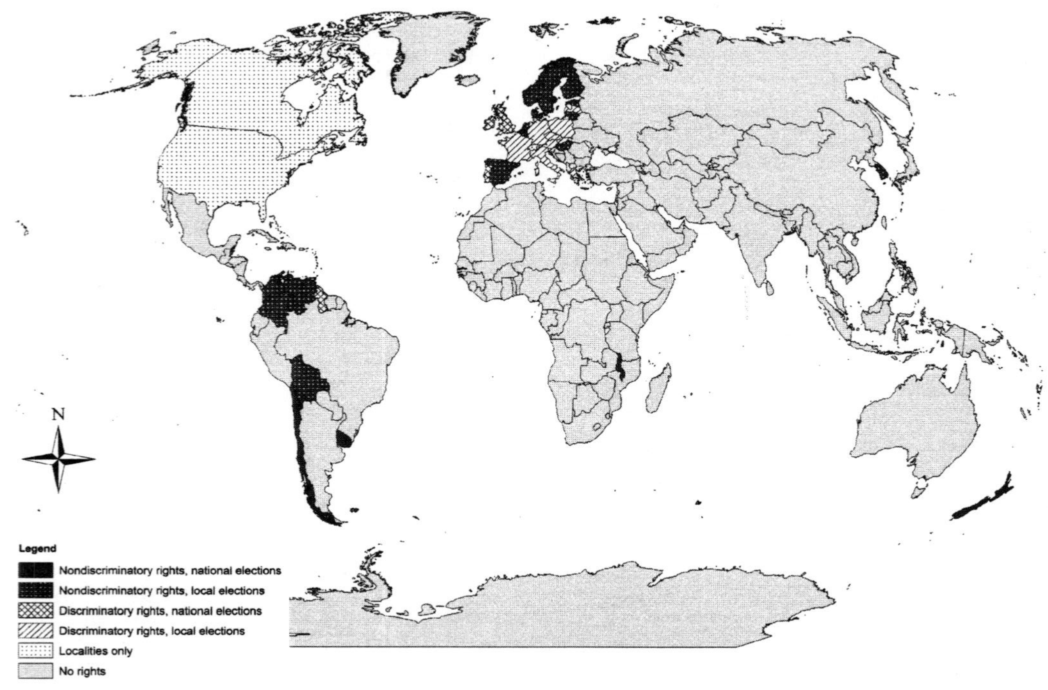

Figure 2.3. World map showing democracies that enfranchised resident aliens in 2006, categorized by the scale and scope of the rights

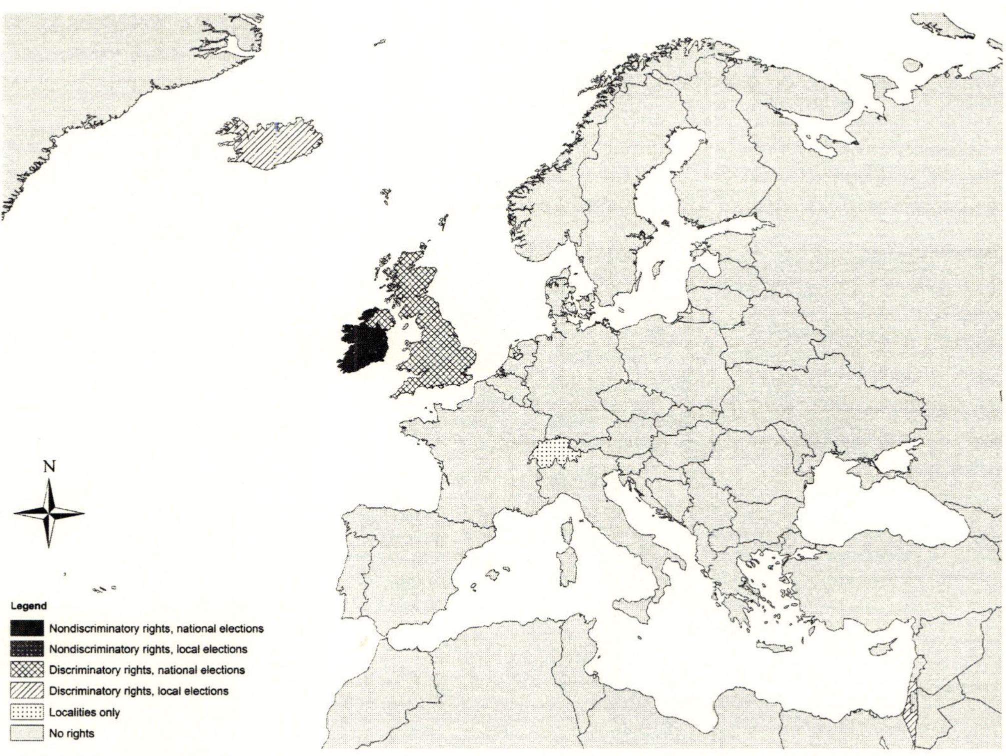

Figure 2.4. Map showing European democracies that enfranchised resident aliens in 1970, categorized by the scale and scope of the rights

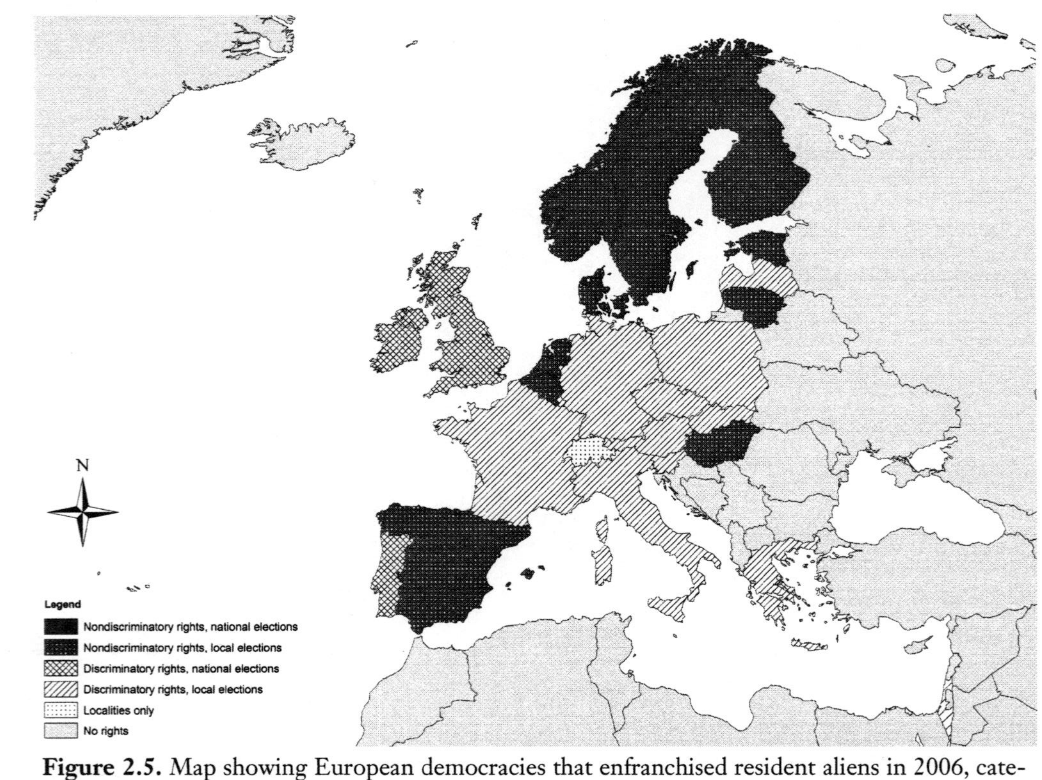

Figure 2.5. Map showing European democracies that enfranchised resident aliens in 2006, categorized by the scale and scope of the rights

maps in Figures 2.2 through 2.5 show, the practice is spreading. This growth explains in part why some scholars have argued that voting rights for resident aliens are an emerging norm of democratic practice. Yet the variety of voting rights regimes that democracies have adopted suggests states exercise discretion over the institutional implementation of the norm. As this empirical overview shows, there is considerable variation in the scope and scale of the rights that states have provided to resident aliens. This variation itself is an important puzzle.

A Typology of Resident Alien Suffrage

The voting rights that aliens have vary widely from state to state in both their scope and cale. For the purposes of this study, the "scope" of resident-alien voting rights refers to the size of the population of enfranchised resident aliens in a given state. Some states extend voting rights to resident aliens of all nationalities, while other states offer the franchise only to resident aliens who are citizens of specific countries. The scope of rights thus captures whether or not the state discriminates based on an alien's nationality. The "scale" of voting rights refers to the types of elections in which resident aliens may vote. In some states, resident aliens can vote only in municipal, local, state, or provincial elections, while in others they have the right to vote in elections for national executive or parliamentary office. Using the scope and scale of voting rights as axes, one can typify states that enfranchise resident aliens into different categories. This chapter categorizes the states that allow resident aliens to vote into six groups:

1. Those states that have no rights
2. Those states in which the national government does not grant a right to vote, but localities, cities, or provinces may offer voting rights to resident aliens for local elections only
3. States in which the national government enfranchises resident aliens for local elections, but aliens must satisfy a nationality qualification
4. States in which the national government enfranchises resident aliens to vote in parliamentary or national elections, but aliens must satisfy a nationality qualification
5. States in which the national government enfranchises all resident aliens irrespective of nationality, but these aliens may vote only in local elections

6. States in which the national government enfranchises resident aliens irrespective of nationality, and these resident aliens may vote in parliamentary or national elections.

It is important to note that states within these categories have important differences as well. Uruguay and New Zealand each allow any resident alien to vote in national elections, for example. Uruguay requires the alien, however, to have resided in Uruguay for fifteen years before qualifying for the franchise, in stark contrast to New Zealand's residency requirement of one year. Likewise, several states have constitutional provisions that permit the legislature to enact laws that would enfranchise resident aliens, but the states have not done so. At least one state (Sweden) has allowed resident aliens to vote in national referenda, even though it normally permits them to vote only in local elections.[10] Figure 2.6 graphs those states that allow resident aliens to vote according to the discriminatory nature of and scale of the rights.

Voting Rights Granted by Localities

In federal systems, local or provincial governments may enjoy the constitutional authority to determine voter eligibility qualifications for their own local elections, and may determine qualifications for national elections as well. In several of these federal states, municipalities or provinces have granted resident aliens the right to vote. Local authorities thus may be important sources of innovation for the political rights of resident aliens.[11] Consequently, several federal states have produced a variety of resident-alien voting regimes that differ not only from other nation-states but from other jurisdictions within the state as well. In this respect, the practice of enfranchising resident aliens is a "bottom-up" phenomenon that emerges first at the local level. Five important examples of resident-alien voting rights emerge at the local level in federal systems: the Federal Republic of Germany, Switzerland, Austria, Canada, and the United States.

In the Federal Republic of Germany, two states and West Berlin established limited voting rights for resident aliens in 1989. Hamburg enfranchised all resident aliens who had resided in the state for more than eight years to vote in local elections, while Berlin required only five years of residency.[12] Schleswig-Holstein also limited the voting of resident aliens to local elections only but further limited these rights

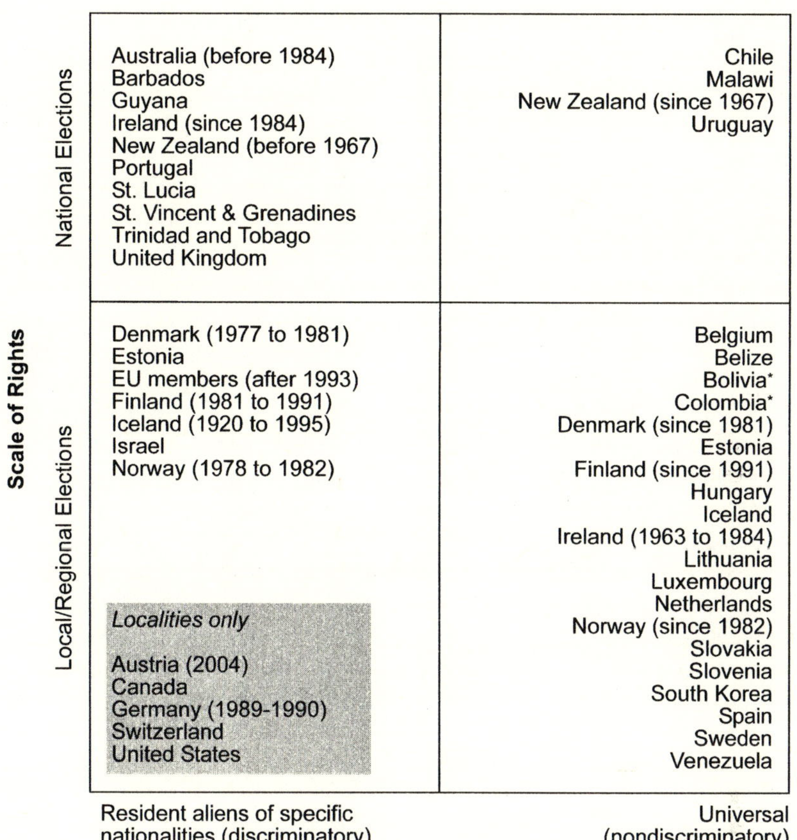

Figure 2.6. The scope and scale of resident-alien voting rights in thirty-eight states. Dates in parentheses indicate the year in which a democracy had a particular voting rights regime. States with asterisks (*) connote those in which the national constitution provides for an act of law to enfranchise aliens but the legislature has not enacted such a law. Sources: Blais et al. 2001; Bauback 2005; Waldrauch 2005; refer to text for other sources.

to Danish, Irish, Dutch, Norse, Swedish, and Swiss residents who had five or more years of residency. The franchise rights in these two German states were short-lived, however; the Federal Constitutional Court ruled in 1990 that both the Hamburg and Schleswig-Holstein laws violated the Basic Law.[13]

Challenges to local resident alien voting laws in Switzerland, by contrast, have survived constitutional scrutiny because Article 39(1) of the Swiss constitution reserves for cantons the explicit power to regulate the exercise of political rights in all cantonal and municipal matters. Two cantons, Neuchâtel and Jura, have constitutions that permit resident aliens to vote. Neuchâtel's practice of alien suffrage dates to 1849 and was restored after a decade-long suspension in the late nineteenth century; Jura's practice dates to its inception as the twenty-third Swiss canton in 1979. In June 2006, Zurich's executive council voted to allow resident aliens to vote in local elections, though opponents of the measure are seeking a referendum to overturn the legislation.[14] Six other cantons have considered but rejected initiatives to enfranchise resident aliens.

In December 2002, Vienna, Austria, adopted a provision to allow all aliens who had resided for five years or more to vote in urban district councils (*Bezirksräte*) but not in elections for Vienna's municipal council (*Gemeinderat*).[15] Austria, like all European Union members, allows all resident aliens who are EU nationals to vote in local elections, consistent with its obligations as a signatory to the Treaty of Amsterdam. Vienna's 2002 initiative significantly broadened these rights by enfranchising legally resident aliens from countries outside the EU. In February 2001, the city's mayor first stated his support for enfranchising non-EU immigrants for local elections though local elected officials divided largely along party lines: left-leaning parties favored the initiative while the right-leaning People's Party and the far-right Freedom Party both opposed it.[16] Despite this opposition, the city-state's government enacted the provision. As in Germany, however, conservative party members challenged the legality of Vienna's provision in federal courts. In June 2004, the Constitutional Court ruled that voting rights for non-EU nationals at any level violate the constitution.[17] Vienna's local initiative thus failed to survive the scrutiny of national courts.

In North America, resident aliens cannot vote in national elections in the United States or in Canada. However, in both nation-states a few jurisdictions have extended voting rights to resident aliens. The Canadian constitution expressly limits voting rights in federal elections to citizens, but in Saskatchewan and Nova Scotia resident aliens with British citizenship may vote in provincial elections.[18] In the United States, a few municipalities allow resident aliens to vote in municipal elections. In New York City, resident aliens with children who attend public schools can vote in school board elections.[19] In May 1994, Arlington, Virginia, also allowed resident aliens with children in public schools to vote in the county's school board election.[20] In Takoma Park, Maryland, by contrast, since 1991 resident aliens have had the right to vote in any civic election, a practice that five other townships in Maryland have since adopted.[21] The Maryland state assembly has endorsed these initiatives by passing the necessary home-rule legislation to make these practices constitutional under state law.[22] In Massachusetts, citizens in both Cambridge and Amherst approved referenda in 1999 to enfranchise resident aliens, though unlike in Maryland the state legislature failed to pass the necessary home-rule legislation to enable the Cambridge and Amherst laws.[23] Several cities have renewed efforts to extend voting rights to resident aliens. In the fall of 2002, the city council of Rockville, Maryland, considered a measure to allow resident aliens to vote, and the mayor of Washington, D.C. once again raised the issue.[24] Migrants' advisory groups in Washington, recently supported the mayor's call.[25] In 2003, the San Francisco board of supervisors considered an initiative to allow resident aliens to vote in municipal school board elections, while the New York City Council is considering amending the city charter to allow resident aliens to vote in all municipal elections, not just school board elections.[26]

The current patchwork of resident-alien voting rights in the United States is a historical anomaly only in its geographic limits. The individual states of the United States have a rich tradition of enfranchising resident aliens that dates from the founding of the republic to the early twentieth century. Raskin and Harper-Ho both observe that historically, states have used alien suffrage to serve a number of different political aims, particularly during the nineteenth century when states had broader authority over matters of citizenship. As westward expansion progressed, territories used the enticement of voting rights to encourage immigrants from Europe to settle and thus speed the territory's admittance to the Union. Similarly, following the Civil War Southern states offered resident aliens the right to vote in order to attract the workers who would replace the slave labor force and to expedite Reconstruction. A second goal was political socialization. Following Wisconsin's lead of enfranchising aliens who had declared their intent to naturalize (so-called "declarant aliens"), during the mid-nineteenth century resident alien voting became a means of educating aliens about the interests and issues of their communities. Other political goals of alien suffrage were less salutary, however, as the process became intertwined with the racial, social, and political divides of the country. Raskin notes that Northern states sought to expand alien suffrage while Southern states sought to limit it, since legislators on both sides believed most immigrants were opposed to slavery. Similarly, Raskin and Harper-Ho both note that the practice of resident alien suffrage was a subtle form of discrimination against other disenfranchised groups like women and African Americans. It is well known that during the nineteenth century race, property, and gender requirements prohibited most American citizens from voting. By giving the vote to propertied immigrant white men, the resident alien franchise underscored that voting was not a right of citizenship.[27] It became an implicit means of reinforcing other discriminatory voter eligibility practices. For these reasons, states continued to discriminate not only against citizens but between resident aliens as well, as they chose to offer voting rights only to European immigrants but not to the burgeoning Chinese immigrant population of California and other western states. In these respects, the nineteenth-century practice of enfranchising resident aliens in the United States was as much about excluding groups from political rights as it was about including them.

Nevertheless, the nineteenth-century practices in the various states of the Union have left a case-law legacy that leads most legal scholars to argue that alien suffrage is neither prohibited nor required by the U.S. constitution. Since the Constitution reserves for states the right to define "electors," furthermore, past practices suggest resident aliens in the United States may legally vote even in elections for national office. For this reason, in the past resident aliens in the United States who voted at the state level could vote in federal elections as well. Thus Aylsworth notes resident aliens voted in every presidential election until 1925.[28] At the height of the practice in the mid 1870s, twenty-two of the thirty-seven states in the Union permitted declarant resident aliens to vote. The Supreme Court has consistently upheld, furthermore, the right of states to determine voter eligibility requirements and has specifically ruled that alien suffrage violates no constitutional provisions. In terms of the United States, then, the question of alien suffrage is purely a political rather than legal one.

As the history of alien suffrage in the United States suggests, the very nature of federalism produces some interesting patterns of alien suffrage both between democracies and within the democratic states themselves. The cases of Switzerland, Austria, Canada, Germany, and the United States suggest that geography provides few obvious explanations for the patterns of passage or rejection of resident alien franchise rights. Schleswig-Holstein's and Hamburg's proximity to the Baltic suggests the influence of Scandinavian norms of resident alien voting along the lines of regimes in Denmark, the Netherlands, Norway, and Sweden, though this cannot explain Berlin, Vienna, or the Swiss cantons of Neuchâtel and Jura (though contiguous to each other, both cantons border on France).[29] Likewise, initiatives to enfranchise legally resident aliens in the United States have sprung up in some of the largest cities—New York City and the suburbs of Boston and Washington, D.C. (though they have failed so far in Los Angeles, San Francisco, and the District of Columbia itself). This is similar to the pattern in the Federal Republic of Germany, where the initiatives took hold in Berlin, Hamburg, and the other Baltic ports of Schleswig-Holstein. In Switzerland, by contrast, three cantons with large cities—Geneva, Vaud (where Lausanne is located), and Bern— all rejected resident alien voting initiatives.[30] These examples all show that voting rights for resident aliens may vary not only between democratic states but within them as well.

Discriminatory Regimes

Several states have enacted voting rights regimes that discriminate based on the resident alien's nationality. In some cases, the nationality criterion reflects historical relationships between a state and its former colonies, such as Portugal's policy of allowing Cape Verdean and Brazilian resident aliens to vote in parliamentary elections.[31] Another important example is Estonia's enfranchisement of its Russian-speaking minority.[32] It is important to note, however, that these "discriminatory" regimes may themselves reflect a latent form of postnational citizenship. The United Kingdom's practice of allowing citizens of Commonwealth nations and the Republic of Ireland to vote in Parliamentary elections reflects the Commonwealth's largely unrealized goal of a common citizenship.[33] Likewise, as the text discusses later, the European Union's Treaty of Amsterdam ensconces voting rights that discriminate in favor of EU nationals who reside in other member states. These examples show that while states may discriminate, the nationality criterion in fact may reflect supranational organizations if not transnational norms of inclusion. In this respect, even discriminatory voting rights for resident aliens may foreshadow the eroding link between citizenship and political incorporation.

Discriminatory Rights for Local Elections

Several states allow resident aliens from their former colonies to vote, but only in local elections. In Portugal, for one, Article 15(4) of the constitution gives resident aliens the right to vote in local elections "subject to reciprocity."[34] Katz notes that these special voting rights are for citizens of Brazil residing in Portugal.[35] In a surprising reversal of the colonial relationship, Estonia has created limited voting rights to accommodate what Laitin calls a "beached diaspora" of native Estonians who speak only Russian.[36] Since the Estonian constitution does not recognize such Russian speakers as citizens, the grant of resident-alien voting rights is one way the government has sought to incorporate this population. However, the right is limited to local elections only and requires the Russian-speaking resident aliens to have established permanent residence. Such resident aliens are not only prohibited from voting in national parliamentary elections, but are also prohibited from joining parties or holding office.[37] These facts suggest the voting rights of Russian-speaking aliens in Estonia are the result of changes in Estonian citizenship law after the demise of the Soviet Union, an event that in effect revoked the citizenship of Russian-speaking residents.

Other states' discriminatory practices may also reflect specific nationality concerns. Since 1950, Israel has allowed resident aliens to vote in local elections, for example, but only those immigrants who come to Israel under the Law of Return but who refuse to take Israeli citizenship.[38] While the Israeli practice does not discriminate based on nationality per se, its dependence on the Law of Return indicates the state discriminates in the allocation of voting rights based on a shared religion.

The European Union has adopted this model for its nationals living in a member state other than the country of his or her citizenship. As discussed below, the Treaty of Maastricht in 1993 required European Union states to allow EU nationals to vote in the local elections and elections for Members of the European Parliament in their place of residence. Nevertheless, to qualify for this right a resident alien must be a citizen of an EU member state. The rights thus discriminate based on nationality. Today all EU members abide by their Maastricht Treaty obligations, though several members had pre-existing voting rights that complied with or exceeded those required by Maastricht. It took several other members some time, furthermore, to reform their laws to comply with this obligation. It was nearly a decade before Italy complied with Maastricht, for example.[39] Maastricht's emphasis on nationality as a qualification for the right to vote has led some scholars to observe that the practice is inherently exclusionary rather than inclusive.[40]

It is worth noting that in a number of the Scandinavian states, all of which today have nondiscriminatory voting rights for resident aliens, these rights emerged from practices that originally discriminated in favor of only a few specific nationalities. When they first enacted voting rights for resident aliens, Norway, Finland, and Denmark all permitted only resident aliens from other Nordic states to vote in local elections.[41] Denmark expanded the right to all resident aliens in 1981, Norway in 1982, and Finland in 1991. All three now require resident aliens to satisfy only a residency requirement.

Discriminatory Rights in National Elections

The voting rights of resident aliens in Portugal, Estonia, and Israel are circumscribed when compared to the broad rights enjoyed by resident aliens from Commonwealth states who reside in the United Kingdom. There citizens of Commonwealth nations and the Republic of Ireland may register to vote in national parliamentary elections. Several other Commonwealth states or former British colonies make similar provisions, including Guyana, Barbados, Jamaica, and several other small Caribbean states.[42] Ireland reciprocates Britain's extension of voting rights to Irish citizens by allowing British citizens to vote in national parliamentary elections (though Ireland also allows resident aliens of any nation to vote in local elections after six months residency).[43] Until 1984, Australia allowed British citizens to vote in parliamentary elections. Though Australia has since rescinded this right, it created a grandfather exception for those British citizens who previously received the franchise. In 1999, this amounted to about 17,000 voters.[44]

Nondiscriminatory Regimes

Nondiscriminatory voting rights regimes are those in which resident aliens do not need to satisfy a nationality qualification for the franchise. These nondiscriminatory rights typically have residency qualifications, however, that in some cases are quite lengthy. Some nondiscriminatory regimes provide the right to vote only in local elections; others provide the right to vote in national and parliamentary elections; and some regimes—like Ireland's and Portugal's—are hybrids because they do not discriminate for the right to vote in local elections, but only resident aliens from specific states qualify to vote in national elections.

Nondiscriminatory Rights for Local Elections

The most common form of resident-alien voting rights today is a nondiscriminatory right to vote in local elections only. Seventeen states allow aliens who satisfy a residency requirement to vote in municipal, provincial, or other local elections; two others (Bolivia and Colombia) make explicit constitutional provision for the national legislature to provide such rights at its discretion. The nondiscriminatory local-rights model differs in important ways in both scale and scope from the discriminatory national and local regimes of states like the United Kingdom, Estonia, or Israel: While it permits voting only in local elections, it does not discriminate among the nationalities of the states' resident alien population. It is also broader in scope than the limited rights offered by jurisdictions in federal states like Switzerland and the United States: It is a right provided by the national government rather than subnational ones, and applies to all municipalities, boroughs, states, or other localities in a given nation-state. In this respect, it is neither geographically discriminatory (as in federal states) nor ethnically or nationally discriminatory. As in all cases of voting rights, however, resident aliens must reside for a given number of years before they can vote in local elections.

This model typifies the resident alien voting rights regimes of Sweden, Denmark, Norway, the Netherlands, Finland, Iceland, Ireland, Hungary, Venezuela, the Republic of Korea, and perhaps Belize. Eight of these states are European democracies. Electoral systems provide no obvious clues. Eight have proportional representation systems, though Ireland, Belize, and South Korea do not. Of the proportional representation systems, all except Venezuela have party-list electoral rules. Belize has a plurality first-past-the-post system, Ireland has a single-transferable-vote proportional representation system, and Venezuela has a mixed-member proportional representation system. The Republic of Ireland first allowed resident aliens to vote in local elections in 1963; today Ireland has the most permissive residency requirement, allowing aliens to vote after only six months residency in the Republic. Sweden enfranchised resident aliens for local elections in 1976, requiring only that the alien voter have resided in Sweden for three years. Denmark followed suit in 1977, requiring only one year of residency, followed by Norway in 1978, which required three years of residency.[45] The Netherlands, in which Rotterdam and Amsterdam first established resident-alien voting rights in 1979 and 1981, respectively, has a longer residency requirement of five years.[46] Another more recent example is Hungary. Upon the collapse of the Soviet Union, the newly constituted legislature passed the Local Elections Act of 1990, which Nagy notes provides voting rights in municipal elections for "non-citizen permanent residents."[47] In 2006 South Korea became the first Asian state to allow resident aliens to vote in local elections.[48]

Interestingly, Iceland has a longer history of resident-alien voting rights, perhaps reflecting its history as a secession state.[49] The history of alien voting rights in Iceland is somewhat convoluted. Article 75 of the 1920 constitution granted voting rights to Danish nationals resident in Iceland, rights that were eventually expanded to other Nordic immigrants.[50] Article 33 of the Icelandic constitution of 1995 stipulates, however, that only citizens can vote. Interestingly, the 1995 constitution accommodates "foreign nationals" who had previous voting rights under Article 75 of the 1920 constitution in a "Temporary Provisions" section at the end of the document.[51] This section effectively grandfathers the resident-alien voting rights that foreign nationals had previously received. In this respect, the Icelandic case is an interesting one: Although the 1995 constitution eliminates resident-alien voting rights, it does so only prospectively for future immigrants to the country.

While Norway, Denmark, and Finland today allow all resident aliens to vote in local elections irrespective of nationality, it is important to recall that these states originally discriminated among immigrants of different nationalities. As Iceland did, Norway, Denmark, and Finland originally extended the alien franchise to immigrants from the Nordic states. In this respect, the alien franchise rights in these states originally were discriminatory. Thus, these rights evolved in scope to encompass all alien residents, not merely those from Nordic states. It is also interesting to note that Norway and Denmark's alien voting rules originally were discriminatory while the Netherlands' and Sweden's were nondiscriminatory. The changing nature of these nondiscriminatory regimes suggest, furthermore, that any analysis should explain not only the existence of voting rights for resident aliens but also how these rights change over time.

Belize, the last state categorized as having nondiscriminatory rights for local elections, offers the franchise in municipal elections only to alien residents of three years or more.[52] Unlike the northern European parliamentary democracies, however, Belize's government is a first-past-the-post plurality parliamentary system, undoubtedly a reflection of its historic relationship with the United Kingdom. Belize's colonial history also begs an important question: Why did Belize opt for the local model instead of the discriminatory national-rights model that typifies other Commonwealth states—the United Kingdom, Barbados, Canada before 1975, and (until 1984) Australia?[53] For this reason, Belize offers an interesting anomalous case: It fits neither the institutional pattern of the northern European democracies, nor the scale of rights typical of other states with historic colonial ties to the United Kingdom.

Nondiscriminatory Rights for National Elections

Four nation-states offer universal voting rights to resident aliens for all elections, local to national: Chile, Malawi, New Zealand, and Uruguay. Prior to 1975, New Zealand allowed immigrants from the United Kingdom to vote in parliamentary elections. Since then, however, any immigrant who has resided in New Zealand for one year may register to vote in national elections.[54] The case of New Zealand, therefore, is the ideal type of resident-alien voting rights: The residency requirement is minimal (only Ireland's six-month requirement is shorter) and the rights are nondiscriminatory—any resident alien who is eighteen years of age or older can register to vote.

Alien suffrage in New Zealand is interesting for two reasons. First is the timing of New Zealand's expansion of voting rights to resident aliens. This occurred in the mid-1970s when the Scandinavian states and the Netherlands first offered the franchise to resident aliens. While the Netherlands, Sweden, Denmark, and Norway used a local-voting approach to alien suffrage, New Zealand opted for national voting rights. The proximate timing of the cases may offer an opportunity to control for as-yet-unspecified transnational or global phenomena, such as norms of "personhood" (in Soysal's words).[55] Second is the hypothesized relationship between colonial history and alien suffrage. States with historical colonial relationships may discriminate in favor of each other's citizens by offering limited voting rights to immigrants from colonial possessions (or from the imperial state). As noted above, this may explain Australia's enfranchisement of British citizens prior to 1984, Portugal's enfranchisement of Brazilians, as well as rights in Canada before 1975 and in other Commonwealth states. A key feature of this practice is, however, their discriminatory rights: States offer voting rights only to specific nationalities as part of a supranational project. Yet New Zealand switched in 1975 from a discriminatory regime to a nondiscriminatory permissive one. Given New Zealand's colonial history, its continuing membership in the Commonwealth, and its geographic proximity to Australia (where the government rescinded the franchise rights of British resident aliens only nine years after New Zealand), New Zealand's permissive alien suffrage regime is an interesting case.

It is important to note that at least in a de jure sense, both Chile and Uruguay also allow any alien to vote in both local and parliamentary elections. Uruguay differs from New Zealand in one substantive way, however. Uruguay's residency qualification is the most exclusionary of any nation-state that allows resident aliens to vote. Only after an alien has resided in Uruguay for fifteen years can he or she qualify for the franchise. This stands in marked contrast with Ireland (which requires only six months of residency to vote in local elections) and New Zealand (which requires only a year of residency to vote in parliamentary elections). While Uruguay's right to vote is nondiscriminatory in a de jure sense, then, its residency qualification raises the question of how other qualifications for the franchise may discriminate against resident aliens. Venezuela also allows resident aliens to qualify for the vote in local elections, but only after ten years of residency. Malawi requires seven years of residency.[56] These residency requirements arguably mitigate the nondiscriminatory nature of the de jure voting rights, and raise issues of comparability with states like New Zealand.

Discrimination through Residency Qualifications

These cases suggest that residency requirements for resident aliens may limit these franchise rights to a very small number. In Chile, Articles 13 and 14 of the Constitution entitle aliens with five years of residency to vote in national parliamentary elections.[57] The Venezuelan constitution (Tit. III, Ch. 4, Art. 64) entitles aliens with ten years of residency to vote in municipal and state elections only, while the Uruguayan constitution (Sect. III, Ch. 2, Art. 78) requires fifteen years of residency.[58] Given that all three states have zero or negative migration rates, it is doubtful that many resident aliens satisfy such onerous residency requirements to qualify for and claim their franchise rights. Furthermore, the status of permanent residency may be a difficult one for many immigrants to obtain. In some instances, this arguably has the consequence of shifting discrimination to a different institutional locus within the state. For example, South Korea's enfranchisement in 2006 of about 6,500 permanent resident aliens who resided in the state for three years or more did not include the country's 500,000 migrant workers who did not qualify for permanent residency status. South Korean law also required resident aliens to meet a property requirement to qualify for permanent residency status.[59] To the degree permanent residency is a qualification for the franchise, then, the rules governing residency status may serve a discriminatory purpose as much as they may include resident aliens in the polity.

It is difficult if not impossible to say when a residency requirement becomes onerous to the point of being restrictive rather than expansive. While Uruguay's fifteen-year requirement clearly curtails the voting opportunities of most aliens, Chile's five-year provision is the same as the Netherlands' residency requirement. The scale of resident alien rights in Chile is greater, furthermore, than in the Netherlands; unlike in the Dutch case, resident aliens in Chile can vote in national elections as well as local or regional elections. So why might one categorize the Chilean case as more restrictive than the Dutch case? Though the Chilean requirements are more permissive in principle, the levels of immigration to Chile mean that in fact far fewer aliens receive voting rights than the Netherlands grants to its resident aliens. While Chile, Venezuela, and Uruguay had near zero or negative immigration rates between 2000 and 2005, the northern European democracies offering nondiscriminatory local rights have net inflows of migrants.[60] Similarly, the number of migrants as a percentage of the total population is much lower in the Latin American democracies. Only 1 percent of Chile's population was migrants in 2002, though Uruguay and Venezuela had slightly higher percentages (2.65 and 4.16, respectively). These figures suggest that the total number of resident aliens eligible to vote is greater in countries that host larger numbers of migrants. While one might argue that the Chilean case parallels the nondiscriminatory national rights of New Zealand, it seems disingenuous to overlook the overall migration levels and net flows of these states as well as their extended residency requirements when categorizing their alien voting rights.[61]

Alien Suffrage in National Constitutions

Curiously, the constitutions of two South American democracies explicitly address the issue of alien suffrage. Colombia's constitution, dating to 1991, stipulates that the legislature may pass an act to allow foreign citizens to vote in municipal or district elections (Tit. II, Ch. 2, Art. 100).[62] The Bolivian constitution (of 1967 as amended in 1994) has a similar clause: The legislature explicitly has the discretion to enfranchise aliens to vote in local elections (Tit. IX, Ch. 1, Art. 220).[63] It is interesting to note not only that these constitutions came into being relatively recently, but also that they explicitly give discretionary power over resident-alien voting rights to the legislatures. However, neither legislature so far has exercised this unique constitutional authority. Nevertheless, the mere fact that constitutional framers considered the issue important begs the question of why they chose to provide for such voting rights.

Resident Alien Voting Rights in International Law

In addition to states that have varying degrees of voting rights for resident aliens, three important pieces of international law address the issue of political rights for resident aliens. One is the Consolidated Version of the Treaty Establishing the European Community, as Amended by the Treaty of Amsterdam of 1997 (hereafter referred to as the Amsterdam Treaty).[64] The treaty amended, consolidated, and reordered the Maastricht Treaty of 1992 to become the legal foundation for common foreign and security policies for the European Community member states and for cooperation among members on issues relating to justice and home affairs. Though the amended and consolidated version changed some of the contentious provisions of the Maastricht Treaty, it preserves an important article that addressed voting rights for EU citizens. Part II, Article 19(1) of the Amsterdam Treaty, echoing Article 8 of the Maastricht Treaty, commits EU member-states to establishing voting rights for those aliens from other EU states who reside in their country. The language reads:

> Every citizen of the Union residing in a Member State of which he is not a national shall have the right to vote and stand as a candidate at municipal elections in the Member State of which he resides, under the same conditions as nationals of that State.[65]

The rights enunciated by the treaty therefore appear to be a hybrid type. It stipulates that member states allow resident aliens to vote only in municipal elections, reflecting the scale of rights typical of the local voting rights regimes used by the Nordic states, the

Netherlands, and others. However, the Treaty also adds a discriminatory nationality requirement; EU member states will extend the right only to EU nationals, not to resident aliens of any nationality. In this respect, the Treaty combines the discriminatory nationality requirements typical of the voting rights regimes of the United Kingdom, Ireland, and Portugal with the restrictive scale of the local regimes of Sweden, Norway, the Netherlands, Spain, and others.

Article 19(1), therefore, is a curious hybrid that defies easy explanation. Given the preexisting heterogeneity of resident-alien voting rights among EU states, it is puzzling that the Treaty articulated this particular set of rights with discriminatory scope and limited scale. It is also puzzling to note that some states quickly revised their voter eligibility requirements to comply with Article 19(1) while others were slow to change (notably Italy).[66] These observations may offer some important insights into the evolution of alien suffrage. The EU member states' resistance to Article 19(1) may help explain, furthermore, a number of important negative cases.

A second important piece of international law is the Council of Europe's Convention on the Participation of Foreigners in Local Life. Shaw notes that the convention, concluded in 1992, establishes a road map for signatories to follow that would lead to the enfranchisement of resident aliens for local elections.[67] Despite the Council's championing of nondiscriminatory rights for local elections, the convention is a weak instrument, with no penalties for signatories' noncompliance. Only eight states have ratified the convention—Albania, Denmark, Finland, Iceland, Italy, the Netherlands, Norway, and Sweden—five of which had preexisting franchise rights that equaled or exceeded those stipulated by the convention. Four other states (including the United Kingdom) have signed but not ratified the convention.[68] Shaw notes, furthermore, that Italy has only partially complied with the convention.[69] All this suggests only modest support among Council members for the convention and its principles.

The final notable piece of international law is the Universal Declaration of Human Rights. Raskin argues that the Declaration is "written in such a way as to leave open the possibility that resident aliens will have the right to vote."[70] Article 21(1) of the Declaration, which enunciates basic political rights, uses the ambiguous term "everyone" instead of "every citizen": It states "Everyone has the right to take part in the government of his country, directly or through freely chosen representatives."[71] Nowhere does the Declaration specify citizenship as a requirement for political rights (or any rights for that matter); it is silent, furthermore, on voter eligibility requirements. While the phrasing of the Declaration falls short of explicit advocacy of alien suffrage, Raskin's argument deserves consideration. It is telling that an important articulation of principals of human rights decouples the ideas of citizenship and political rights. In this respect, the Universal Declaration of Human Rights approximates the historical condition of many states granting at least some resident aliens the right to vote and participate in elections.

Raskin also notes that the International Covenant on Civil and Political Rights of 1966 contrasts with the Universal Declaration of Human Rights by explicitly confining the right to vote to citizens.[72] Article 25 (subsections a through c) uses the term "citizen" when articulating a vision of political rights.[73] The contrast with the Universal Declaration of Human Rights illustrates that international human rights agreements arguably have competing and contradictory conceptions of the political rights of noncitizens.

Negative Cases: States That Have Rejected Alien Suffrage

A number of states have either considered franchise rights for resident aliens but failed to offer them, or rescinded voting rights they had extended previously to resident aliens. Though these failed cases vary over time, they offer both an important theoretical counterweight and observations against which to test hypotheses. These negative observations fall into two categories: states whose governments considered resident aliens voting rights but failed to adopt them (hereafter referred to as "failed cases") and states that rescinded alien voting rights ("rolled back" cases).

The failed cases include France, Japan, Latvia, and jurisdictions within Switzerland and the United States—because the latter two are federal nation-states, innovation among their constituent jurisdictions has resulted in both positive and negative examples of municipalities adopting voting rights for resident aliens. France first considered resident alien voting in 1981, when the Parti Socialiste (PS) first proposed an initiative to enfranchise resident aliens. Rath reports that the PS measure faced widespread opposition.[74] The Assemblé Nationale considered another measure to enfranchise resident aliens in 2000, but the measure failed due to constitutional concerns and opposition from the Sénat.[75]

Latvia and Japan's consideration of voting rights for resident aliens suggest that the state faces international pressures when considering voting rights for resident aliens. Kashiwazaki reports that in 1990, eleven permanent resident Korean nationals in Japan sought from a Japanese court the right to vote in national elections.[76] Five years later the Japanese supreme court ruled that the right to vote is reserved for Japanese nationals, but also held that the Diet has constitutional authority to enact legislation enfranchising resident aliens if it so chooses. In 2000, the Diet considered but tabled such legislation despite the championing of such voting rights by the South Korean government. In Latvia, the parliament rejected a measure to permit the state's resident aliens to vote in local elections despite pressure from the European local governments' Chamber of Regions and from the Latvian Human Rights committee.[77]

By contrast, the federal democracies of Switzerland and the United States present numerous cases of resident alien voting initiatives at the local level that have failed to win popular support. Seven other cantons have considered but rejected similar measures.[78] Similarly, the success of the Takoma Park initiative and its replication in other Maryland hamlets, not to mention the rights of resident aliens to vote in New York's school board elections, belies the difficulties that resident alien voting initiatives have faced elsewhere in the United States. In the early 1990s, activists in Los Angeles, San Francisco, and Washington, D.C., tried to adopt voting-rights measures similar to the one established in Takoma Park. San Francisco voters considered such a ballot initiative in November 2004. In all three cases municipal voters failed to approve the measures.[79] Similarly, though the voters in Amherst and Cambridge, Massachusetts, elected by referenda to extend voting rights to resident aliens, the Massachusetts State legislature failed to enact the necessary home-rule legislation that would have enabled the Amherst and Cambridge initiatives. It is interesting to note, furthermore, that in both the Swiss case and in the United States large urban areas have rejected, for the most part, alien suffrage initiatives while smaller municipalities or cantons have enacted such measures. This pattern contrasts, furthermore, with the Federal Republic of Germany's brief history of alien suffrage, which occurred in the largely urban *länder* of Hamburg and West Berlin.[80]

These are interesting counterexamples to those democracies that allow aliens to vote. For example, resident alien voting initiatives in France and Belgium have faced strong opposition even as similar measures in the Netherlands, Norway, Denmark, and Sweden at the same time faced little or no opposition. What explains this variation within Europe? The case studies in chapter 6 explore this question.

The failed cases in federal systems raise another important question: Is the variation in outcomes within a nation-state caused by the same mechanisms that cause the observed variation among nation-states? In these respects, the failed cases may present important crucial cases for a model that seeks to explain variation in voting rights for resident aliens. The patterns in which migrants settle within a democracy may affect the outcome of resident alien franchise initiatives within federal states.[81] For this reason municipalities, cantons, *länder*, or states with large immigrant populations may be more likely to enact alien suffrage.

Australia, Canada, and the United States present important cases of rolled-back alien voting rights that contrast with the failed cases. As noted above, in 1984 Australia eliminated the voting rights of British citizens resident in Australia (though it grandfathered the rights of those British citizens who resided in Australia prior to January 25, 1984). Canada similarly rescinded voting rights for resident aliens who were citizens of Commonwealth states in 1975, though Nova Scotia and Saskatchewan have at least de jure rights to allow British subjects to vote in provincial elections.[82] Though of a different historical period, the United States' rollback of resident-alien voting rights was of an even greater scale. Raskin and Harper-Ho both argue that the shift in immigration sources from Northern Europe to Southern Europe and Asia, when coupled with the xenophobia that followed the First World War, caused most states of the Union to reconsider granting voting rights to declarant aliens.[83] As Aylsworth noted, from a high of twenty-two states in 1875, the member states of the United States had disenfranchised all resident aliens within the country, a remarkable reversal given what the scope and scale of resident alien rights once had been.[84] It would be easy to dismiss the United States' rollback as belonging to another era, or as the product of a historically unique confluence of war and intolerance. Such a dismissal ignores, however, historical parallels between the 1900s and the 1980s and 1990s in the composition and size of immigration to the United States.[85] So why did the states rescind the rights in an era of mass migration from non-European states when localities today once again are extending the rights in a similar era?

Finally, it is important to note three other potential negative observations. The case of the Federal Republic of Germany is difficult to categorize. Is it a failed case or a rolled-back case? On the one hand, three German *länder* did extend franchise rights to specific resident aliens, but on the other, the Federal Constitutional Court ruled these rights unconstitutional a year later, implying that enfranchised resident aliens never consolidated these political rights. Given that the German courts never established the legality of alien suffrage, it seems reasonable to treat the German case as a failed observation rather than an instance of rolled-back rights. The other difficult case is that of the United Kingdom. Since the eligibility of resident aliens to vote is tied to an intergovernmental organization—the Commonwealth—the roll of resident aliens eligible to vote in parliamentary elections ebbs and flows with the membership of the Commonwealth. Although the UK's rules of eligibility may not have changed over the years, resident aliens theoretically may lose their voting rights through no action of their own. In this respect, as the case of the United Kingdom shows, the discriminatory aspect of these voting rights can cut both ways: It can exclude resident aliens from voting as arbitrarily as it may include them. This and the other cases of roll-back illustrate, furthermore, an important and perhaps theoretically interesting phenomenon: Resident aliens may be the only voters in consolidated democracies to lose the franchise. Whereas voting rights for citizens, women, minorities, and other previously excluded groups are now sacrosanct, states apparently may legitimately rescind the voting "rights" of resident aliens.[86]

Why Enfranchise? A Preview

Legal scholars who have explored the expansion of voting rights for resident aliens have proffered a number of explanations for variations in such rights. The common variables to their analyses are levels of immigration and associated xenophobic backlashes; the historical and legal evolution of national conceptions of both citizenship and of voting rights; and, in Raskin's words, "evolving international norms of community based democracy and human rights."[87] In this respect, the hypothesized causes of alien suffrage range from historical path-dependent processes to national institutions and international norms. While the next chapter derives explicit hypotheses, it is worth previewing that discussion by exploring what a number of researchers have written about the cases this chapter presents.

Alien suffrage rights are inescapably embedded in a broader institutional and legal framework of general voting rights. For this reason, franchise opportunities for resident aliens in many countries evolve as other electoral institutions and franchise rights change. Harper-Ho and Raskin both explain the variation over time of alien suffrage in the United States as a product in part of broader debates about the gender, race, and property requirements for voter eligibility.[88] Contrasting the recent alien voting rights successes in the United States to the failed initiatives in the Federal Republic of Germany, Neuman explains the differences in part by citing historically divergent conceptions of citizenship and democratic legitimacy.[89] Unlike in the United States, courts in Germany historically have viewed the right to vote as a collective, rather than individual, right. This right is tied historically, furthermore, to a conception of German nationality as an ethnic construct; the right to vote is not only a collective right of the nation, it is a collective right of the *German* nation.[90] The absence of alien suffrage rights in Germany:

> …reflects the particular historical development of nationhood in Germany, where the rise of a linguistic and cultural nationalism at the beginning of the nineteenth century led to an emphasis on nationality rather than residence as a crucial factor in defining a polity.[91]

A historically exclusive conception of the nation proscribes voting by resident aliens in the German case. Therefore, the franchise rights of resident aliens depend upon not only the franchise rights of other members of the polity but on historically contingent constructions of the polity itself. Chapter 6 explores how these historical institutional factors shape the political opportunities for resident aliens today.

Scholars also cite changes in the size and composition of immigration, and the corresponding social backlashes, to explain variations in the voting rights of resident aliens. Harper-Ho attributes the end of alien suffrage in the United States in the 1920s to both the shift in the ethnicity of the immigrant population (from northern European to southern European and Asian nationalities) and to the xenophobic backlash that followed the First World War.[92] Raskin comes to a similar conclusion.[93] The absolute level of immigration, independent of its ethnic composition, may also explain the variations among the states that enfranchise resident aliens. Neuman, for one, argues that the expansion of alien suffrage is inversely related to the level of immigration.[94] Those European states that have expanded the rights are those with lower proportions of resident aliens, while those states with the highest proportion of resident aliens—including France, the United Kingdom, Belgium, and Germany—have either discriminatory or no voting rights whatsoever for their resident aliens.[95]

Finally, these scholars also cite the importance of international factors as well. Neuman argues, "As the interdependence of national economies deepens and regional 'common market' arrangements multiply, more nations (including the United States) may be called upon to rethink the question of alien suffrage."[96] Similarly, Raskin cites "evolving international norms of community-based democracy and human rights" as one explanation for the emergence of resident-alien voting rights in several American municipalities.[97] He thus sees alien suffrage as a local response to transnational processes and emerging global norms: "the unification of national economies into a global market system at the end of this century undermines the salience of national identity and increases the historical importance of defining a citizenship of place and locality."[98] He calls this redefined citizenship a "polity of presence."[99] Such a radical redefinition of basic concepts as *citizenship* and the *body politic* may reflect the deterritorializing impact of modern global trading relationships, in which labor and capital migrate unhindered across national borders but political and social rights do not. The "straitjacket of nation-state citizenship" is incapable, Raskin argues, of accommodating the fundamental political rights of those who participate in and sustain these widening transnational processes.[100] In this respect, emerging global norms of community-based democracy encourage municipalities and localities to enfranchise resident aliens.[101] The globalization of the marketplace may have created a localized response that is transforming traditional conceptions of citizenship, participatory government, and democratic legitimacy.

These hypothesized explanations for alien suffrage are complex and somewhat contradictory. Raskin cites emerging global norms for community-based participatory democracy, while Harper-Ho and Neuman cite xenophobia to explain the curtailment of resident-alien voting rights. When will global norms of participatory democracy override popular backlash to immigration? Similarly, Neuman cites different historical traditions of citizenship to explain variations in alien suffrage. Under what conditions will national institutions or historical conceptions of citizenship rights yield to emerging global norms? Furthermore, not all municipalities within federal states respond to these norms in the same way. Given the same institutional legacies and conceptions of citizenship, why have some municipalities in the United States, or cantons in Switzerland and provinces in Canada, enfranchised resident aliens while others have not? Clearly, the global norms of community-based democracy that Raskin identifies, or historical conceptions of the nation that Neuman identifies, are not sufficient to create resident-alien voting rights. Other factors must explain the wide variation. These questions demonstrate the need to consider what other scholars have written about the state's incorporation of its migrant population. The following chapter undertakes such a consideration of the hypothesized causes of variation in the state's treatment of resident aliens.

Implications for the Research Design

Table 2.1 lists a sample of democracies around the globe that have some form of voting rights for resident aliens. These cases represent about one in four of the world's democracies. Yet those democracies that do extend voting rights to resident aliens vary considerably in both the scope and scale of those rights.

Given this variability among the states that enfranchise resident aliens, and given the limited number of observations, it is unclear whether or not a single model can explain all the variation among the cases. There are a number of possible research strategies. One is to conduct a comparative analysis of a smaller set of states, perhaps the members of the European Union since several EU democracies allow aliens to vote.[102] Such a comparative case-study design would allow the researcher to control for some variables, such as the role of Article 19(1) of the Treaty of Amsterdam. It would also allow variation in the type of voting rights states grant, since, using the typology developed in this chapter, the EU member states represent three of the models of resident-alien voting rights (discriminatory local, discriminatory national, and nondiscriminatory local rights). With so few observations, however, such a comparative design may not be able to test the number of divergent hypotheses that nationalist and transnationalist scholars put forth.[103] It is also unclear how one would select a "representative" set of cases given the numerous hypothesized causal factors.

An alternative design would use the universe of democracies to test hypotheses. While such an approach would allow for greater generalization, it faces the challenge of explaining such wide variation among democracies for a relatively rare if growing practice. A universal test faces the additional problem of conflating new and consolidating democracies with those that have long traditions of representative government. It is unclear, in other words, whether using all democracies as the study's population captures a representative set of states. In these respects, the choice of the states to examine is a difficult one between general but valid findings or specific findings that may not be generalizable due to sampling and degrees-of-freedom problems.

Table 2.1.
Sample of States That Have Enfranchised Resident Aliens

State	Localities, local or national rights?	Nationality requirement?
Australia	National	British citizenship (rescinded 1984)
Austria	Local	EU citizenship
Barbados	National	Commonwealth citizenship
Belgium	Local	None
Belize	Local	Commonwealth citizenship
Bolivia	Constitutional	—
Canada	Localities	Commonwealth citizenship; provinces only
Chile	National	None
Colombia	Constitutional	—
Denmark	Local	None
Estonia	Local	None
Finland	Local	None
France	Local	EU citizenship
Germany	Local	EU citizenship
Guyana	National	Commonwealth citizenship
Hungary	Local	None
Iceland	Local	Grandfathered rights from 1920 constitution; current law requires citizenship
Ireland	Local/National	Only British citizens allowed to vote in national elections
Israel	Local	Qualification tied to Law of Return
Italy	Local	EU citizenship
Latvia	Local	EU citizenship
Lithuania	Local	None
Luxembourg	Local	None
Malawi	National	None
Netherlands	Local	None
New Zealand	National	None
Norway	Local	None
Portugal	Local/National	Only Brazilians allowed to vote in national elections
St. Lucia	National	Commonwealth citizenship
St. Vincent & Grenadines	National	Commonwealth citizenship
Slovakia	Local	None
Slovenia	Local	None
South Korea	Local	None
Spain	Local	None
Sweden	Local	None
Switzerland	Localities	None
UK	Local/National	EU citizenship for local elections; Commonwealth citizenship for national elections

(Continued)

Table 2.1. (*Continued*)
Sample of States That Have Enfranchised Resident Aliens

United States	Localities	Municipalities only; previous states' rights rescinded
Uruguay	National	None
Venezuela	Local	None

In the second column, "localities" refers to subnational governments that grant voting rights to resident aliens, while "local" refers to voting rights given by the national government but only for local or regional elections.

A second challenge is that of measuring the voting rights of resident aliens in a given state. Does the typology developed here validly capture the differences in resident-alien voting rights between states? It may not, given a number of states that seem to defy easy classification. For example, Ireland allows resident British nationals to vote in parliamentary elections, and resident aliens of any nationality to vote in local elections. Therefore, Ireland's voting rights include both discriminatory and nondiscriminatory features. Another important question is whether or not the de jure constitutional provisions of some states create de facto rights for resident aliens. The cases of Venezuela and Uruguay most explicitly raise this issue. A related question is the number of resident aliens who actually vote in each state—data that is difficult to find. Despite these concerns, however, the next chapter argues that a ranking of the subject states on the criteria of scope and scale of voting rights is a reasonably valid measure of the national or transnational citizenship practices of a state.

To meet these challenges, this study adopts a time-series cross-section (TSCS) research design. While scholars of citizenship politics have produced a number of valuable and detailed studies, to my knowledge none has conducted a broader cross-section test of the competing explanations for differences in how democracies incorporate their resident aliens. The small sample sizes of these case studies necessarily limit their generality. As Coppedge argues, their "thick concepts and theories are unwieldy in generalizing or rigorously testing complex hypotheses."[104] If scholars of citizenship politics are to build mid-range theories, they need to complement case research with rigorous quantitative comparative analysis. To my knowledge, few researchers have utilized such a research design.[105] Yet such studies tend to obfuscate and oversimplify the richness of citizenship politics. For this reason, this study complements its large-*n* quantitative analysis with case studies of enfranchisement initiatives in Germany, the Netherlands, and Belgium. The quantitative analysis informs these case studies: Chapter 6 illustrates how the findings of the TSCS study can inform our case research.

The surprising number of states that allow resident aliens to vote suggests, however, that such a study is overdue. The next chapter reviews the literature on citizenship and political incorporation to derive hypotheses to explain why some states enfranchise their resident aliens while others do not. Chapter 4 develops the TSCS research design. Rather than conducting a small-n comparison of European democracies or a large-n study of all democracies, this study instead opts to examine over time the policies of twenty-five democracies, a population derived on the basis of their number of resident aliens and their democratic longevity. While the time-series cross-section research design has unique methodological challenges, such a design provides an important complement to the existing body of case study research on the political incorporation of migrants.

The history of suffrage movements shows that citizens and states rarely extend voting rights in the absence of social unrest, war, and agitation by excluded social groups. Alien suffrage has occurred, by contrast, with relatively little violence. This is perhaps the most provocative of the many questions this empirical overview has raised. While the study has posed several questions about the democratic practice of enfranchising aliens, however, so far it has left them unanswered. The next chapter begins a systematic investigation of these questions by deriving hypotheses from the nationalist and transnationalist literature. Informing these hypotheses is a shared commitment to a basic question: Why do states vary in their policies and practices for the incorporation of resident aliens? As this chapter has demonstrated, the variation among those democracies that enfranchise resident aliens is considerable. A key task for nationalists and transnationalists—and by extension this study—is to explain not only the surprising number of states that allow their resident aliens to vote but also the different ways in which they do so.

3

—————

Nationalism and Transnationalism:
Hypotheses on the Political Incorporation of Resident Aliens

Many social scientists have written about the state's political incorporation of its resident aliens. One may broadly categorize their explanations into two schools of thought, the nationalist and the transnationalist theses. These theses differ in their emphasis on domestic versus international and transnational influences of state policies, and in their emphasis on nationality as an explanation for the incorporation opportunities for migrants. Reflecting the heritage of political rights theorists such as T. H. Marshall and Stein Rokkan, nationalist scholars generally give explanatory primacy to factors within the state, from political culture and institutions to contestation between societal groups. As the name suggests, scholars of nationalism argue that conceptions of the "nation" continue to drive the state's organization of its polity and its treatment of resident aliens. Transnationalist scholars offer a corrective to the nationalist thesis by calling attention to international and transnational influences on the state's treatment of resident aliens. Transnationalists argue that intergovernmental treaties and organizations, burgeoning transborder nongovernmental groups, and transnational claims-making by migrants constrain the discretion states have over the ways they incorporate resident aliens. Consequently, transnationalists assert, states have moved away from conceptions of the polity based on the "nation" and toward a more inclusive, multinational polity. They argue emerging institutions for the political incorporation of migrants reflect new transnational norms of inclusion that, broadly, are "postnational." This chapter explores the nationalist and transnationalist theses in greater detail and derives seven hypotheses that may explain why democratic states have chosen to enfranchise their resident aliens.

Nationalism and Transnationalism: An Overview

A number of social scientists draw a distinction between nationalist and transnationalist arguments about the sources of the state's incorporation policies. In his analysis of Canada's policies toward its resident aliens, Galloway makes a distinction between nationalist and "postnationalist/multicultural" politics.[1] Koopmans and Statham break multiculturalism and postnationalism into two distinct categories to identify three models of citizenship politics.[2] Indeed, the tension between national and transnational citizenship practices informs a number of recent surveys of citizenship policies.[3] Yet the frequency with which social scientists throw about the terms "nationalism" and "transnationalism" is a cause for some confusion. Researchers often use the terms to refer to the policies or citizenship practices of a given state. Multinational societies that encourage immigration and have low barriers to naturalization, such as New Zealand, sometimes are called "postnational" democracies. Other researchers (such as Neuman) use the terms "nationalist" and "transnationalist" to refer to bodies of social science scholarship on the causes of state citizenship policies.[4] In this sense, the terms refer to theories rather than state practices. For the purposes of this study, "nationalism" and "transnationalism" refer to two bodies of scholarship rather than to specific state practices. The nationalist and transnationalist theses diverge on two important points: the level of analysis at which each locates the causes of state citizenship policies, and on the implications of state practices for the relationship between the "nation" and the political community. It is important to note, however, that there is considerable crossover between the two bodies of scholarship. Many scholars see a mix of domestic and international sources of state policies, and argue for a nuanced conception of the evolving relationship between the state, the nation, and the body politic. Their work is an important reminder that the nationalist/transnationalist distinction is a continuum rather than a dichotomy.

The Nationalist Thesis

The nationalist thesis argues that the historical relationship between the nation and the state, as manifested in culture, institutions, and practices, principally drives the state's policies for the incorporation of resident aliens. This thesis encompasses arguments by traditional political development scholars like Marshall, Rokkan, and Lipset; collective action theorists like Freeman and Money; and political culture arguments like Brubaker.[5] Marshall argues that states gradually extend political rights to social groups only after these groups gain the civil and legal protections with which to make claims for political participation. To Marshall, enfranchisement thus is the result of claims-making by citizens who enjoy civil but not economic or political rights. By contrast, Rokkan and Lipset reject Marshall's unilinear argument.[6] Instead, they argue European states incorporated social groups at different times due to variations in their state formation histories and their medieval institutional legacies. By this line of reasoning, political rights depend upon each state's unique history of institutional development.

Collective action theorists explain variations in citizenship politics, by contrast, as a product of political institutions and the pulling and hauling among interest groups. Freeman and Money both argue that the tendency of immigrants to reside together creates both pro- and anti-immigration groups within electoral districts.[7] Using this analysis Money explains variations in immigration quotas in Australia, France, and Great Britain. Similarly, Joppke and Aleinikoff both argue that national constitutional regimes and domestic political considerations shape the opportunities for national courts to extend legal protections to resident aliens.[8] Klausen explains differences in the social, economic, and political rights of resident aliens as a product of the state's need to police claimants for welfare benefits.[9] Citizenship policies, therefore, reflect the organizational challenges and institutional constraints that immigrant groups face. This approach argues that migrants are conceptually indistinct from any other interest group, at least in terms of the claims they make on the state.

Political culture is another important influence on citizenship politics. Brubaker, for one, explains the greater rate of naturalization among France's aliens than among those in Germany as the product of different "cultural definitions of citizenry" embedded in competing legal traditions of jus soli in France (citizenship by birth) and jus sanguinis in Germany (citizenship by decent or ancestry).[10] Similarly, Hammar notes the importance of the historical relationship between the nation and state.[11] For example, because in France the state formed before the nation did, Hammar argues, France developed an inclusive, multinational conception of French citizenship. By contrast, because the German nation preceded the centralized state, Germany historically has emphasized an ethnically and linguistically defined, exclusive conception of the nation. Barrington similarly cites the importance of ethnic versus political and national versus multinational conceptions of the state.[12] These arguments show cultural variables not only reflect the historical path of the state's and nation's evolution, they also infuse contemporary understandings of political membership and incorporation.

Though nationalist scholars differ in their emphasis on material, cultural, and institutional variables, they share a commitment to explanations of citizenship politics that understand the political community as a product of the historical relationship between the nation and the state. Just as immigration quotas and naturalization policies reflect unique national cultures, local interest group politics, or state formation histories, then, a nationalist analysis of voting rights for resident aliens would cite these factors to explain the differences among states in voting rights for resident aliens. These factors reinforce the historical linkage between the nation and the state. This hegemony of the "nationalist logic" is apparent in the continued central role of the state in constructing, maintaining, and regulating membership in the polity.[13]

The Transnationalist Thesis

The transnationalist thesis explains state citizenship policies and practices, by contrast, as a product of transnational or global processes that weaken the historical linkage of the nation to the state. The transnationalist thesis also includes a broad range of perspectives, though all share the argument that international and transnational processes transform not only the politics of citizenship within states, but also the authority, capacities, and legitimacy of the state as well. Castles and Davidson summarize the transnationalist thesis well:

> Globalization erodes the autonomy of the nation-state, undermines the ideology of distinct and relatively autonomous cultures, and causes the increasing mobility of people across borders.... These new factors destabilize traditional ways of balancing the contradictions that always beset the nation-state model: the contradiction between the inclusion and exclusion of various groups, between the rights and obligations of citizenship, and—most important—between political belonging as a citizen and political belonging as a national.[14]

Some political theorists argue similarly that the economic, social, and political incorporation of resident aliens reflects a new Kantian cosmopolitanism in which "relations between individuals transcend state boundaries, and in which an order based on relations between states is giving way to order based at least in part on universal laws and institutions."[15] This argument echoes Soysal's thesis that emerging global norms of "universal personhood" have enshrined human rights in international institutions and transformed the sources of civil protections for citizens and resident aliens alike.[16] Rather than states being the guarantors of individual social, economic, and political rights, Soysal argues, states now enact protections and rights codified in international institutions and agreements like the Universal Declaration of Human Rights, the International Covenant on Civil and Political Rights, and the International Labour Organization.[17]

A second important argument of the transnationalist thesis, advanced by scholars such as Hammar and Layton-Henry, is that states have developed institutional alternatives to citizenship to accommodate the large influx of migrant labor that their increasingly global economies require.[18] Hammar discusses "denizen rights," or the body of legal, social, and political rights that permanent foreign residents enjoy in several states in Europe and North America.[19] Castles and Davidson argue that states increasingly have adopted a model of "quasi-citizenship" in which citizens and permanent aliens enjoy nearly identical rights but the state maintains—and even nurtures—symbolic and formal distinctions between citizens and aliens.[20] Similarly, Bauböck talks about "transnational citizenship."[21] While the terminology that Hammar, Castles and Davidson, and Bauböck adopt differs, their arguments are similar: States have pursued innovative alternatives to citizenship to address the democratic contradictions posed by their growing population of resident aliens.

To transnationalist scholars, this emergence of innovative institutions for resident aliens is one of three consequences of these various transnational forces.[22] These institutional innovations include not only voting rights for resident aliens but an emergent international norm supporting "plural nationality"—the practice of individuals holding the citizenship of more than one state.[23] A second consequence, the transnationalist thesis asserts, is that resident aliens and immigrants have changed their strategies for making social, economic, and political claims on the nation-state. Rather than pursuing their needs through the traditional institutions and resources that are available to citizens, resident aliens increasingly make claims by appealing to their "home" states (that is, their states of citizenship) for support, or by appealing to international law and norms. Sassen notes that when immigrants seek redress from national courts, they increasingly cite international law as the basis for their claims.[24] International law has recently recognized, furthermore, the legal standing of individuals and non-governmental organizations (NGOs), enabling them to pursue claims against states in international courts.

This pattern of claims-making by resident aliens results, according to the transnationalist thesis, in a third fundamental change in citizenship politics. The nation-state now faces multiple levels of governance and participation in its making of citizenship and immigration policies. Local governments increasingly adopt policies and practices, for example, that may conflict with the national state's citizenship policies. This may be why several U.S. municipalities allow resident aliens to vote, while some Japanese municipalities have adopted measures that are more liberal than the central government's policies and practices.[25] The nation-state also faces transnational and international actors that increasingly seek to influence its citizenship policies. Barrington argues that European international organizations played a crucial role in the citizenship policies of the Baltic republics during the 1990s, while Kashiwazaki cites the role of international treaty obligations in liberalizing Japanese practices.[26] While states today maintain juridical sovereignty over their political communities, this line of reasoning suggests, they face a new web of constraints both from supranational and subnational actors. Although states may remain the instruments through which resident aliens receive their economic, social, and political rights, this is because:

> International law still protects sovereignty and has the state as its main object, but the state is no longer the only subject in international law. In addition to all its other functions, it becomes an institutional apparatus of a transnational order based on human rights.[27]

State sovereignty thus is being challenged simultaneously from "above" (by international and nongovernmental organizations) and from "below" (by rights activists and immigrants themselves).[28] Increasingly, political communities are constructed through transnational processes rather than through state-centered processes; these multiple levels of participation in the construction of the polity imply both that the historical linkage between the nation and the state has weakened, and that states themselves have less authority.

Voting Rights for Resident Aliens:
Nationalism or Transnationalism?

The state's enfranchisement of resident aliens provides an important test of both the transnationalist and nationalist theses. It is a useful test of the nationalist thesis because it presents an apparently radical redefinition of citizenship and a challenge to the state's exercise of sovereignty over its polity. It is an important test for the transnationalist thesis because the state nevertheless remains the principal institution for the allocation of individual rights and opportunities, particularly for those of aliens. While many transnationalist scholars cite the extension of the vote to resident aliens as evidence of denizen rights or quasi-citizenship, of institutionalized human rights, or of norms of democracy, the variation among the cases raises doubt about the transnationalists' explanations.[29] How can states that face a common set of emerging norms of human rights and democracy adopt such divergent institutions? Likewise, the fact that many of the states that extended resident aliens voting rights did so during the 1960s and 1970s raises the question of whether voting rights preceded both the emergence of global norms and the explosive growth of international organizations and NGOs.

While these observations call into question the expectations of the transnationalist thesis, however, it is also unclear whether the traditional linkages of the nation and the state cited by nationalist scholars can explain the emergence of voting rights for resident aliens. Collective action theorists explain well the delimiting of social and economic rights for resident aliens, but they may not be able to explain cases of expanding the franchise. The historical and institutional variables that Rokkan and Marshall cite seem unable, furthermore, to explain the patterns of enfranchisement of resident aliens.[30] How can states with similar political development such as France and Denmark take different paths to resident alien voting?[31] While cultural and rational choice theorists explain these differences as a consequence of shared understandings of nationhood or of the political geography of migrant settlement, these explanations are not obvious a priori. The practice of enfranchising resident aliens thus challenges both the nationalist and the transnationalist theses.

It is important to note those scholars who are sensitive to both nationalist and transnationalist explanatory variables. At least five studies have used both transnationalist factors and the cultural and institutional variables of the nationalist thesis to explain the state's citizenship practices. Barrington explains variations in the treatment of the Baltic republics' Russian-speaking minorities as a product both of how societies conceive of the nation and of the influence of international organizations.[32] Similarly Laitin's comparison of the incorporation of the "beached diaspora" of Russians in four post-Soviet republics constructs a model that combines individual incentives to assimilate with macro-level factors such as the historical patterns of empire-republic relationships.[33] Kashiwazaki argues that the interplay between Japanese scholars, leaders of resident alien groups, and Japan's accession to international human rights conventions has resulted in the expansion of civil, economic, and political rights of aliens in Japan.[34] Aleinikoff and Klusmeyer explicitly link voting rights for resident aliens to cultural understandings about the meaning of citizenship, reciprocity agreements among states, and supranational political integration in the European Union.[35] These works exhibit considerable sensitivity to the interaction between nationalist and transnationalist factors. Both transnationalist and nationalist scholars recognize, furthermore, a degree of variation among the citizenship politics of nation-states. While some states remain wedded to "differentialist" practices that draw a legal or substantive distinction between citizen and immigrant populations, others have adopted multicultural approaches to citizenship and resident alien incorporation.[36] A central question, therefore, is under what conditions will exclusionary, ethnically-based nationality practices emerge in a nation-state, and under what conditions will inclusive, multinational practices emerge. To date, most scholarship on citizenship has failed to answer this question for two reasons. First, most of the existing research relies upon a single or small number of case studies, making generalizations difficult and highly debatable.[37] Second, much of the scholarship has failed to test systematically the relative influence of domestic, cultural, and international variables side-by-side.[38] The nationalist-transnationalist debate will benefit from a study that tests their competing hypotheses across a larger number of observations.

An analysis of voting rights for resident aliens speaks to more than just the theoretical disagreements between nationalist and transnationalist scholars. The dialogue between these schools of thought has implications for international relations theory's broader understanding of the effects of transnational processes on state sovereignty. Given the ubiquity of globalization theorists today, and the apparent willingness of many to proclaim the transformation if not the "retreat" of the nation-state, the state's policies to construct its political community present a crucial test of the state's hypothesized loss of autonomy.

Hypothesized Causes of Political Incorporation

The nationalist thesis argues that nothing in the recent evolution of citizenship policies represents any change in the meaning of state sovereignty or in the capacities of the nation-state. Because states construct their polity through citizenship policies, they retain both juridical sovereignty over their citizenry and the de facto authority to determine the political, social, and economic rights of their resident alien populations. The transnationalist thesis rejects this line of thinking. Ironically, both the nationalist and the transnationalist theses attribute an important role to the state in the politics of citizenship: as a guardian of national myths of identity, or as an enactor of global norms of inclusion. They differ, however, in their emphasis on the sources of state policies and on the implications of state practices on the historical relationship of the state to the nation. Nationalists see citizenship practices as reinforcing this relationship, while transnationalists see citizenship practices as changing it.

Of course, many states combine elements of nationalist and transnationalist policies and practices. This is true even of voting rights for resident aliens: Rights that discriminate based on nationality arguably reflect a nationalist logic and tradition.[39] Likewise, international organizations may reinforce the power of nationalist logic through "supranational" citizenship policies, such as those of the European Union and the Commonwealth of Nations. An important question, therefore, is under what conditions will the state pursue differentialist instead of assimilationist practices? The literature on citizenship politics offers several important hypotheses about when the state is likely to enfranchise permanent residents, whether or not these rights will discriminate among nationalities of migrants, and when initiatives to enfranchise permanent residents will fail.

Nationalist Hypotheses

The nationalist thesis emphasizes three sources of citizenship practices—cultural, institutional, and geographic. Brubaker's distinction between the legal traditions of jus soli and jus sanguinis is the most important cultural explanation.[40] Likewise, Barrington argues that variations in the immigrant incorporation regimes are due in part to two understandings about the relationship of the nation to the state: whether the nation is ethnically defined or politically defined, and whether the state is culturally defined as a nation-state or a multinational one.[41] Hammar's seminal study also emphasizes the importance of culturally-defined myths about the nation: whether or not the state views the institution of citizenship as membership in the nation, or membership in the state.[42] Together, these understandings about the relationship between the nation and the state have profound consequences for the political incorporation of migrants. In Germany, for example, until 2000 the tradition of jus sanguinis meant that children born on German soil did not automatically receive German citizenship. As a consequence, the political rights of immigrants—or more importantly, the lack thereof—were passed down through the generations. By contrast, Aleinikoff and Klusmeyer argue that because the principle of jus soli allows children of resident aliens to become citizens, voting rights for resident aliens are less imperative in jus soli states.[43]

Germany may be the extreme case. In most states citizenship policies contain a mix of both jus sanguinis and jus soli practices. States with strong traditions of jus soli, like the United States and France, nevertheless often follow the jus sanguinis practice of offering citizenship to children born overseas to their citizens. For cultural scholars, the important question is the degree of historical emphasis on one of the two legal traditions. They argue that jus sanguinis states tend to view immigration as "temporary"; to have higher barriers to naturalization; and to take fewer steps to provide civil, economic, and political rights to resident aliens. States with a jus soli tradition tend by contrast to have easier naturalization regimes, to be receptive to cultural and ethnic differences, and to provide a broader range of rights to resident aliens. One might expect jus soli states to be more likely to offer aliens the right to vote. Conversely, however, Aleinikoff and Klusmeyer suggest that jus sanguinis democracies are more likely to offer voting rights precisely because aliens are less likely to naturalize.[44] To jus sanguinis states, voting rights may be an institutional alternative to naturalization. The distinction between a tradition of jus soli and one of jus sanguinis thus captures important differences in the cultural understandings of the relationship between the nation and the state. It offers an important hypothesis:

Hypothesis 1(a): States with a jus sanguinis tradition are less likely to enfranchise resident aliens than are states with a jus soli tradition.

Nationalist scholars also identify institutional factors to explain variations in the citizenship policies of states. Aleinikoff argues courts tend to be more receptive to immigrants' claims for rights, while legislatures tend to be illiberal in their making of immigration policies.[45] Similarly, Joppke finds the role national courts play in making citizenship policies explains in part why the historical evolution of immigrants' rights has reversed the sequence that Marshall identified.[46] Yet in at least two cases, an activist judiciary has overturned legislation that enfranchised aliens—in the Federal Republic of Germany in 1990 and in Austria in 2004. The role of the judiciary, therefore, is an important hypothesis to test:

> **Hypothesis 1(b):** States with activist courts are more likely to enfranchise resident aliens than states with weak or inactive judiciaries.

The political economy of social welfare also may be an important determinant of the political rights of resident aliens. While many nationalist researchers argue that the civil, social, and political rights of resident aliens tend to be bundled together, Klausen makes a counterintuitive argument about the nature of such rights.[47] She takes a collective action approach to assert that immigrants' rights vary according to the type of rights resident aliens claim: Because social rights are fundamentally a private good, states must police claimants. This naturally makes these goods more exclusive. Thus, expansive social programs ironically may foreclose resident aliens' opportunities for incorporation. In this respect, social rights may be inversely correlated with political rights. Klausen notes that citizenship practices in the Nordic states tended to be exclusionary during the era of the welfare state, but became more inclusive as these states have scaled back social welfare programs during the 1990s. Therefore, the political economy of welfare is a third nationalist hypothesis:

> **Hypothesis 1(c):** States with extensive social welfare programs are more likely to enfranchise resident aliens than are states with fewer social rights.

Several scholars also have highlighted the importance of partisan factors. Hammar, for one, argues that within Europe social democratic parties typically have passed the legislation that enfranchises resident aliens.[48] He argues that parties of the left tend to gain from voting rights for resident aliens while rightist parties lose. Similarly, Howard finds that left-of-center governments typically liberalize the rights of immigrants while right-leaning governments resist the expansion of the rights of immigrants.[49] Joppke similarly argues, "The political left, true to its universalist vocation, generally supports de-ethnicized [nondiscriminatory] citizenship rules, which lower the threshold of citizenship acquisition for immigrants."[50] On at least one occasion, by contrast, a left-leaning government has backed down from its plans to extend aliens the right to vote. In 1981, the Parti Socialiste in France backed down from a campaign promise to enfranchise France's noncitizens.[51] The role of political parties is an important fourth nationalist hypothesis:

> **Hypotheses 1(d):** States in which leftist parties control the government are more likely to enfranchise resident aliens, while states whose governments are controlled by rightist parties are less likely to enact voting rights for resident aliens.

Together, nationalist authors explain variations in citizenship policies and practices as a consequence of immigrant groups articulating their claims for rights through the traditional institutions that tie the nation to the state: the courts, political parties, and social entitlements. The institutions that nationalists cite are the same factors, furthermore, that characterize political contestation among citizens. In this respect, the claims of resident aliens for rights are contested largely in the same manner as the claims of any other societal group.

Transnational Hypotheses

To explain the emergence of voting rights for resident aliens the transnationalist thesis cites the ways in which sending states and transnational factors shape and help redefine the polity of host states. Three relevant factors are the role of sending states' governments in organizing their émigrés for political activity in their host states; the role of global civil society and international NGOs in the advocacy for political rights for minorities and resident aliens; and a host state's commitment to human rights.

It is the hallmark of transnational citizenship politics that the states from which migrants emigrate play an important role in their political organization and interest articulation when they settle abroad. To capture this dynamic, Guarnizo makes an important distinction between "transnationalism from below" and "transnationalism from above."[52] Whereas scholars and politicians alike commonly recognize that immigrants maintain transnational ties to their home domiciles, to their families, and to other transnational networks—that is, transnationalism from below—sending states increasingly seek "to construct a 'deterritorialized' state that will retain the loyalties of emigrants, keep them under political control, and use them to advance sending-state interests."[53] Sending states may seek to maintain émigré loyalty for a variety of reasons, from the financial (the importance of remittances to foreign exchange) to the political (the importance of transnational influence networks in national elections), but the emerging practice is the same: Sending states facilitate their émigrés' political participation in both their host state and their home state.[54] In his analysis of immigrants in the United States, DeSipio for one argues that these practices "seek to reshape the relationship between the sending country and the émigré.... The goal of these policies is to create an interest group in the United States that is sensitive to the needs of the sending country."[55] For this reason, Mexican candidates for national office often campaign in the United States; Dominican political parties even maintain offices in New York City. Similarly, the South Korean government has made voting rights for Korean nationals an important part of its diplomatic relationship with Japan.[56] The Turkish government plays a similar role in the organization of Turkish nationals who reside in Germany.[57]

These forms of transnational political participation result in a number of innovative political institutions for a sending state's émigrés. Both Guarnizo and Ramirez argue, for example, that Mexico adopted dual-citizenship policies in 1997 precisely because it wanted to encourage Mexicans residing in the United States to naturalize there without fear of losing their legal rights or status in Mexico.[58] All these examples suggest a revision to Hirschman's classic formulation: émigré loyalty comes at the price of both exit (migration and return) and voice (political rights both at home and in the host state).[59]

It is less clear what role sending states play in the advocacy for voting rights for resident aliens, but the question merits further investigation. The participation of sending states in the organization of resident aliens may be a necessary but not sufficient condition for the expansion of their political rights. The organizational and advocacy roles of sending states may be ineffective if migrants are geographically dispersed in the host state, or if the host state's judiciary is deferential to the legislature. In this respect, the role of sending states may interact with the geographic and institutional variables identified by the nationalist thesis.

Sending states may not organize their émigré populations, furthermore, if they have no financial or political incentive to do so. Guarnizo notes that the Dominican Republic works to aid

Dominican expatriates in the United States largely because Dominican parties compete for their absentee votes.[60] Without a competitive party system, contested elections, or absentee ballots, sending states may provide little or no aid to their emigrants abroad. The political institutions of sending states, thus, may affect the likelihood of voting rights in host states.

An important hypothesis, therefore, is that the participation of the sending state in the political organization of migrants will predict the citizenship policies of the host state. It is extremely difficult, however, to derive meaningful measures of transnational influences among host and sending states. Much of the problem arises from differences among democracies in how they enumerate their populations of resident aliens. The democracies of this study vary considerably in how they define and count their populations of resident aliens.[61] Without comparable measures, it is difficult if not impossible to identify which sending states may participate in the political organization of migrants. Should one examine transnational patterns between foreign citizens and their sending states, foreign-born individuals and their states of birth, or between immigrants and their states of citizenship? Should one examine all sending states, or only those that send the most individuals (be they foreign citizens, foreign-born, migrants, or some other ethno-national group)? For a large-n study such as this one, the challenge of identifying a valid and reliable measure of the transnational organization of migrants group is considerable.

This book chooses instead to explore the relationship between geography and the voting rights of resident aliens. It assumes that one may find evidence of the transnational organization of migrants by looking at the practices of a democracy's neighbors. A simple fact of migration is that resident aliens are more likely to come from nearby states than from those far away. Likewise, nearby states have fewer barriers to organizing their émigré communities in a given democracy than do those sending states that are located on other continents. Mexico presumably has had more success organizing its expatriates in the United States than has Indonesia, for example. To explore transnationalism, therefore, one may hypothesize that the practices of neighboring states will be a significant predictor of the practices in a given democracy:

Hypothesis 2(a): States that border on other states that enfranchise resident aliens are more likely to extend voting rights to aliens. States

that do not border on other states that enfranchise aliens are less likely
to do so.

The transnationalist thesis argues that international organizations
play an important role both in constraining states' citizenship policies
and in expanding the social, economic, and political opportunities for
resident aliens. Both governmental and non-governmental international organizations take interest in states' citizenship policies precisely because these policies can have international consequences:
They can lead not only to civil strife and to subsequent refugee flows,
they can also lead to tensions between states and to territorial divisions. IGOs and NGOs, therefore, play an important role in moder-
ating those citizenship policies and practices that may exclude
minorities and resident aliens. Barrington argues that the Council of
Europe, the Conference for Security and Cooperation in Europe
(later the Organization for Security and Cooperation in Europe), and
Helsinki Watch played important roles in shaping the citizenship
policies of the newly independent Baltic republics.[62] He argues that
these bodies not only kept Latvia's and Estonia's policies from being
more discriminatory than they otherwise would have been, but also
that the Council of Europe became an advocate for local voting rights
for Estonia's Russian-speaking resident aliens. Likewise, Kashiwazaki
argues that Japanese accession to UN conventions on human and
minority rights caused it to reform its citizenship laws and to accept a
growing number of refugees from Indochina.[63] Sassen argues that
instruments of the international human rights regime such as the
Universal Declaration of Human Rights not only enable individuals
and NGOs to seek legal recourse in international courts against
nation-states, they also provide national courts with the legal basis to
challenge or change domestic citizenship laws.[64] Even the United
States Supreme Court increasingly has referred to international law
in its immigration law decisions; this practice of comparative consti-
tutionalism appears to be a growing feature of the Court's decisions.[65]
Soysal similarly argues that emerging global norms of "personhood"
constrain the freedom of states to treat resident aliens differently than
they treat citizens.[66] Of course, states may create de jure social, economic, and political rights for resident aliens that lack substance;
Martiniello contends this is precisely the case with local voting rights
for EU nationals.[67] Yet even the enactment of symbolic rights can
"break with the dogma that the franchise must be strictly tied to
national citizenship."[68] In this respect, even symbolic voting rights

demonstrate the importance of international organizations, norms of human rights, or norms of democracy. Empowered by these norms and international legal conventions that give them standing, international and transnational organizations increasingly have asserted their influence over the state's policies and practices for the incorporation of resident aliens.

> **Hypothesis 2(b):** States that are committed to international human rights institutions are more likely to allow substantive voting rights for resident aliens. States that do not commit to international human rights institutions are less likely to enact voting rights for resident aliens.

> **Hypothesis 2(c):** States that are permeated by NGOs are more likely to allow substantive voting rights for resident aliens. States that are less receptive to NGOs are less likely to enact voting rights for resident aliens.

Because the variables identified by transnationalist scholars are located in the relations between states and transnational processes, one might expect that states will increasingly converge around a set of common practices toward citizens and resident aliens. Indeed, the importance of emerging international norms and practices has led transnationalist scholars to argue that plural nationality is becoming an accepted norm of citizenship, and that political rights increasingly are grounded in residency, "membership in the polity," or "personhood" rather than citizenship or nationality.[69] While the state may remain the locus of the enactment and disbursement of rights of resident aliens, its policies increasingly reflect the claims-making of transnational actors within its borders, the requirements of international governmental and non-governmental organizations, and emerging international human rights norms. At the extreme, these processes may reverse the historical relationship between the nation and the state; rather than the state constructing the nation through citizenship policies, a polyglot, transnational polity reconstructs an inclusive, postnational state.

Conclusion: Convergence or Heterogeneity?

By locating the sources of state policies in the international system, the transnationalist thesis argues states face a common set of causal factors. This implies an important expectation: States will converge around a common practice. This "convergence hypothesis" is one crucial test of the transnationalist hypothesis, particularly since the empirical overview of chapter 2 suggests not only considerable heterogeneity between states that have and have not enfranchised their resident aliens, but also variation in the scope and scale of rights among those states that do allow resident aliens to vote. This variation among the cases suggests the transnationalist hypotheses derived in this chapter may tell only part of the story. The very fact that states have enfranchised resident aliens challenges, however, the expectations of the nationalist thesis. Why has nationalist logic prevailed in some states but not in others? Thus, voting rights for resident aliens are an important test for both the nationalist and transnationalist theses.

While these hypotheses are not an exhaustive list of the possible explanations for why states enfranchise resident aliens, they locate possible causes in a diverse set of political practices. These include political culture, interest group contestation, legislative and judicial institutions of the state, the international human rights regime, NGOs, and even in the relations between democracies that send migrants and those that receive them. In this respect, the nationalist and transnationalist theses locate explanations in a continuum from state-level to system-level variables. Unlike most previous analyses of the rights of resident aliens, this study explicitly tests systemic and state-level factors within the same model. The next chapter develops the population of states for this study as well as the measures with which to test the nationalist and transnationalist hypotheses.

4

___

Study Population, Measures, and Estimation Strategy

Because the transnationalist thesis emphasizes the significance of systemic and transnational factors, an important question is whether or not their explanations obtain across a broad range of democratic states. Likewise, the transnationalist emphasis on the growth of international instruments of human rights and of global civil society suggests that since these factors have grown during the era of globalization, we should observe changes over time in the ways in which states incorporate their resident aliens over the last half century. Surprisingly, however, transnationalist researchers so far have eschewed studies that test their arguments across either a broad population of democracies or over time, as have nationalist researchers. One goal of this book, therefore, is to use a research design that tests broadly the systemic and dynamic explanations offered by transnationalist researchers.

To do so, this study uses a time-series cross-section (TSCS) research design to test the hypotheses developed in the previous chapter. This chapter identifies the population of democracies for the study, develops the study's dependent variables, and identifies measures for the nationalist and transnationalist hypotheses. The chapter also elaborates the functional forms of the models used to test these hypotheses and delineates the methods used to specify the models. Chapter 5 analyzes the findings and discusses their implication for the debate between the nationalist and transnationalist theses.

Population of the Study

This study looks at a large population of democracies to test the generalizability of the transnationalist and nationalist arguments. It

65

chooses as its population those established democracies that have significant populations of migrants. For two important reasons, this study looks only at established democracies rather than a population that includes newer, transitional democracies. First, transitional democracies may yet restrict political rights and civil liberties. It is an irony of political development that democratic reversals may result from the sudden universalization of rights in transitional democracies. Rokkan, for one, argues that historically, states that have undertaken the sudden universalization of voting rights have suffered from frequent reversals of democratic rights.[1] Second, it is arguably not valid to compare the political incorporation of migrants in transitional democracies to that in established democracies. Since citizens themselves have only begun to enjoy democratic rights in these transitional states, it is disingenuous to investigate whether or not these states offer political rights to resident aliens as well. The very fact that voting rights are relatively novel in many transitional states raises serious questions about the validity of comparing these states to democracies with well-developed institutions, practices, and civil societies. While normatively important and theoretically interesting, the political incorporation of resident aliens may be of less importance to the governments of emerging democracies than is the consolidation of institutions, the nurturing of democratic values and civil society, and the prevention of autocratic revanchism. The political rights of migrants are thus a fine-grained feature of democracy. Inclusion of emerging democracies in the study would risk conflating democracies with substantially different histories of political development and institutions for the incorporation of their migrant populations. One may safely assume that transitional democracies are less likely to enfranchise aliens, given their nascent civil societies and the challenges of consolidating the rights of their citizens. For these reasons, this study defines its population as the community of established democracies with significant populations of resident aliens.

How does one distinguish between "emerging" and "established" democratic states? Surprisingly there is no consensus among those political scientists who study democratic transitions. However, one commonly employed measure is the Gastil index, a combined measure of a state's political rights and civil liberties that Freedom House has measured for each state since 1972–1973.[2] For example, Norris defines a "democracy" as a state with a Gastil political rights score of 4 or less at the time of her study.[3] Norris's measure does not suffice for this study, however, for two reasons. First, it ignores the civil liberties component of the Gastil index, which may skew the sample.

For example, since 1990 Ethiopia, Jordan, Kuwait, and Liberia (among others) each scored less than 4 on the political rights index at least once—and hence are democracies by Norris's criterion—but never scored less than 4 on the civil liberties index. Second, Norris's practice of using a state's political rights score only for a given year fails to account for whether or not the state has experienced a recent regime change or a sudden increase or decline in rights and liberties. "Snapshot" measures of democracy do not capture whether democratic rights and liberties have existed over time, and thus fail to distinguish between transitional and established democratic states. It is possible, for example, for a state to be coded a "democracy" one year but not the next—indeed, by Norris's criterion Cambodia and Indonesia were democracies for a year during the 1990s. Thus, the practice of using single-year scores on only the political rights component of the Gastil index is neither valid nor reliable: It fails to discern both democracies from non-democracies and emerging from established democratic states.

This study uses two alternative criteria to define the population of established democracies. Rather than relying on single-year scores, it uses composite ten-year scores for both the Gastil index and the POLITY scores recorded in the Polity IV dataset.[4] Like the Gastil index, the Polity IV dataset measures the democratic properties of each state, but uses more refined measures of democratic institutions.[5] An "established" democracy may be defined as a state that has scored either (a) 4 or less on the combined Gastil indices for every year from 1990 to 1999 inclusive; or (b) 9 or 10 on the POLITY variable for every year from 1991 to 2000 inclusive without a change in regime.[6] This requirement follows Lijphart's selection of democracies based on continuous democratic practice and durable institutions, though the ten-year criterion of this study is less rigorous than the nineteen-year criterion Lijphart uses.[7] Forty-three democracies satisfy either the Gastil or the POLITY criterion.

Included among these democracies are a number of states that have relatively small populations and may be geographically isolated (such as the island nations of the Pacific). Diamond, who defines small democracies as those with populations of fewer than one million, argues these "microstates have little scope to influence the direction of many other countries."[8] Norris similarly excludes democracies with fewer than three million citizens.[9] This study splits the difference between Diamond and Norris, and restricts the population of the study to those democracies with greater than two million citizens. Using the population figures for 2000 from the United Nations

Population Division, twenty-eight of the forty-three established democracies have populations of two million or more.[10]

Of these twenty-eight democracies, three have insignificant populations of migrants. One may define a "significant" population of migrants as (a) one million or more resident aliens, or (b) a population of migrants greater than or equal to 1 percent of the state's total population, based on the United Nations' 2002 population data. Three states—Bolivia, Jamaica, and Papua New Guinea—are thus excluded from the population of established democracies. This results in a population of twenty-five established and large democracies that have experienced significant immigration. Table 4.1 lists these states. In 2000, more than 60 percent of the world's migrants who resided in democratic states lived in these twenty-five countries.[11]

It is important to note that, as defined, this population excludes a number of states with sizeable populations of migrants. Argentina, India, Pakistan, Poland, the Republic of Korea, Russia, South Africa, Turkey, and Ukraine each host migrant populations greater than one million, but do not consistently score high enough on either the Gastil index or the POLITY score to qualify as "established" democracies. Likewise, some democracies have migrant populations that are a large percentage of their overall population, but either have fewer than two million citizens (for example, Luxembourg and Estonia) or are transitional democracies (Latvia, Lithuania, and Kyrgyzstan). This population excludes, furthermore, three states that currently enfranchise at least some resident aliens. Iceland has fewer than one million citizens, Venezuela is a transitional democracy, and Colombia's resident migrants are less than 1 percent of its total population.

One might argue these selection criteria favor nationalist explanations, since transitional democracies are precisely those states that are most responsive to the pressures of international organizations. These transitional states may actively solicit advice and support from international organizations or international NGOs as they develop their democratic institutions. If so, by focusing only on consolidated democracies the study is likely to find support only for the domestic factors that the nationalist thesis identifies. Yet one could make an opposite argument as well: The large number of European Union democracies in the population (fifteen of the twenty-five states are EU members) favors transnationalist expectations. One might expect EU democracies to exhibit greater sensitivity to the systemic and transnational pressures emphasized in transnationalist arguments, not only because these states have subordinated areas of sovereignty to EU institutions, but also because these democracies are home to large, mobile, politically assertive communities of resident aliens who are likely to organize themselves transnationally. In the end, the decision to exclude transitional democracies is a reasonable one that favors neither one set of arguments or the other. As discussed below, furthermore, the study includes a variable for EU membership to assess the impact of transnationalist factors independent of European Union effects. For these reasons, the twenty-five democracies in the study's population represent a fair test of nationalist and transnationalist arguments.

Table 4.1. Population of the Study

Australia	Italy
Austria	*Japan*
Belgium	Netherlands
Canada	New Zealand
Costa Rica	Norway
Denmark	Portugal
Finland	Spain
France	Sweden
Germany	Switzerland
Greece	United Kingdom
Hungary	United States
Ireland	Uruguay
Israel	

States that had no voting rights for resident aliens between 1960 and 2004 are listed in italics.

Dependent Variables: Voting Rights for Resident Aliens

The voting rights for the resident aliens of the states in the study vary widely in both their scale and scope. As noted in chapter 2, the "scope" of these rights refers to the size of the resident alien population to which the state extends voting rights. Some states allow all resident aliens to vote while others extend rights only to aliens of specific nationalities. In other words, the scope characterizes the discriminatory nature of the voting rights. The "scale" of these rights refers to the types of elections in which resident aliens can vote, from local or municipal elections to parliamentary elections. This study operationalizes one measure of voting rights for resident aliens as an ordinal dependent variable categorized according to the scope and scale of rights.

This typology distinguishes six possible categories of the ordinal dependent variable: (0) the state does not enfranchise resident aliens; (1) only municipalities or local governments, but not the national government, offer the franchise to resident aliens; (2) the state has discriminatory voting rights for local elections only, but granted by the national government and hence a nationwide right; (3) discriminatory voting rights for national elections; (4) nondiscriminatory rights for local elections; and (5) nondiscriminatory rights for national elections. One may order these rights according to, first, the number of number of resident aliens who receive the franchise, and second, the degree to which the state "unbundles" voting rights. One feature of voting rights for resident aliens is that some democracies have restricted the practice to voting in local elections only. These states have effectively unpacked the right to vote into distinct subsets of rights—the right to vote in local elections is not the same as the right to vote in national elections. In other words, states conceive of the franchise as a body of rights rather than a single right. One way to order observations of the dependent variable, therefore, is to determine whether or not an alien has the full body of voting rights, or only some unbundled element of it.

For these reasons, discriminatory rights for national elections rank as a lower order than nondiscriminatory rights for local elections, since the later enfranchises a greater number of resident aliens. Nondiscriminatory rights also reflect what Joppke calls the "de-ethnicization" of rights for immigrants from groups outside narrow constructions of cultural, ethnic, linguistic, or religious similarity.[12] Of course, one might argue that voting rights in parliamentary elections, even if those rights discriminate in favor of specific nationalities, may have a greater influence on national politics and hence one should rank them higher than nondiscriminatory local rights. In other words, one might argue orders three and four should be reversed. Discriminatory rights reflect a broader nationalist logic, however, because the rights are contingent upon the resident's nationality while nondiscriminatory rights reflect the inclusive norms of transnationalism. In this sense, the ordinal measures are ranked not just according to the number of resident aliens who are enfranchised but also according to their relative emphasis on attributes of national identity, ethnicity, or language as a qualification for the franchise. In this way, the proposed ordering of the dependent variable seeks to capture a spectrum from differentialist to inclusive practices in order to test the competing nationalist and transnationalist hypotheses.

Of the twenty-five states in this study, currently two have no voting rights for resident aliens (category 0). In three federal states (Canada, Switzerland, and the United States), the national government offers no political rights for resident aliens, but local or sub-federal governments have enfranchised aliens (category 1). Three Nordic states (Finland, Norway, and Denmark) originally offered local voting rights only to other Nordic citizens. These, therefore, are cases of discriminatory local rights. Likewise, since the Treaty of Maastricht in 1993, all EU member states have had discriminatory voting rights for local elections (category 2). Five states have had discriminatory national rights (Ireland, the United Kingdom, Australia, Canada, and Portugal), though Australia and Canada have since rescinded their national voting rights (category 3). Today, Belgium, Denmark, Finland, Hungary, the Netherlands, Norway, Spain, and Sweden have nondiscriminatory local voting rights (category 4).[13] Two states, New Zealand and Uruguay, currently offer nondiscriminatory national voting rights for resident aliens (category 5).[14] Table 4.2 lists the observed cases against the six categories of the dependent variable.

Since the type of voting rights may not be inherently ordinal, the study estimates a second model with a binary dependent variable. This dependent variable measures whether a democratic state has some voting rights for its resident aliens or none at all. This measure presents an additional problem, however. How should one code those states like Switzerland in which the national government does not extend rights but one or more local governments do (that is, measure 1 of the ordered dependent variable)? To assure valid comparisons across the study's population, these states are coded as having no voting rights for resident aliens. Therefore, the binary variable tests whether or not a state's national government grants voting rights to resident aliens.[15] This second measure of the dependent variable thus allows the study to test for the sensitivity of the model to different measures of the dependent variable, and avoids problems raised by the few democracies in which only localities allow resident aliens to vote.

Measures for the Independent Variables

To test nationalist versus transnationalist explanations for voting rights for resident aliens, the study derives measures of the independent variables for this study from the four nationalist and three transnationalist hypotheses developed in chapter 3.

Table 4.2. The Subject States, as Ranked by the Ordered Dependent Variable

Nondiscriminatory Rights, from National Government

4. To Vote in Local Elections	*5. To Vote in National Elections*
Belgium (2004 to present)	New Zealand (1975 to present)
Denmark (1981 to present)	Uruguay (1991 to present)
Finland (1991 to present)	
Hungary (1991 to present)	
Ireland (1963 to 1984)	
Netherlands (1982 to present)	
Norway (1982 to present)	
Spain (1985 to present)	
Sweden (1976 to present)	

Discriminatory Rights, from National Government

2. To Vote in Local Elections	*3. To Vote in National Elections*
Austria (1996 to present)	Australia (until 1984)
Belgium (1994 to 2003)	Canada (until 1974)
Denmark (1977 to 1980)	Ireland (1984 to present)
Finland (1981 to 1990)	New Zealand (until 1975)
France (1994 to present)	Portugal (1976 to present)
Germany (1994 to present)	United Kingdom
Greece (1994 to present)	
Israel (1950 to present)	
Italy (1994 to present)	
Norway (1978 to 1981)	

Rights from Local Governments

1. To Vote in Local Elections
Canada (1975 to present)
Germany (1989)
Netherlands (1979 to 1981)
Switzerland (1849 to present)
United States (1968 to present)

No Rights

0. No Rights	
Australia (1984 to present)	Italy (before 1994)
Austria (before 1996)	Japan
Belgium (before 1994)	Netherlands (before 1979)
Costa Rica	Norway (before 1978)
Finland (before 1981)	Spain (1978 to 1984)
France (before 1994)	Sweden (before 1976)
Germany (before 1989, 1990 to 1994)	United States (circa 1920 to 1968)
Greece (before 1994)	

Numerals for each category are the ordinal ranking of the group of observations. Dates in parentheses next to state names are the dates during which the state belonged to that category.

Nationalist Hypotheses

Nationalist explanations emphasize the importance of historical traditions of citizenship, state institutions, welfare policies and enforcement, and the influence of parties within governments. Each of these hypotheses reflects a "nationalist" logic because they identify processes that reinforce a group identity and shared understanding of the "nation" based upon shared ethnicity, language, religion, history, or locality.

Birthright Citizenship: Hammar, Brubaker, Neuman, and Barrington each argue that the state's political incorporation of migrants depends in part upon cultural understandings of the relationship between the nation and the state.[16] Brubaker argues that a state's citizenship policies embody these understandings through the legal doctrines of jus sanguinis (citizenship by blood) and jus soli (citizenship by birth). States of the jus sanguinis tradition generally do not grant citizenship to the children of resident aliens, resulting in an exclusion from political rights that is passed down through generations of resident aliens. Because jus soli states offer citizenship to the children of resident aliens, by contrast, those states tend to have more expansive incorporation regimes than jus sanguinis states. Hypothesis 1(a) captures this argument.

While many states combine aspects of both jus soli and jus sanguinis laws and practices, for the purposes of testing nationalist versus transnationalist hypotheses the important question is the state's relative emphasis on jus sanguinis versus jus soli practices. Adams proposes distinguishing between states strictly based on whether or not the state grants birthright citizenship to children of resident aliens.[17] Following her method, this study operationalizes this hypothesis as a binary variable. States that grant citizenship to children born to resident aliens are coded as 1; states that do not are scored a 0. In the event a state offers birthright citizenship but requires one parent to have citizenship, the state is coded a zero. Likewise, states that offer birthright citizenship only to third-generation children of resident aliens are coded as a zero. Adams, Kondo, and Weil offer the best information on birthright citizenship; their work covers twenty-two of the twenty-five states in the study.[18] For Hungary, the study relies upon Nagy's discussion, which notes that the government offers birthright citizenship only to stateless children.[19] Hungary thus is coded it as a 0. Both Costa Rica and Uruguay are coded as allowing birthright citizenship based on the author's reading of their constitutions.[20]

Nationalist scholars have noted that jus soli states typically have offered a broader range of rights and opportunities to their resident aliens than jus sanguinis states have. Likewise, Brubaker notes that jus soli states typically have higher naturalization rates than jus sanguinis states.[21] These findings give rise to opposite expectations about the effect of birthright citizenship on the voting rights of resident aliens. One might expect that jus soli states are more likely to extend voting rights to resident aliens. A counterintuitive argument, however, is that jus sanguinis states may use "denizen rights" (in Hammar's memorable term) like limited voting rights to incorporate aliens without extending to them the full body of citizenship rights. Voting rights may represent, in other words, a procedural and substantive alternative to naturalization. Aleinikoff and Klusmeyer suggest, for one, that because jus sanguinis states offer fewer opportunities for naturalization, they may be more likely to offer the franchise to resident aliens, not less so.[22] Thus one might expect them to be more likely to enfranchise their resident aliens. The study tests both of these expectations. Statistically, one would expect a significant and positively signed coefficient if indeed jus soli states are more likely to enfranchise aliens; a significant and negative coefficient would be consistent with Aleinikoff and Klusmeyer's suggestion that jus sanguinis states may be more likely to extend voting rights to resident aliens.

Judiciary versus Legislature: Hypothesis 1(b) asserts that states in which national courts are traditionally deferential to the legislature are less likely to enfranchise resident aliens. Therefore, the role of the judiciary may have profound impact on the political rights that resident aliens may or may not enjoy. Differing national judicial and legislative institutions, histories, and immigration law make problematic any cross-sectional comparisons of judicial and legislative approaches to immigration policy. A research design that traces the evolutions of citizenship laws in twenty-five states also faces considerable research costs. This project consequently uses an alternative measure that is both less costly and more generalizable, if less detailed about specific migration policies. Lijphart's index of judicial review measures the strength of the judicial review in twenty-three of the study's states based upon, first, the presence or absence of judicial review and, second, three degrees of the courts' activism in asserting authority over legislative matters, with higher values indicating greater activism.[23] Lijphart's data covers the judicial activism in the twenty-three states from 1945 to 1996. For 1997 to 2004, I assign each state the judicial activism scores they received in 1996.

For the two states of this study not included in Lijphart's analysis (Hungary and Uruguay), the study replicates his methodology. Fortunately, both states are easily coded. Of Hungary's constitutional courts, Howard writes:

> Because of its legal tradition, Hungary has a considerable advantage among the countries of Central and Eastern Europe. The Hungarian court is strikingly active and "has in fact been characterized as the most powerful constitutional court in the world."[24]

Likewise, Utter and Lundsgaard find Hungary's constitutional court to be similar in design and activism to Austria's constitutional court, a judiciary that Lijphart scores as a 3.[25] On these grounds, Hungary is coded as having an active constitutional court, or a 3 on Lijphart's scale. While Uruguay has a de jure constitutional court, by contrast, it is largely unassertive and ineffective. Skaar explains the failure to prosecute human rights violations in Uruguay as incomplete judicial reform.[26] For this reason, Uruguay is scored as having no effective judicial review (a 1 on Lijphart's scale).

Because nationalist scholars have noted the activism of courts in the extension of civil and economic rights to migrants, one might expect that states with activist judiciaries are more likely to enfranchise their aliens. There are good reasons to suspect, however, that the opposite expectation may also hold. For one, issue areas may matter: Judiciaries may be more deferential to legislatures on the political incorporation of migrants than they have been on issues of civil and economic rights. For another, activist judiciaries are not necessarily progressive ones: They may use judicial review to enforce conservative conceptions of nationality. Consequently, while nationalist scholars expect activist judicial review to correlate positively with the voting rights of resident aliens, the study tests the opposite expectation as well. Statistically, one would expect a positively signed coefficient if activist courts expand the voting rights of aliens; a negatively signed coefficient would indicate activist courts delimit these rights.

Welfare Spending: Hypothesis 1(c) relates the rights of resident aliens to the state's welfare policies. A number of nationalist scholars have argued that democracies tend to bundle social, economic, and political rights together: That is, states that offer civil and social protections to aliens are more likely to offer them political rights as well. By contrast, Klausen has argued that a state's social spending is inversely related to the incorporation opportunities that the state offers to resident aliens.[27] Are democracies with extensive social welfare programs more or less likely to enfranchise their resident aliens? To test this hypothesis, the study measures the state's welfare spending for each year from 1960 to 2004. Huber, Ragin, and Stephens offer several different measures of welfare spending; one is social security transfers as a percentage of gross domestic product.[28] Because this measure traces spending as a percentage of GDP, it allows easier comparison both across subjects and over time without having to correct for inflationary effects. Thus this measure is most useful in a TSCS study. Huber, Ragin, and Stephens' dataset covers twenty-three of the twenty-five from 1960 to 2004.[29] For the remaining two states, the study follows Huber, Ragin, and Stephens' methodology and constructs the social spending data from the International Labour Office's annual *World Labor Report*.[30] The ILO has not published the *Report* in recent years, however. Consequently, the study relies on data from the Organization for Economic Cooperation and Development, the European Commission, and the International Monetary Fund for observations between 2001 and 2004.[31] The study uses a linear interpolation routine to impute values for missing yearly observations for each subject state.[32]

Partisan Composition of Government: Hypothesis 1(d) seeks to test whether differences between left- and right-leaning parties explain why states enfranchise resident aliens. One can use Blais, Blake, and Dion's proposed measure of the partisan composition of governments to test these expectations. They suggest measuring the difference between the percentage of cabinet seats held by parties of the left and those held by parties of the right.[33] The study uses left-right coding of parties and governments compiled by Armingeon et al., who use Blais, Blake, and Dion's measure for twenty-one of the twenty-five states in the study (all except Costa Rica, Hungary, Israel, and Uruguay).[34] For the remaining four states, the study relies on party composition of government data from Beck et al., who code observations through 2000.[35] This provides coverage for all states and all years in the study except for Israel from 1960 to 1974 and for Costa Rica, Hungary, and Uruguay since 2000. Woldendorp, Keman, and Budge's provide scores for the composition of the Israeli government during these years, which one can normalize to the Blais, Blake, and Dion scale.[36] For years subsequent to 2000, the study replicates Blais, Blake, and Dion's methodology using government cabinet data from official sources.[37]

Positive scores on Blais, Blake, and Dion's scale indicate a cabinet composition favoring parties of the left, while negative scores indicate a composition favoring parties of the right. A finding of significance and a positive coefficient would support the expectation that left-leaning parties are more likely to enfranchise resident aliens.

Transnational Hypotheses

The transnationalist thesis emphasizes the influence of international factors and transnational actors on the opportunities for incorporation resident aliens have. These include the roles of international governmental and non-governmental organizations as advocates for the political rights of resident aliens; a state's commitment to human rights; and the participation of sending states in the organization of the political activity of their migrants in host states.

Neighborhood Effects and Transnational Organization: Guarnizo coined the phrase "transnationalism from above" to capture the practice of sending states maintaining and nurturing ties to their emigrants.[38] Though he argues that states do this to maintain the loyalties of emigrants and to use them to advance their interests, one consequence is that sending states advocate to host states greater opportunities for social, economic, and political rights for resident aliens.[39] For these reasons, the domestic politics of sending states may have an impact on the organization of migrant groups in host states. Finally, remittances from migrants may be an important economic incentive for sending states to participate in the political organization of their migrants. Hypothesis 2(a) captures these arguments.

How does one measure these transnational factors? The number of source states for migrants in the states in this study is conceivably large and prohibitive. Since each state in this study's population likely has resident aliens from numerous sending states, there are considerable research costs to investigating whether or not each sending state has organized migrant groups in each subject state. The inquiry is complicated, furthermore, by the fact that the study's observations are host states, but this variable conceptually measures attributes of sending states. Host states differ widely, furthermore, in how they report their populations of aliens. The standards democracies use to enumerate and report their resident aliens have changed over time as well.[40] Reliable measures of "aliens" thus are unavailable for a TSCS study. For the purposes of this study, one cannot easily measure the transnational organization and advocacy of migrant groups by analyzing the demographic composition of each democracy's population of resident aliens.

It is equally difficult, furthermore, to measure directly the efforts of sending states to organize migrants in each of the twenty-five states in the study. One technique researchers have employed is to measure the incentives for sending states to organize their migrants rather than their actual efforts. For example, several scholars cite the growing importance of remittances to national economies as one reason why sending states may become advocates for the rights of their overseas citizens.[41] Unfortunately, the data on remittances suffer from problems of validity and reliability, particularly in a TSCS study. The International Monetary Fund's *Balance of Payments Statistics Yearbook* reports remittance outflows from each state, but the data is unreliable for two reasons.[42] First, because the IMF relies upon states to report their data, the *Yearbook* contains no data for states (including Australia and the United Kingdom) that do not report remittance flows to the IMF. Second, since 1960 the IMF has changed several times its recommended methods of accounting for remittances.[43] Therefore, the data on remittances is unreliable both across the democracies in this study and over time.

These practical research limits require the study to make assumptions about which sending state or states to examine for each host state in the study's population. To simplify the analysis, one may assume that these transnational factors arise among states that are geographically proximate. This is a reasonable assumption: Resident aliens are more likely to have emigrated from states that are nearby than ones that are distant. Likewise, if transnational advocacy for migrant rights is important, then states' practices should be correlated: What a democracy chooses to do should predict the practices of its neighbors. For these reasons, the study uses a measure of the effects of neighboring countries proposed by Beck.[44] He suggests measuring the spatial relationships among subject states in cross-sectional studies by using a variable that is the mean score of the dependent variable for each state that borders a subject state. Thus, for Germany, for example, its score on this neighborhood variable is the mean score in a given year of the nine states that border it (the Netherlands, Belgium, Luxembourg, France, Switzerland, Austria, the Czech Republic, Poland, and Denmark). Since it is likely that transnational networks influence states over time, the analysis lags this neighborhood effects variable one year.[45] Though this variable does not directly measure transnational organizations and advocacy per se, it has both lower research costs and greater reliability for this study's TSCS design.

The Influence of IGOs and NGOs: Several scholars argue that international and non-governmental organizations influence state policies toward resident aliens. Hypotheses 2(b) and 2(c) suggest that transnational processes transform the meaning and practice of the state's sovereignty over its political community.

There are two measures to capture the influence of treaties, IGOs and NGOs. The first is an ordinal measure of each state's commitment to relevant international treaties and agreements on human rights and the rights of migrants. Soysal singles out several relevant agreements: the Universal Declaration of Human Rights (UDHR), the International Convention on Civil and Political Rights (ICCPR), and the European Convention on Human Rights.[46] Sassen cites UN resolution 45/158, the International Convention on the Protection of the Rights of All Migrant Workers and Their Families.[47] Sikkink identifies several relevant agreements and NGOs, including the UN Commission on Human Rights, the Inter-American Convention on Human Rights, Amnesty International, and the Ford Foundation.[48] For simplicity, the analysis focuses on three prominent institutions: the ICCPR, the International Covenant on Economic, Social, and Cultural Rights (or ICESR), and the respective regional agreements, such as the Inter-American Convention on Human Rights, that seek to protect the rights of migrants. Following Simmons's method, the study constructs a variable that scores each state according to whether or not it has ratified the ICCPR, the ICESR, or the appropriate regional human rights agreement.[49] The analysis follows Simmons's technique of assigning each state a score of 0 if it has taken no action on a specific instrument, +1 if it has signed but not ratified the instrument, and +2 if it has signed and ratified the instrument. This variable thus ranges from 0 to 6 with 0 indicating the state has acceded to no relevant covenants, and 6 representing full ratification of all three instruments. By measuring the commitment to international human rights of each state for each year in the study, one can measure the degree to which the growth of the international human rights regime has influenced the state's policies toward the political incorporation of resident aliens. Figure 4.1 presents the commitment of the states in this study to the international human rights regime by plotting the mean and median scores of this variable for the study's population for each year from 1960 to 2004.

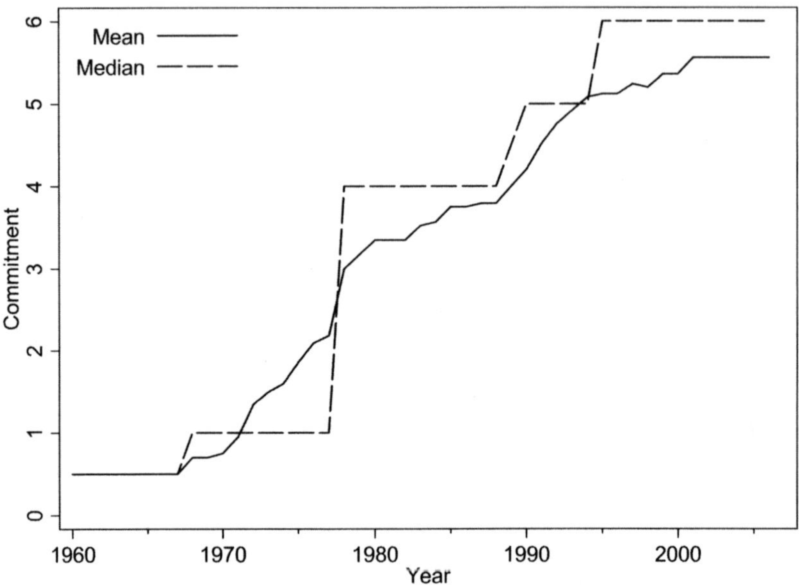

Figure 4.1. Mean and median values of the commitment to human rights for the study's population, 1960 to 2004.

Undoubtedly the organization and scope of principled issue-networks varies widely both among the twenty-five states in this study and over time. This variation defies easy measurement and raises problems of comparison across nation-states. Rather than tracing the formation of such networks directly, the study uses Anheier's suggestion to measure the density of international non-governmental organization membership in each of the twenty-five democracies.[50] Anheier defines membership density as the number of international NGOs with at least one member in the state, per one million population. Because this measure is highly skewed toward states with small populations, Anheier and Stares recommend using the log of this measure, a recommendation this study follows to account for differences in population size. This measure allows for direct comparison of the density of INGO networks across states. Anheier and Stares construct this measure using data from the Union of International Association's *Yearbook of International Organizations*.[51] This data is available for each of this study's democracies for each year from 1984 to 2004. For years prior to 1984, the UIA reports figures only for 1960, 1966, 1977, and 1981. Since the numbers of NGOs reported by the UIA generally are increasing, the analysis uses a linear interpolation to impute values for the missing observations.[52] Figure 4.2 plots the average and median log density of INGO membership of the study's population for each year from 1960 to 2004, illustrating the growth of NGOs.

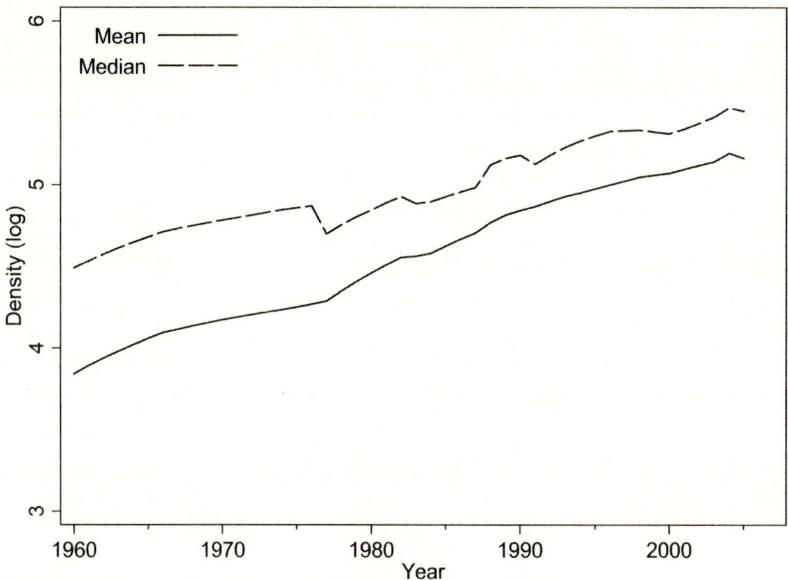

Figure 4.2. Mean and median values of the density of international NGOs for the study's population, 1960 to 2004.

Control Variables

There are a number of possible factors that may confound the hypothesized relationships between the study's independent and dependent variables. To avoid inferring significant affects that may arise due to spuriousness, the study incorporates six control variables. These account for the electoral systems of the subject states, membership in the EU and the Commonwealth of Nations, the political development of each state in the study, and temporal trends within the time series.

Membership in the European Union: Given the large number of European states in the study, one concern is whether or not voting rights for resident aliens are a "European" phenomenon. There are three reasons to suspect the observations of EU democracies may be correlated. First, the EU's recent treaties (Maastricht and Amsterdam) require member states to allow resident aliens from other EU states to vote in local elections. Second, several EU states including Spain and Portugal grant voting rights to resident aliens of other states that reciprocate the rights to Spanish or Portuguese resident aliens. To the degree these states are sources of intra-European migration, this is an explicit, de jure interdependence of observations. Finally, the number of European states in the study's population (sixteen of the twenty-five democracies), and the fact the states with the longest history of resident alien voting are European, suggest the institution of voting rights for resident aliens may emerge out of the processes of European integration. If so, the proposed cultural and institutional variables in the model may be correlated, making estimates of significance biased. This multicollinearity likely will hide any significant effects that may exist.[53] This control variable will assess whether or not a state's membership in the EU predicts its voting rights practices. For each country-year observation in the study, the models use a dummy variable to code whether (scored as a 1) or not (scored as a 0) the state is a member of the EU. With this coding, a positively signed significant coefficient would indicate that EU membership increases the likelihood of enfranchising resident aliens.

Membership in the Commonwealth of Nations: Likewise, a number of Commonwealth states have or have had voting rights for citizens of other member states.[54] This practice may reflect the influence of attempts to establish a "Commonwealth citizenship" in the 1940s.[55] More generally, Howard argues that former colonial powers tend to have generally liberal policies toward immigrants from their former colonies.[56] To control for the effects of membership in the Commonwealth, the analysis uses a dummy variable indicating whether (1) or not (0) the state belonged to the Commonwealth.

Electoral Systems: With emphasis in proportional representation (PR) electoral systems on the inclusion of minority groups, one might expect that states with PR systems are more likely to enfranchise resident aliens than those with first-past-the-post systems. This dummy variable codes each state according to whether it is a PR or semi-PR system (1), or a majoritarian system (0). The study use data from Lijphart and from Beck et al. to code this variable.[57]

History of Political Development: Rokkan argues that the timing of the enfranchisement of citizens depends upon a state's history of development.[58] He asserts "the stronger the [state's] inherited traditions of representative rule, the slower, and the less likely to be reversed the process of enfranchisement and equalisation."[59] Similarly, Howard argues that states that democratized earlier (in the nineteenth century) tend to have inclusive immigration policies that are based on civic rather than ethnic criteria.[60] Since these arguments explicitly relate the rights of resident aliens to the pattern of the state's formation, an important question is whether or not the state's path of political development might explain variations in the enfranchisement of resident aliens. The analysis measures the subject states on two factors Rokkan identifies: whether or not a state has a strong tradition of representative rule, and whether or not the state seceded from another state.[61] Given the difficult nationality questions arising from secession, one might argue that secessionist states are more likely to enfranchise resident aliens—or perhaps less so, as the case of Latvia suggests. The models use two dummy variables. One represents the state's formation history: center-formed states are coded a 1, while secessionist states are a 0. The other dummy variable measures the state's history of representative rule. Those states with a strong tradition of representative rule are coded 1, while states with histories of absolutist rule are coded as a 0. Rokkan's analysis covers thirteen of the twenty-five democracies in the study. For the remaining twelve democracies, the study codes their histories of representative rule and state formation using POLITY scores from the nineteenth and early twentieth century as recorded in the Polity dataset.

Temporal Trends: The study seeks to explain change in the voting rights practices of the twenty-five democracies from 1960 to 2004. To test whether or not the model explains variation in voting rights practices over time (as well as between democracies) it includes a time-counter variable. This counter variable is constructed so that it is centered on 1982, the midpoint of the time series of the study, and varies from –22 to +22. The counter is negative for each year prior to 1982 and positive for each year after 1982. The value of the counter variable thus measures the given observation's distance in time from the study's midpoint: Hence, an observation for 1985 is scored a +3 on the time counter, while an observation for 1960 is scored –22. This control variable assesses whether or not there is temporal variation the model fails to explain. If the counter is significant and negative, for example, it indicates an unexplained trend before 1982; a significant and positive finding indicates unexplained variation over time after 1982.

Longitudinal Coverage

Most of these measures are available for all states in the study's population from 1960 to 2004.[62] Huber, Ragin, and Stephens note that for the measurement of social security transfers, the data before 1960 is sporadic and unreliable.[63] Likewise, the UIA has not published any data on international NGOs before 1960. For these reasons of data availability, this study uses 1960 as the first year of observation of the study's population of democracies. These states represent not only a geographically diverse sample (including the South Pacific, Asia, Europe, North and South America) but also negative cases (Costa Rica and Japan) as well as reversals (Australia and Canada). The observations for the study are country-years, or one observation of a subject state in a given year. The analysis examines all states in the study from either 1960 or the year in which the state became a democracy. Five of the subject states became democracies after 1960. Greece is coded as becoming a democracy in 1975, Portugal in 1976, Spain in 1978, Uruguay in 1985, and Hungary in 1990. The study has 1,021 possible observations, though the unavailability of data for some variables results in 981 complete observations with which to test hypotheses.

Model Specification and Methods of Estimation

For the time-series cross-section design this study uses (which the literature often labels "TSCS"), specification and estimation face a number of potential problems that can affect the bias and efficiency of estimates.[64] These problems can lead the researcher either to be overconfident in his or her inferences, or to make the wrong inferences. Beck has demonstrated that the TSCS researcher can solve a number of the problems of estimation of TSCS models with a proper specification of the model.[65] However, for reasons the text identifies later, Beck's proposed specification in fact overcorrects for the problems of TSCS designs. If so, then his proposed specification is likely to find no significant effects when in fact some may exist. For this reason, this study opts for a middle-of-the-road estimation strategy that neither ignores the problems of TSCS studies nor overcompensates for them at the cost of incorrectly accepting a false hypothesis. The common use of robust standard errors is the most feasible estimation strategy, given this study's design.[66]

The analysis uses this strategy to estimate two sets of models: one set with an ordered dependent variable, and one with a binary dependent variable. By differentiating between discriminatory and nondiscriminatory rights for aliens, on the one hand, and the right to vote in local elections versus national elections, on the other, the study has constructed an ordered dependent variable with which to test the nationalist and transnationalist hypotheses. Because this ordering is not a generic one, the study estimates a second class of models with a binary dependent variable that distinguishes between states with voting rights for resident aliens and those that have none. For both dependent variables, the model is re-estimated with different subsets of independent variables to test the sensitivity of findings to model specification.

Problems with TSCS Designs

TSCS research designs are common in political science. A number of researchers have used TSCS designs with ordered or binary dependent variables.[67] For example, democratic peace researchers have used TSCS designs to investigate ordinal levels of nonmilitary conflict between pairs of democracies.[68] Although political scientists have used TSCS research designs for many years, however, only relatively recently have they paid attention to a number of problems with the estimation of such models. Beck and Katz first called attention to the problems of estimating TSCS designs with ordinary least squares (OLS) or feasible generalized least squares (FGLS) estimators.[69] Yet Beck and Katz's method, though now commonly accepted and utilized in TSCS studies, is not appropriate for this study's design.

Three Problems with OLS or FGLS Estimators in TSCS Studies

Beck and Katz show that TSCS designs inherently have a number of features that violate the classical OLS assumptions about the residuals (or "error term").[70] For OLS estimates to be unbiased and efficient, the error terms must be independent and identically distributed. (A researcher also assumes the dependent variable is continuous, which clearly is not appropriate for this study—more on this later.) Since the error process is simply the sum of omitted variables, this assumption is equivalent to presupposing the model is completely specified:

The modeler proceeds as if the model endogenizes all causal variables. This strong assumption of homoscedasticity is a requirement if OLS estimators are to be unbiased and efficient. However, for three reasons, TSCS studies typically violate this assumption.

First, TSCS studies typically suffer from panel heteroscedasticity, or as Beck and Katz explain "variances of the error process differ from unit to unit."[71] In a TSCS design, to satisfy the condition of homoscedasticity, the researcher must assume that the error process is the same for each unit in the study. Needless to say, this is a very strong assumption that most TSCS researchers choose not to make. In the context of this study, the omitted variables that make up the error process likely differ among the democracies in this study. Since it is highly unlikely this study endogenizes all relevant variables, the error process for the United States likely differs from that of Costa Rica or Hungary, for example. This is panel heteroscedasticity.

Second, TSCS research designs often suffer from contemporaneous correlation of the error terms within a given time period.[72] In some panel designs, such as medical research when the units of analysis are randomly selected patients, contemporaneous correlation is not a serious issue since it is unlikely that the error processes of any two patients are correlated. In TSCS studies of international politics, however, the error processes of two states (or more) may be highly correlated in any given year. For example, in comparative studies of economic performance, states that trade with each other likely will have highly correlated economies and hence correlated error processes. As Beck has pointed out, contemporaneous correlation in international relations often arises from geography: States that border each other likely will engage in international processes such as trade or migration that, if not controlled for in a TSCS design, will give rise to contemporaneous correlation.[73] This type of error is a serious concern for this study for three reasons. First, the geographic proximity of a number of the states in the study suggests that international processes may create contemporaneous correlation. Second, the fact that migration occurs between the study's subject states raises the possibility that reciprocal flows of migrants may create correlation between the study's panels. Third, the study is explicitly interested in the transnational organization of migrants; this is another way of saying the study is interested in testing the hypothesis that observations are correlated both contemporaneously and over time. Indeed, the border effects variable, which measures the spatial processes among democracies in the study, is effectively the hypothesis that contemporaneous correlation occurs.[74] Thus the study needs explicitly to account for this possibility.

The third violation of the assumption of homoscedasticity arises in many time-series designs. Serial correlation is a common problem in designs in which the researcher takes repeated observation of a subject or subjects at regular intervals over some period of time.[75] In a TSCS design, unit-specific serial correlation means that the error process for a given unit in a given time period is correlated to the error process for one or more previous time periods. It is easy to see why serial correlation plagues TSCS studies. Since the observer determines the periodicity of observation for either theoretical or practical reasons, the intervals between observations likely will differ from the temporal processes that occur within the error term. In comparative economic studies, for example, multiplier effects of economic stimulus may take several years to enlarge an economy. If such a study took quarterly or yearly observations, it would suffer from serial correlation. This hypothetical example is illustrative, furthermore, of how serial correlation may occur in this study. Since this study is explicitly interested in how the state's social security expenditures may influence the opportunities resident aliens have for political incorporation, it likely has serial correlation since changes in social security spending may take several years to work through national economies.

As Beck and Katz show, an important consequence of these three violations of the assumption of homoscedasticity is that OLS or FGLS estimators understate the parameters' standard errors. Since the value of the test statistic of an estimate is inversely related to the estimate's standard error, this underestimation leads to overconfidence in the estimates and hence a greater chance of finding significant effects when in fact no such effects occur (which is known as type I error). Beck and Katz have shown that the overconfidence of FGLS estimators is a function of the number of time periods (T) and the number of units (N) in a TSCS study.[76] In the worst case of a small N and small T, FGLS can understate the true variability of an estimator by 30 to 100 percent. In other words, Beck and Katz show that TSCS researchers using OLS or FGLS estimators typically have found significant effects where there is none.

Corrections for TSCS Problems

Until Beck and Katz first called attention to the problems of panel heteroscedasticity, contemporaneous correlation, and unit-specific serial correlation, researchers often ignored these problems.[77] Since 1995, however, most TSCS researchers have adopted one of two methods: using "fixed effects" models to endogenize panel heteroscedasticity, or Beck and Katz's proposed technique for calculating panel-corrected standard errors, or PCSEs.[78]

Fixed-effect models assume that there are unobserved or unmeasured predictors of a study's dependent variable that are unique to a given panel, or in Green, Kim, and Yoon's terms, "fixed unobserved differences" between countries in TSCS studies of international relations.[79] In pooled TSCS studies, such unobserved effects can result in panel heteroscedasticity. Fixed-effects models correct for these unobserved effects by estimating a unique intercept for each panel in a TSCS study. Unfortunately, as Green, Kim, and Yoon note, fixed-effects estimation techniques work well only for large data sets with measures that vary considerably (or are "discordant") over time.[80] When independent variables have little or no longitudinal variation, they contribute no information to the regression.[81] Since fixed-effects regression is inefficient and uses many degrees of freedom, longitudinally invariant data may lead to standard errors that are large. If so, researchers are likely to find no significant effects when some may exist (type II error). Fixed-effects estimation would be highly inefficient for this research design, given the model's use of longitudinally invariant measures. For example, of the 981 country-year observations in this study, the dependent variable changes only twenty-five times. Likewise, the control variables for political development and electoral systems also change infrequently if at all. Given these peculiarities of the study's data and measures, fixed-effect estimation is likely to produce standard errors that are so large that they are likely to result in type II errors. In other words, fixed-effects modeling risks the opposite inferential error (type II) than a pooling strategy (type I). What then should the researcher do? Green, Kim, and Yoon conclude that "fixed-effects regression shoulders the burden of proof: a dearth of time-series information would lead us to accept the adequacy of pooling."[82] This conclusion is pertinent to those TSCS studies—including this one—that endogenize variables that measure relatively invariant features of a state, such as its electoral system or its history of political development.

The second method to address common problems in TSCS studies, panel-corrected standard errors (PCSE), uses regression residuals from OLS to estimate the contemporaneous covariance matrix for a given TSCS design. Using Monte Carlo experiments, Beck and Katz have shown this technique produces the correct standard errors for FGLS estimates in TSCS studies with panel heteroscedasticity and contemporaneous correlation.[83] However, PCSE techniques work only when the model seeks to explain a continuous dependent variable. Because PCSE uses OLS residuals to estimate contemporaneous variance-covariance matrix, it requires the use of OLS estimators. Since the use of OLS to estimate binary or polychotomous dependent variables leads to heteroscedasticity, panel correction techniques are not an option for such model specifications. As Beck notes, political methodologists know very little about corrections for common error-term problems in TSCS studies with ordinal or binary dependent variables.[84]

Thus, PCSE estimation is inappropriate for studies with ordered or binary dependent variables. Researchers that have estimated ordered or binary dependent variables with data structures that are longitudinally invariant typically have used one of two techniques. On the one hand, many simply have acknowledged they know nothing about panel heteroscedasticity or unit-specific serial correlation.[85] On the other hand, some have used robust standard errors to minimize the likelihood of type I error. This technique uses each cluster in a TSCS study as a "super observation" in the covariance computation, thus increasing substantially the estimated standard errors.[86] Simmons, for one, has opted to estimate an ordinal dependent variable using an ordered probit model with robust standard errors that are adjusted for "clustering" on each country in her study. She argues that this technique substantially increases the estimated standard errors and "reduces the likelihood of inferring effects where in fact there are none."[87] While the Simmons technique does not explicitly account for unit-specific serial correlation or contemporaneous correlation among panels, it represents an important approach to avoiding underestimation of variances, particularly when a given research design lacks the necessary independent data to estimate a large number of corrective parameters. One can supplement Simmons's use of robust standard errors, furthermore, with a model specification that explicitly endogenizes contemporaneous correlation. Although this specification does not account for within-panel serial correlation, it corrects for two of the three common problems of TSCS studies.

Beck has argued that panel-correction techniques typically treat problems with error processes in TSCS studies as "nuisances" for which the modeler needs to correct.[88] The same can be said of Simmons's approach to TSCS models with ordinal dependent variables. Beck advocates instead that political scientists treat problems with TSCS error terms as processes to endogenize within the model. Since the error term of the model is simply the sum of omitted variables, Beck argues the modeler can seek to endogenize those processes that give rise to panel heteroscedasticity, contemporaneous correlation, and unit-specific serial correlation. In other words, Beck advocates political scientists treat problems with TSCS designs through their choice of model specification rather than through corrections at the time of estimation. The study follows Beck's advice in principle by choosing a number of specifications that control for some spatial effects and serial correlation. The analysis does not use Beck's particular specification, however. This is because Beck's proposed specification requires a considerable number of degrees of freedom, which are not available from this study's data.

Specification of the Models

While Beck's recommendations for model specification are straightforward and simple to implement, they make considerable demands on the data that may in fact overestimate standard errors for parameters of interest. To correct for country-specific serial correlation, he recommends using a lagged observation of the dependent variable and to correct for country-specific effects with country dummies. For contemporaneous correlation, Beck argues researchers should explicitly model the spatial relationships among units that give rise to contemporaneous correlation. In studies of international politics, Beck argues researchers should include a spatial variable that equals the "weighted sum of the [lagged] dependent variable of all other [adjacent] units."[89] Since this study explicitly seeks to understand the spatial organization of the democracies in the population, earlier in the book the analysis developed just such a lagged spatial variable as a measure of border effects (hypothesis 2(a)). As also noted earlier, the study seeks to investigate a number of factors that may give rise to panel heteroscedasticity. The models have included variables that account for the history of political development in each of the twenty-five democracies, for the differing national conceptions of citizenship, and for differing legal institutions. By including both domestic and international variables, furthermore, the models explicitly investigate panel-specific attributes. While no model can endogenize all possible sources of panel-specific heteroscedasticity, it is reasonable to assume the independent and control variables account for most of the panel-specific effects in the model.

Unfortunately, Beck's proposed corrections would greatly increase the number of variables in any model. For the twenty-five democracies and forty-five years of observation in this study, Beck's proposals to add country-specific and time-period–specific dummies to the model will add seventy dummy variables to the thirteen variables of theoretical interest. Since the study has only 981 observations in the study, these eighty-three variables will reduce the degrees of freedom and increase the estimated variances of the theoretical parameters. The demands of Beck's specification thus increase the likelihood of overestimating the true variance, and consequently finding no significant effects when in fact some may occur. While Beck's techniques are useful for TSCS designs with more time periods, more cross sections or greater variability of the dependent variable, for this particular study they are too demanding of the data.

The analysis chooses instead to use Simmons's technique of pooling the TSCS observations and using robust estimates of standard errors. While this technique does not explicitly model the sources of panel heteroscedasticity, contemporaneous correlation, and serial correlation as Beck's specification does, it does not ignore these problems either. Rather, it avoids underestimating the variances of the coefficients causal parameters, and hence overconfidence in estimates, by using a larger estimate of variance. For this reason, Simmons's technique errs on the side of a finding of no significance. While it does not explicitly address the problems that Beck and Katz have identified, Simmons's technique avoids the overestimation of variances that will result from using Beck's proposed correction. In addition, the model has explicitly endogenized a spatial variable that corrects for contemporaneous correlation through geography. The models thus correct both for contemporaneous correlation and panel heteroscedasicity, though not within-panel serial correlation. While it is not an ideal solution, this specification has fewer costs than Beck's proposals.

Formal Representation of the Models

The conceptual specification of the study's models is:

$$VR_t \sim f \left(\begin{matrix} JUS, JREV, SSX_{t-1}, PARTY, HR, NGO, BORDER_{t-1}, \\ EU, PR, COMMON, FORMHIST, REPHIST, TIME \end{matrix} \right)$$

where VR_t is the ordinal score of a state's voting rights for resident aliens in a given year t. The above specification is simply a specific statement of the general functional relationship $y \sim f(\beta x)$. The four nationalist variables are JUS (the jus soli versus jus sanguinis variable), $JREV$ (strength of judicial review), SSX_{t-1} (social security transfers as a percentage of GDP, lagged one year), and $PARTY$ (partisan composition of government). The three transnationalist variables are *HR* (commitment to human rights), *NGO* (density of NGO membership), and *BORDER*$_{t-1}$ (the measure of border effects, lagged one year). The model also includes six control variables—*EU* (European Union membership), *COMMON* (membership in the British Commonwealth), *PR* (proportional representation electoral system), *REPHIST* (history of representative government), *FORMHIST* (center-formed or secessionist state), and *TIME* (the time counter). These control variables correct for panel heteroscedasticity and contemporaneous correlations among the independent variables in a given year, and test for temporal trends across the study's time series. This results in a general specification of the model:

$$(4.1)\ y^{*}_{i,t} = \alpha + \beta x_{i,t} + \varepsilon$$

where $y^{*}_{i,t}$ is the latent, unobserved dependent variable for country i at time t and $x_{i,t}$ is the vector of hypothesized explanatory and control variables. One can estimate the specification in equation (4.1) using a standard ordered probit model with robust standard errors, or a probit model for the dichotomous dependent variable. For both dependent variables, the analysis estimates six different models to test the sensitivity of findings to specification.

For both sets of models, the discussion in the next chapter relies on standard levels of confidence for statistical tests. Because one concern is the sensitivity of the study's findings to the choice of an ordered dependent variable, one may assume that some factors may be significant when estimating the ordered dependent variable but not when estimating the dichotomous dependent variable. One therefore wants the tests of significance to capture these marginally significant factors in order to distinguish them from factors that do not approach significance. Consequently, the following discussion uses the 0.05, 0.01 and 0.001, levels of confidence for all statistical tests.

The analysis complements each of these model specifications with the interpretation and presentation techniques proposed by King, Tomz, and Wittenberg.[90] In brief, King, Tomz, and Wittenberg use the information available from a model's variance-covariance matrix to simulate full distributions for each hypothesized independent and control variable in a model. Once a researcher has full distributions, he or she can present the uncertainty associated with each independent variable. The researcher can also use the distributions to set causal variables of interest at prespecified values and then see how they will affect a model's findings. In other words, using King, Tomz, and Wittenberg's methods, one can set the birthright citizenship variable to "1" (i.e., a jus soli state) to see how the how strong an effect this variable has on the probability of observing one or more realizations of the dependent variable. Therefore, these techniques not only communicate the point estimates typical of output from ordered probit analysis but also convey the uncertainty associated with the point estimates. As the next chapter shows, this ability to set causal variables at specific values of interest allows a researcher to explain a number of the surprises that emerge from the ordered probit analysis.

Conclusion

With these measures of the nationalist and transnationalist variables one can test the hypothesized causes of the state's enfranchisement of resident aliens. Whenever possible the study has endeavored to use measures developed by other scholars on the assumption that these measures are more reliable and will allow this study to present its findings using a shared foundation of knowledge. Yet it is important to note that most of the preexisting measures are for testing the nationalist hypotheses. This is due in part, no doubt, to the fact that states collect and report data on their national attributes such as their social security expenditures and their partisan politics. Few states gather data on transnational phenomena, however; it is the burden of social scientists to gather the data that may measure these transnational flows. The study has endeavored to derive measures of transnationalism that not only are valid and reliable but that also have manageable research costs. As this chapter has argued, existing measures of transnationalism are necessarily compromises of costs, validity and reliability.

The next chapter turns to the findings of the ordered and binary models. The estimations produce a number of significant and surprising findings in the debate between the nationalist and transnationalist thesis. Neither thesis explicates entirely why some democracies have extended the franchise to resident aliens. The findings of the ordered probit analysis paradoxically highlight both the importance of a large-*n* study to test hypotheses and the insufficiency of such designs to explain contrary findings. Chapter 7 returns to this point.

5

Statistical Findings

Do nationalist or transnational factors explain why democratic states extend the right to vote to their resident aliens? This chapter begins to answer this question by presenting the results of the models developed in the previous chapter. In brief, the models offer some support both for nationalist and for transnationalist arguments. By estimating several models using differing subsets of independent variables as well as the ordinal and binary dependent variables, the chapter explores the sensitivity of the statistical findings to choice of model specification. These alternative specifications produce similar results, illustrating the robustness of the study's findings. The chapter then analyzes the relative impact of the significant causal factors on the choices democracies make. Building on these findings, the analysis discusses the implications of these findings for the debate between the nationalist and transnationalist theses.

The Ordered Probit Model

Table 5.1 presents the findings of the estimation of the full ordered probit model (listed as model 1). A quick glance at model 1 shows some support for the nationalist hypotheses but only weak support for the transnationalist hypotheses. Three of the four nationalist variables are significant, while only the border effects measure of the transnationalist hypotheses is significant. The birthright citizenship and welfare expenditure variables are significant in the direction predicted by much of the nationalist literature. As suggested by the work of Brubaker but contrary to Aleinikoff and Klusmeyer's supposition, jus soli states are significantly more likely to offer their aliens the right to vote than jus sanguinis states are.[1] The positive coefficient of the welfare-spending variable affirms the expectation that democracies with extensive social and civil rights for their aliens are more likely to have broader political rights. This finding contrasts with Klausen's argument that extensive welfare programs lead to the closure of the political rights of migrants.[2]

It is important to note that two of the four nationalist variables produce surprising findings. Hammar has argued that governments composed of parties of the left are more likely to enfranchise resident aliens than are those composed of parties of the right.[3] Similarly, Joppke and Howard have argued that left-leaning parties tend to have more liberal citizenship policies.[4] Since the measure of the partisan composition of government is the difference between the percentage of seats held by parties of the left and those held by parties of the right, Hammar's expectation would be that the coefficient for the partisan variable would be significant and positive. Model 1 in Table 5.1 shows, however, that the partisan variable has no significant effect. In other words, governments composed of left-leaning parties are no more likely to offer aliens the right to vote than right-leaning governments. This is a surprising finding. Another surprising finding is the impact of judiciaries. Nationalist scholars have suggested that because courts have assertively extended civil and social protections to resident aliens, they may be more likely to extend voting rights as well. Yet it is apparent from model 1 that the opposite holds true in the case of voting rights. The negative coefficient for the strength of judicial review shows that voting rights are inversely related to judicial activism: States with activist judiciaries are less likely to offer voting rights to resident aliens, not more so. These are both surprising findings that the case studies in the next chapter explore in greater detail.

Only one of the three transnational variables is significant, suggesting the transnationalist thesis performs weakly in the ordered probit model. It is interesting to note that a democracy's commitment to human rights does not predict its voting rights practices. Neither does its permeation by international nongovernmental organizations. One significant variable is important, however. The neighborhood effects measure this study uses as a proxy for transnationalism—the mean value on the dependent variable of a democracy's neighbors—is positive and significant. This illustrates that democracies that enfranchise aliens tend to cluster together: It is no coincidence, for example, that Sweden borders on three states (Denmark, Norway, and Finland) that also provide their resident aliens voting rights. This has two important implications, one methodological and the other theoreti-

Table 5.1. Estimated Effects of Nationalist and Transnational Factors, Ordered Probit Analysis

	1. *Full Model*	2. *Full Model, unadjusted standard errors*	3. *Controlling only for time trend*
$N =$	981	981	981
$P > chi^2 =$	< .001	< .001	< .001
Log likelihood =	−1162.15	−1162.15	−1234.22
Pseudo R^2 =	.2578	.2578	.2118
Explanatory Variable	**Estimated Coefficient (standard error)**		
Nationalist Hypotheses			
1(a) Birthright citizenship	1.489***	1.489***	1.534***
	(0.362)	(0.107)	(0.416)
1(b) Strength of judicial review	−0.522**	−0.522***	−0.460*
	(0.195)	(0.060)	(0.200)
1(c) Social security expenditures, lagged 1	0.126**	0.126***	0.070*
	(0.034)	(0.011)	(0.031)
1(d) Party of government	−0.219	−0.219***	−0.201*
	(0.113)	(0.056)	(0.098)
Transnational Hypotheses			
2(a) Accession to international human rights agreements	0.048	0.048	−0.049
	(0.094)	(0.034)	(0.097)
2(b) Density of NGOs	0.122	0.122*	0.198
	(0.139)	(0.059)	(0.128)
2(c) Mean DV score of bordering states, lagged 1	0.391***	0.391***	0.347*
	(0.107)	(0.040)	(0.144)
Controls			
EU dummy	−0.708	−0.708***	—
	(0.370)	(0.103)	
Commonwealth dummy	0.578	0.578***	—
	(0.420)	(0.130)	
PR dummy	0.039	0.039	—
	(0.644)	(0.177)	
History of representative institutions dummy	0.231	0.231*	—
	(0.325)	(0.102)	
Center-formed state dummy	−0.355	−0.355***	—
	(0.270)	(0.096)	
Time trend	−0.009	−0.009	0.010
	(0.016)	(0.006)	(0.017)

*=significant at 0.05; **=significant at 0.01; ***=significant at 0.001

Table 5.1 (continued)

	4. *Nationalist factors only, plus time trend*	5. *Nationalist factors plus controls and time trend*	6. *Transnational factors only, plus time trend*	7. *Transnational factors plus controls and time trend*
$N =$	985	985	1,006	1,006
$P > chi^2 =$	< .001	< .001	< .001	< .001
Log likelihood =	−1293.75	−1232.03	−1416.98	−1330.62
Pseudo R^2 =	.1757	.2150	.1164	.1703
Explanatory Variable	**Estimated Coefficient (standard error)**			
1(a) Birthright citizenship	1.584*** (0.358)	1.509*** (0.329)	—	—
1(b) Strength of judicial review	−0.606*** (0.136)	−0.608*** (0.177)	—	—
1(c) Social security expenditures, lagged 1	0.087** (0.030)	0.133*** (0.035)	—	—
1(d) Party of government	−0.136 (0.122)	−0.127 (0.108)	—	—
2(a) Accession to international human rights agreements	—	—	−0.079 (0.086)	0.044 (0.084)
2(b) Density of NGOs	—	—	0.356** (0.120)	0.357* (0.176)
2(c) Mean DV score of bordering states, lagged 1	—	—	0.340* (0.138)	0.338** (0.116)
EU dummy	—	−0.503 (0.389)	—	−0.184 (0.341)
Commonwealth dummy	—	0.586 (0.411)	—	0.893 (0.729)
PR dummy	—	−0.095 (0.510)	—	0.139 (0.834)
History of representative institutions dummy	—	0.284 (0.394)	—	0.413 (0.364)
Center-formed state dummy	—	−0.136 (0.319)	—	−0.169 (0.305)
Time trend	0.014 (0.019)	0.010 (0.017)	0.027* (0.013)	0.019 (0.013)

* = significant at 0.05; ** = significant at 0.01; *** = significant at 0.001

cal. First, as is common in TSCS studies the democracies in this study are spatially correlated. This variable thus serves to correct for the correlations among panels that are common in TSCS studies, giving one greater confidence in the importance of the other significant effects found in the model. A second important implication is that this spatial correlation suggests some neighborhood effects in the spread of voting rights for resident aliens. A given democracy's enfranchisement of its resident aliens is predicted by its neighbor's practices. An important theoretical question is, therefore, how this process works: Does it arise from transnational actors, demonstration effects, or some interstate process? We'll return to this question later.

Finally, none of the six control variables is significant in model 1. This suggests that the hypothesized independent variables explain much of the observed variation in the voting rights practices of the study's twenty-five democracies. There is no unexplained temporal trend in the observed variation of the voting rights practices of the study's democracies, as the nonsignificance of the time counter variable shows.

To test the sensitivity of these findings to model specification, the study conducts six other ordered probit estimations on subsets of nationalist and transnational factors. Table 5.1 compares the full model to these alternative specifications (labeled models 2 through 7). Model 2 estimates the full model with unadjusted standard errors rather than robust standard errors adjusted for clustering within panels. This estimation strategy clearly shows how without adjustments, the estimated variances are much smaller. Consequently, the risk of finding significant effects when none exists is much greater. For this reason, one should discount the findings in model 2; the subsequent discussion focuses on models 1 and 3 through 7.

The results show several factors perform consistently despite differences in model specification. The measures for birthright citizenship and strength of judicial review are significant and signed consistently in all four models (1, 3, 4, and 5). Likewise, the measures for commitment to human rights and for border effects behave consistently in the different specifications. In all four models (1, 3, 6, and 7), the measure of border effects is significant and positive; in none of the four models is the measure of accession to human rights instruments significant. Similarly, control variables appear to perform consistently in the differing specifications. The dummies for proportional representation systems, Commonwealth states, and political development (representative institutions and center-formed states), all are not significant in any specification. Only one model (model 6) finds unexplained variation over time, though this is unsurprising given that model 6 is the most parsimonious of the models. Altogether, ten of the full model's thirteen variables behave consistently across the differing specifications, illustrating the relative robustness of these variables.

One nationalist measure deserves scrutiny. In all four models, the measure of the partisan composition of government has an inverse relationship with the dependent variable. Nevertheless, the party variable is significant in only one of the four models (model 3). This finding of the direction of effect is consistent with an earlier study that found partisan factors to be significantly and negatively related to voting rights for resident aliens.[5] Nevertheless, it is worth considering why the party variable is significant in only one of the four models estimations presented in Table 5.1. One possible explanation is that the current study updates the data from the previous study: Whereas the earlier study included data for democracies only through the year 2000, the estimations in Table 5.1 include data through 2004. The addition of observations from 2001 to 2004 thus appear to affirm the party variable's negative relationship to voting rights but to cause it to switch from a significant finding to a finding of no significance.[6] It is important to note, furthermore, that this change in significance reflects the arbitrary convention of using a probability of .05 as the threshold for significance. In the earlier study, the party variable was significant at $p = .040$. With the additional data used in the models in Table 5.1, the significance test in the full model for the party variable produces a probability of $p = .054$. One can draw two conclusions from this behavior of this variable. First, it is important to be cautious about inferring effects from partisan factors. Second, even a finding of no significance is conceptually important given the findings of previous researchers—it is surprising to find no differences between left-leaning and right-leaning governments. The analysis returns to this point in chapter 7.

The only transnational factor that behaves inconsistently across the different specifications is the measure of the density of NGOs. This factor is significant in the hypothesized direction in models 6 and 7. Model 6 is the most parsimonious model, however, including only the three transnational factors and the time control. Given this spare model, one suspects this estimate is biased due to the omission of significant factors. In the other two models that are more fully specified (1 and 3), this factor is not significant. On the question of the estimated effect of NGO density, then, one can conclude the finding of the full model is probably unbiased. Since "overfitting" is less statistically problematic than omitting relevant variables, the fully specified model informs my subsequent discussion of findings.

It is important to note, finally, the impact of the European Union control variable. EU membership does not appear to cause democracies to enfranchise their aliens. Though the reasons for this finding are not apparent, there is a possible theoretical explanation. Because EU citizens receive the body of rights embedded in EU institutions based on their citizenship in a member state, some might argue the process of European integration is an inherently nationalistic one.[7] Clearly, EU rights are discriminatory: Under Article 19 of the Treaty of Amsterdam, for example, EU nationals residing in an EU state but outside their country of citizenship can vote for their member of the European Parliament. However, non-EU resident aliens cannot. Furthermore, only citizens of EU member states can become citizens of the European Union. In this respect, the constitution of a "European" citizenship depends heavily on the citizenship practices of the individual EU nations, which can be highly nationalistic and differentialist. EU citizenship is, in Martiniello's words "supranational" rather than postnational.[8] The European integration project thus is a discriminatory one. Carter, for one, concludes that the exclusionary nature of EU citizenship "suggests that regional integration may be a barrier to developing a genuinely global citizenship."[9] Likewise, Aleinikoff and Klusmeyer cite EU political integration as an important source of discrimination in the allocation of political rights to resident aliens.[10] This may explain why the ordered probit model finds that EU states are no more likely to enfranchise their resident aliens than other states.

To understand the relative effects of these significant explanatory variables in the ordered probit model, one can use the simulation techniques developed by King, Tomz, and Wittenberg to discern how relative changes in the explanatory variables will affect specific outcomes of the dependent variable.[11] These techniques allow a researcher to simulate the probability of a specific outcome of a model given theoretically interesting values of explanatory factors. Two outcomes of model 1 are of particular theoretical interest: that the state will offer voting rights of some sort (irrespective of the rights' discriminatory nature or the type of election in which aliens can vote), and that the voting rights will be nondiscriminatory.[12] The simulation assumes that all other explanatory and control variables assume their mean values. Table 5.2 presents the results of this analysis.

These results show the strength of nationalist factors on voting rights for resident aliens. Democracies with birthright citizenship policies are twice as likely to have some form of voting rights for their resident aliens as are jus sanguinis states. Likewise, jus soli states are eight times more likely to have nondiscriminatory rights than are jus sanguinis democracies. The marginal effect of the strength of judicial review is also telling. States with no judicial review are three times more likely to enfranchise resident aliens than are democracies with the most active courts. Surprisingly, democracies without judicial review are almost twice as likely to have nondiscriminatory rights as those democracies with even the weakest judicial review. Table 5.2 also simulates the changes in probabilities arising from the effect of the party composition of government variable. Relative to birthright citizenship and judicial review, partisan factors make only a little difference on whether or not a state has voting rights for resident aliens and on whether or not those rights discriminate on the basis of an alien's nationality. Governments composed of parties of the right only are 15 percent more likely to have some form of resident-alien voting rights as are left-leaning governments. Right-leaning governments are almost twice as likely to have nondiscriminatory rights, although in absolute terms these probabilities are small. This suggests partisan factors have little to no impact either on the probability of any rights or on whether or not such rights discriminate based on nationality.

The importance of the social security transfers also is interesting. Clearly, democracies with large welfare programs are more likely to offer the right to vote to their resident aliens. However, the marginal effect of welfare spending on the scope of those rights varies. Democracies that spend 15 percent or less of their gross domestic product on welfare benefits are unlikely to have nondiscriminatory rights. Conversely, democracies that spend 20 percent or more of their GDP on welfare benefits are two and a half times more likely to have nondiscriminatory rights. This finding affirms the nationalist argument that democracies tend to bundle political rights of migrants with economic benefits: States with extensive welfare programs are more likely to have broader political rights.

The simulation results also illustrate the relative impact of neighborhood effects. Democracies whose neighbors on average have some voting rights for their aliens are more likely to enfranchise their own resident aliens. This effect is considerable: Even those democracies whose neighbors on average have only local rights are 25 percent more likely to have some form of voting rights as those democracies with no neighbors who enfranchise aliens. Though the neighborhood

**Table 5.2. Simulated probabilities of voting rights,
ordered probit analysis**

Factor	Probability of of any rights ($y > 0$)	Probability of non-discriminatory rights ($y = 4$ or 5)
Birthright citizenship?		
No	.46	.04
Yes	.91	.35
Judicial review		
No judicial review ($x = 0$)	.92	.42
Weakest judicial review ($x = 1$)	.84	.24
Strongest judicial review ($x = 3$)	.32	.02
Partisan composition of government		
Right-leaning government ($x = -1$)	.74	.13
Moderate government ($x = 0$)	.66	.10
Left-leaning government ($x = 1$)	.58	.07
Social security transfers:		
10 percent of GDP	.42	.03
15 percent of GDP	.66	.09
20 percent of GDP	.85	.24
25 percent of GDP	.95	.47
Neighbors have:		
no rights ($x = 0$)	.54	.05
local rights ($x = 2$)	.80	.20
national rights ($x = 3$)	.89	.32

Simulated probabilities of any form of voting rights for aliens and for nondiscriminatory rights, ordered probit analysis. All other factors are assumed to take their mean values.

effect has weaker impact on the discriminatory nature of these voting rights, it is nevertheless considerable. If a democracy's neighbors on average have even local voting rights, that democracy is four times more likely to have nondiscriminatory rights than one whose neighbors do not have any voting rights. Although the other transnational factors are not significant, the impact of the measure of border effects suggests that nevertheless there is some transnational process that affects the ways states incorporate their resident aliens.

The ordered probit analysis largely has affirmed the importance of nationalist explanations, though the surprising findings about the impact of activist judiciaries and the nonfinding about partisan control of governments suggest that nationalist explanations are insufficient. It is apparent that shared conceptions of citizenship and nationhood, as captured in the birthright citizenship variable, contribute significantly to a democracy's decision regarding whether or not to enfranchise its aliens. Surprisingly, a democracy's commitment to human rights agreements does not affect whether or not it chooses to extend the right to vote to its resident aliens. Neither does the permeation of international NGOs within a democracy affect the practice of enfranchising resident aliens. Nevertheless there may be some transnational process influencing the practices of democracies, since the model's measure of neighborhood effects is significant and positive. Because these findings support the nationalist thesis but offer less support to transnationalist arguments, it is important to consider the degree to which the choice of an ordered dependent variable contributes to these findings that favor nationalist arguments.

The Probit Model

Since the ordering of the dependent variable in the ordered probit analysis is neither natural nor necessarily obvious, the study estimated a probit model with a binary dependent variable for the same population of democracies over the same period, from 1960 to 2004. To simplify the analysis, the models look at the voting rights practices of only national governments. For the binary variable, those democracies in which only local or regional governments offer voting rights are coded as negative observations. The results of this probit analysis appear as model 1 in Table 5.3.

It is apparent that, for the most part, the binary probit model confirms the findings of the ordered probit model. It provides strong support for the nationalist thesis. The measures of birthright citizenship and social security expenditures are significant. Likewise, of the three transnational variables, only the measure of neighborhood effects is significant. It is interesting, furthermore, that as in the ordered probit analysis, the measures of a democracy's commitment to human rights and its permeation by international NGOs are not significant. The probit model disagrees with the ordered probit model, however, over the importance of judicial review. In the probit model a democracy's strength of judicial review does not significantly affect whether or not a democracy enfranchises resident aliens. Model 1 thus produces similar statistical findings as the ordered analysis with the exception of the measure of judicial review.

Table 5.3 also lists several alternative specifications of the probit model. As in the ordered probit analysis, model 2 estimates effects using unadjusted standard errors and likely suffers from overestimating the significance of factors; the subsequent discussion disregards

Table 5.3. Estimated effects of nationalist and transnational factors, probit analysis

		1. *Full Model*	*2.* *Full Model, unadjusted standard errors*	*3.* *Controlling only for time trend*
	N =	981	981	981
	P > chi^2 =	< .001	< .001	< .001
	Log likelihood =	–298.89	–298.89	–368.56
	Pseudo R^2 =	.5457	.5457	.4399
	Explanatory Variable	**Estimated Coefficient (standard error)**		
Nationalist Hypotheses	1(a) Birthright citizenship	0.988* (0.451)	0.988*** (0.174)	1.429*** (0.430)
	1(b) Strength of judicial review	–0.436 (0.255)	–0.436*** (0.099)	–0.286 (0.052)
	1(c) Social security expenditures, lagged 1	0.127 (0.052)	0.127*** (0.020)	0.064 (0.048)
	1(d) Party of government	–0.303 (0.168)	–0.303*** (0.089)	–0.337** (0.128)
Transnational Hypotheses	2(a) Accession to international human rights agreements	–0.143 (0.096)	–0.143** (0.054)	–0.315* (0.146)
	2(b) Density of NGOs	0.378 (0.215)	0.378*** (0.093)	0.301 (0.211)
	2(c) Mean DV score of bordering states, lagged 1	1.076*** (0.304)	1.076*** (0.129)	1.021*** (0.198)
Controls	EU dummy	–1.152* (0.560)	–1.152*** (0.193)	—
	Commonwealth dummy	0.078 (0.640)	0.078 (0.227)	—
	PR dummy	–1.315 (0.672)	–1.315*** (0.246)	—
	History of representative institutions dummy	0.852 (0.457)	0.852*** (0.158)	—
	Center-formed state dummy	0.181 (0.513)	0.181 (0.147)	—
	Time trend	0.039 (0.024)	0.039*** (0.009)	0.049* (0.024)
	(constant)	–1.952 (1.588)	–1.952*** (0.547)	–1.553 (1.422)

* = significant at 0.05; ** = significant at 0.01; *** = significant at 0.001

	Table 5.3 (*continued*)			
	4.	*5.*	*6.*	*7.*
	Nationalist factors only, plus time trend	*Nationalist factors plus controls and time trend*	*Transnational factors only, plus time trend*	*Transnational factors plus controls and time trend*
$N =$	985	985	1,006	1,006
$P > chi^2 =$	< .001	< .001	< .001	< .001
Log likelihood =	−492.45	−315.92	−455.52	−352.91
Pseudo R^2 =	.2558	.5225	.3274	.4789
Explanatory Variable	**Estimated Coefficient (standard error)**			
1(a) Birthright citizenship	1.365** (0.464)	1.299*** (0.375)	—	—
1(b) Strength of judicial review	−0.440* (0.195)	−0.505* (0.207)	—	—
1(c) Social security expenditures, lagged 1	0.077 (0.045)	0.139** (0.044)	—	—
1(d) Party of government	−0.235 (0.158)	−0.170 (0.142)	—	—
2(a) Accession to international human rights agreements	—	—	−0.307* (0.122)	−0.135 (0.102)
2(b) Density of NGOs	—	—	0.354 (0.197)	0.546*** (0.166)
2(c) Mean DV score of bordering states, lagged 1	—	—	0.965*** (0.225)	1.008*** (0.246)
EU dummy	—	−0.737 (0.414)	—	−0.452 (0.483)
Commonwealth dummy	—	−0.128 (0.701)	—	0.369 (0.780)
PR dummy	—	−1.078 (0.665)	—	−1.223* (0.572)
History of representative institutions dummy	—	1.152* (0.494)	—	0.981* (0.454)
Center-formed state dummy	—	0.172 (0.439)	—	0.310 (0.421)
Time trend	0.024 (0.024)	0.035 (0.023)	0.060** (0.019)	0.057** (0.019)
(constant)	−0.396 (1.018)	−0.676 (1.270)	−0.954 (0.911)	−1.904** (0.646)

* = significant at 0.05; ** = significant at 0.01; *** = significant at 0.001

this model. Models 3 through 7 illustrate the sensitivity of the statistical findings to choices of variables. As the table shows, only four of model 1's thirteen variables behave consistently across the different specifications. Of the nationalist factors, birthright citizenship is significant and positive in all four specifications. The strength of judicial review is significant and negative in two of the four specifications. Likewise, the social security expenditure and party variables appear sensitive to choices about model specification. These inconsistencies suggest caution when inferring effects from these nationalist factors. Likewise, of the transnational factors only the border effects variable behaves consistently across specifications: in all four models, it is significant and positive, suggesting the presence of some transnational factors. A state's commitment to international human rights agreements is significant in both models 3 and 6, though the estimated direction of effect is opposite the expectation. Statistically it appears as if a state's commitment to human rights makes it less likely to enfranchise aliens. As there is no theoretical reason to explain such a statistical finding, one may conclude that this is a one-tailed test. Thus, the significant and negative finding is conceptually a finding of no significance.

As with the ordered model, the analysis assesses the relative importance of the significant factors in the probit model. Table 5.4 presents the results of this analysis. These simulated probabilities largely affirm the analysis of the ordered model presented in Table 5.2. The birthright citizenship measure is a strong predictor of the voting rights practices of the study's democracies. States that offer birthright citizenship to children of their resident aliens are about 27 percent more likely to give their resident aliens the right to vote. Though the probit model found that the strength of judicial review is not a significant predictor, Table 5.4 includes the simulated probabilities for this variable to facilitate comparison with the ordered probit analysis. As Table 5.4 shows, democracies without any judicial review are nearly 30 percent more likely to offer their aliens some voting rights than are those states with the most assertive courts. The measure of a state's social security expenditures also exhibits effects similar to its impact in the ordered probit model. States that spend 20 percent or more of their GDP on welfare are almost 40 percent more likely to offer their aliens the right to vote as are those democracies that spend 10 percent or less on welfare. It is clear that, as in the ordered probit analysis, nationalist factors explain much of the observed variation in voting rights practices in the binary probit model.

**Table 5.4. Simulated Probabilities of Voting Rights
for Aliens, Probit Analysis**

Factor	Probability of voting rights ($y = 1$)
Birthright citizenship?	
No	.63
Yes	.90
Judicial review	
No judicial review ($x = 0$)	.92
Weakest judicial review ($x = 1$)	.87
Strongest judicial review ($x = 3$)	.63
Social security transfers:	
10 percent of GDP	.52
15 percent of GDP	.75
20 percent of GDP	.90
25 percent of GDP	.96
Neighbors have:	
no rights ($x = 0$)	.41
local rights ($x = 2$)	.96
national rights ($x = 3$)	.99

All other factors are assumed to take their mean values.

There are some neighborhood effects in the binary model, suggesting that, as in the ordered analysis, there may be some transnational process that affects the variation of the voting rights practices of the study's democracies. Those democracies with neighbors that have even local rights are twice as likely to enfranchise their resident aliens. This spatial effect is similar in magnitude to the impact of neighborhood effects in the ordered model. Together these findings provide important confirmation of at least one transnational factor: The democracies that enfranchise their aliens are geographically clustered together, indicating that transnational or systemic processes may be influencing state practices.

Clearly, the probit analysis is consistent with many of the findings of the ordered probit analysis. Both models provide considerable support for nationalist arguments, differing however on the importance of parties and on the effect of national judiciaries. The probit and ordered probit analyses concur on the significance and direction of effect of the birthright citizenship and social security transfers measures. While both models provide only limited support for the transnationalist thesis, they both find significant neighborhood effects among the study's democracies. They concur on the strength and direction of this effect, furthermore. Finally, the simulated distributions for the significant parameters show that the two models largely concur on the marginal impact of the three significant variables that are common to both. Together, the probit and ordered probit models suggest considerable robustness of the findings.

Table 5.5 compares the performance of each variable in the two models.[13] These results suggest only limited sensitivity of the data to the researcher's choice of estimator. The two models produce identical results with the exception of the nationalist measure of the strength of judicial review. The models concur on twelve of the thirteen variables. This suggests that the findings of significant nationalist and transnational factors—as well as important findings of no significance—are reasonably robust. It also demonstrates that the model specification performs reasonably well irrespective of the data problems typical of TSCS studies and of the choice of estimator.

Table 5.5. Comparison of Significant Factors, Ordered Probit Versus Probit Analysis

	Model	
Variable	Ordered probit	Probit
Nationalist		
Birthright citizenship*	+	+
Strength of judicial review	−	n/s
Social security spending*	+	+
Partisan composition of government*	n/s	n/s
Transnational		
Neighborhood effects*	+	+
Commitment to human rights*	n/s	n/s
Density of NGOs*	n/s	n/s
Control		
European Union member (one-tailed)*	n/s	n/s
Commonwealth member*	n/s	n/s
Proportional representation*	n/s	n/s
History of representative institutions*	n/s	n/s
Center-formed state*	n/s	n/s
Time trend*	n/s	n/s

Comparison of each variable's significance and direction of effect in the ordered probit and probit models, full specifications. Each model was estimated with robust standard errors adjusted for clustering on each country. Asterisks (*) indicate those variables on which the two models concur on the significance and the direction of effect.

Conclusion

In the models presented in this chapter, the nationalist factors have performed well. The transnational factors do not perform as well against either the ordered or the binary dependent variable, though the models find that a democracy's practices for its enfranchisement of aliens are predicated in part upon the practices of its neighboring states. Clearly, democracies that extend voting rights to their aliens are clustered together. This fact suggests the importance of transnational or international factors that the analysis fails to capture. This is unsurprising: Statistical models tend obscure the richness of the politics of citizenship today. For this reason, the following chapter offers three case studies that trace the influence of nationalist and transnational factors on the enfranchisement policies of three democracies. There is another reason, furthermore, to use qualitative research to understand the politics of enfranchising immigrants. As the statistical results show, the factors that most influence the probability of enfranchisement are precisely those particularistic, historically conditioned factors that are unique to each nation-state. To understand, then, how shared conceptions of nationality may affect the enfranchisement of resident aliens, or how partisan competition and national courts play a role, qualitative research is a necessary complement to large-n statistical analysis. Toward this end, the following chapter explores the debates over the enfranchisement of resident aliens in three European states: Belgium, the Netherlands, and Germany.

6

Case Studies:
Political Incorporation and
Historical Institutionalism

Up until now the extension of voting rights has always been a positive thing in Dutch history. There have always been positions stating why such an extension should perhaps not put into effect, but after a few years one could not imagine it being otherwise anymore.

—Dutch Member of Parliament Peter Lankhorst
of the Politieke Partij Radikalen (PPR)

Elections in which foreigners can vote cannot convey democratic legitimacy.

—The German Federal Constitutional Court,
The Guardian, November 1, 1990

In the big cities, the immigrants run the city councils....Now that they are going to give them all the right to vote, they will take over the smaller towns too. Pretty soon, we won't be the boss in our own country anymore.

—A Belgian truck driver, *Christian Science
Monitor*, February 3, 2004

This chapter explores the debate in three states over the enfranchisement of resident aliens. The statistical analysis in chapter 5 suggests the importance of nationalist factors in explaining why states enfranchise resident aliens. Statistically speaking, birthright citizenship is a significant predictor, as nationalist scholars hypothesize. Yet two nationalist factors perform opposite of the expectations: Conservative parties are no less likely to extend the franchise than are left-leaning ones, and activitist judiciaries are less likely to enfranchise aliens, not more so. In contrast, the statistical analysis found little support for transnationalist factors, though the finding of significant

111

spatial correlation among the states in the population suggests there are unobserved transnational processes at work. How can one explain these surprising findings? Clearly one must look beyond the large-*n* statistical analysis for a qualitative assessment of why states enfranchise resident aliens. This chapter looks at three such states: the Netherlands, the Federal Republic of Germany, and Belgium.

These three case studies present interesting riddles. Why would the Netherlands enfranchise resident aliens with little difficulty in the 1980s, while Belgium experienced three decades of debate and abortive legislation before enacting local voting rights for resident aliens in 2004? Why did Hamburg and Schleswig-Holstein's experiment with local voting rights in 1989 fail to survive the constitutional scrutiny of the German Federal Constitutional Court? The answers to these questions lie in the shared, historical understandings of the meaning of "citizenship" in each of the three states. That is, as in all states, citizenship in Belgium, the Netherlands, and Germany is an institution embedded in the unique historical experiences and societal conflicts of each state. To understand the different patterns of political incorporation of resident aliens, then, one must first understand how these conflicts have molded the institution of citizenship. This is consistent with the statistical findings of the importance of birthright citizenship in the enfranchisement of resident aliens.

The following analysis uses a controlled comparison of three states to explore the impact of cultural conceptions of citizenship on the political incorporation of resident aliens. The chapter looks at the Netherlands, Germany, and Belgium for three reasons. First, all three states are founding members of the European Union. Martiniello, for one, has argued that EU institutions impose citizenship rules "from above" and constrain the citizenship policies of member states.[1] Indeed, as noted in chapter 2, the Treaties of Maastricht (Article 8B) and Amsterdam (Article 19(1)) stipulate that member states must establish voting rights in local elections for aliens from other EU member states who reside in their countries.[2] Because the three cases are all EU member states, one can assess the importance of the historical deep structure of citizenship while controlling for EU institutional factors. Second, the Netherlands, Germany, and Belgium, each have proportional representation (PR) electoral systems. Because PR systems arguably emphasize the representation of minority groups, one might expect that states with PR systems would be more likely to enfranchise resident aliens than majoritarian states. Not only do PR systems embody civic norms of accommodation of minority groups, they also may create electoral incentives for parties to enfranchise societal groups who may favor one party or another. Several scholars have argued that left-leaning parties tend to have more inclusive policies toward resident aliens, though the statistical findings in chapter 5 suggest otherwise.[3] Because all three subject states are PR systems, however, the cases control for this rival hypothesis.

The third reason to examine the experiences of the Netherlands, Germany, and Belgium is that the three states vary considerably in the voting rights they provide to resident aliens. In the 1980s, the Netherlands first adopted voting rights for aliens of any nationality who satisfied a residency requirement. Though there was some controversy, the Dutch parliament pursued this initiative with relatively little public opposition; and the practice has enjoyed broad popular support in the Netherlands. In Belgium, by contrast, opponents repeatedly blocked initiatives to enfranchise resident aliens, a debate that has recurred in Belgium regularly since the 1970s. Only in 2004 did the government finally succeed in extending the vote to resident aliens. Finally, Germany neither succeeded in adopting voting rights for aliens, as the Netherlands did, nor suffered from the protracted debate that Belgium endured. Rather, in 1990 the German Federal Constitutional Court struck down the laws enacted by three *länder* governments to enfranchise aliens in local elections.

To understand the divergent experiences of these three neighboring states, one must first explore how each society understands the meaning of "citizenship." These understandings in turn reflect the unique historical paths of political developments of each state and society. The historical nature of these institutions is significant in two respects. First, historically conditioned understandings of citizenship explain why the Netherlands has pursued a relatively assimilationist policy on voting rights while Germany and, until recently, Belgium have excluded aliens from the franchise. Second, one can understand the recent change in Belgium—as well as Germany's decision in 2000 to enact jus soli provisions in its citizenship laws—as the product of changing historical circumstances at the turn of the millennium.

The Netherlands

Citizenship in the Netherlands reflects what Stuurman has called the "communitarian-liberal" model of citizenship.[4] Although the Netherlands shares many of the jus soli and republican principles of the French conception of citizenship, the two models differ considerably in their views of the nature of the rights of individuals. As Stuurman argues, the liberal-republican model of citizenship that typifies French policy conceives of rights as naturally adhering to individuals. This emphasis on individual rights rejects the idea that communities—whether religious, ethnic, or linguistic—should enjoy "quasi-rights" based on group identity. In the liberal-republican model, the only group identity that legitimates political rights is the Republic itself. Inherent in the French model is an illustrative paradox. Because it rejects discrimination based on group attributes, French policy not only allows for the possibility of immigrant assimilation to French society irrespective of ethnic or linguistic origins, it also expects such assimilation. This paradox of republican tolerance was evident recently, for example, in the Muslim *foulard*, or headscarf, controversy in France.

Though the Netherlands shares a similar liberal and jus soli heritage with France, the Dutch conception of citizenship attributes greater importance to community rights.[5] The Netherlands' history includes a strong tradition of representative government at the local and provincial level, and of progressive and stable enfranchisement.[6] Dutch citizenship policy reflects three important historical legacies: religious tolerance of the Reformation and the seventeenth century, the Batavian Revolution of 1795, and the cosmopolitanism of the Netherlands' colonial heritage. Together these experiences explain the broad Dutch policy of multiculturalism and tolerance toward noncitizens.

Prak provides a definitive account of how the Batavian Revolution of 1795 took the traditions and rules of local representation and institutionalized them at the state level.[7] Prior to 1795, each of the United Provinces maintained its own laws and practices for membership in the political community. A citizen of Gelderland may not have any rights, for example, if he or she moved to Utrecht. Because of the commercial nature of some of the provinces, furthermore, many (particularly Holland) had a considerable number of residents who were born in other nations. Several provinces allowed non-natives to purchase citizenship with its attendant rights, including the right to vote. Although this practice was undeniably discriminatory based on individual wealth, it nevertheless reflects the provinces' conception of the political community as a multiethnic, communal construct rather than a linguistic or ethnic one. When Napoleon's armies invaded the provinces in 1795, they brought with them a liberal-republican template for citizenship. This model reflected the *citoyen* conception of membership in the political community that found powerful expression in Jacobite France. To estab-

lish a "Dutch" citizenry from the disparate provinces, France instrumentally defined a "Dutch" citizen as any citizen in one of the seven
provinces. Given the heterogeneous and multiethnic quality of
provincial citizenship, then, the Batavian Revolution *ab initio* created
a polyglot Dutch citizenship that paradoxically emancipated individual rights from ethnicity and religion (as had occurred in France), yet
tied them to communal identities.

Dutch citizenship is unique, then, in its combination of French
republican liberalism, Protestant religious toleration, and colonial
multiculturalism. The historic emphasis in Dutch liberalism on community rights finds expression in the state's policies for the incorporation of immigrants even to this day. The Netherlands' decision to
enfranchise resident aliens is particularly illustrative of this shared
conception of Dutch citizenship. The cities of Rotterdam (in 1979)
and Amsterdam (in 1981) first introduced noncitizen voting in local
elections. As two large and historic centers of trade and commerce for
the Netherlands, both cities had large populations of foreign citizens
in the late 1970s.[8] Like many other municipalities throughout
Europe, furthermore, Rotterdam and Amsterdam experienced a
period of voluminous immigration during the 1960s and 1970s.
Combined with Surinamese and other immigrants from former
Dutch colonies, the two cities faced a yawning inequality between
their citizenry and their growing populations of noncitizens.
Rotterdam and Amsterdam chose enfranchisement as a means to
broaden the integration of aliens into civic life. Three years later, the
Dutch Parliament extended the right to vote in local elections to any
alien who had resided in the Netherlands for five or more years.[9]

Two aspects of the Netherlands' enfranchisement of noncitizens deserve emphasis. First, voting rights for the Netherlands'
resident aliens reflected a broader Dutch integration policy that
emphasized community rights rather than individual rights. This
policy "was set up aimed at emancipation of the official categories
of ethnic minorities, with the objective of elevating the ethnicized
groups to equal social status with the indigenous groups in Dutch
society."[10] The policy sought not only to broaden political rights
through the franchise, but also to reform naturalization laws. Here
then is evidence of Stuurman's communitarian-liberal model of citizenship rights. Second, as Jacobs notes, the Netherlands' example
is marked by two surprising factors: an absence of agitation for
rights among immigrant groups themselves, and a degree of consensus on enfranchisement across the spectrum of Dutch political
parties and their leaders.[11] The left-leaning Social Democrats

(PvdA), the Christian Democrats (CDA), and the right-wing VVD all supported the 1985 bill to enfranchise noncitizens at the local level. Rath finds that this broad partisan coalition reflected a broad elite consensus favoring enfranchisement.[12]

The enfranchisement of resident aliens in the Netherlands, then, was an elite-led process characterized by broad societal and partisan support. The absence of political controversy reflects broader Dutch norms of political consensus, and its absence of a nationality qualification reflects the communitarian-liberal model of community-based rights. Both the decision to enfranchise aliens and the politics surrounding it illustrate, then, the Netherlands' unique historical experiences as a multiethnic, pluralist society of diverse communities. The absence of controversy in the Netherlands is all the more striking when juxtaposed with the experiences of Germany and Belgium.

The Federal Republic of Germany

Germany's policies for the incorporation of noncitizens reflect the ethno-linguistic conception of nationhood that Brubaker illustrated so memorably.[13] In contrast with the French republican-liberal model of citizenship, German law and policy reflects a conception of the polity as a pre-political ethnic and linguistic community rather than a construct of the state itself. In practice, German law attributes rights to the German nation as a social collectivity rather than to individuals as political beings.[14] This conception is institutionalized in German citizenship law through its historical emphasis on the doctrine of jus sanguinis. Before the state adopted jus soli practices in 2000, an individual joined the political community through descent rather than by his or her place of birth. An important consequence of this emphasis is Germany's incorporation policies: Though the state provides extensive social and economic rights for resident immigrants, these policies typically reinforce the distinction between citizens and noncitizens rather than erase them. This is true in German law as well as in popular political discourse. The myth of the "guest worker" (*gastarbeiter*)—of "temporary" immigrant laborers who, despite decades of residence in Germany, will return someday to their countries of origin—is a telling example of how powerfully the distinction between citizens and aliens shapes popular dialogue on issues of immigrant incorporation. These shared understandings of German citizenship help explain why the German experiment with the alien franchise was so short-lived.

Why does Germany's citizenship law emphasize ethnic and linguistic criteria, whereas other states in the jus soli tradition emphasize residential criteria? Brubaker asserted that it reflects Germany's history of political development.[15] For centuries, Germans were a linguistic and (to a lesser extent) religious community without a state. Upon unification in 1870, federal law reinforced the notion of a "German" as one who spoke the language and descended from another German. The process of German unification may explain, furthermore, the "ethnicization" of German citizenship policies.[16] Although there is no necessary reason why the historical discontinuity between nation and state should require an ethnic definition of belonging, Preuss argues that the ethno-linguistic conception of citizenship enabled elites to control the process of political unification without mass participation.[17] In this sense, unification and ethnicization of citizenship are inextricably related, with consequences for contemporary citizenship politics in Germany.

Other scholars have explored the implications of this cultural conception of nationhood for German political development and citizenship policies, so it is not necessary to belabor the point.[18] It is interesting to consider, however, Joppke's argument that postwar German history ironically reinforced the notion of the German nation as an ethnic community rather than a political construct:

> While in principle delegitimized by its racist aberrations under the Nazi regime, ethno-cultural nationhood was indirectly reinforced and prolonged by the outcome of World War II, with the division of Germany and the scattering of the huge German diasporas in communist Eastern Europe and the Soviet Union. Against this backdrop, the Federal Republic defined itself as a vicarious, incomplete nation-state, home for all Germans in the communist diaspora.[19]

Not only did the postwar division of Germany give renewed emphasis to an ethno-cultural conception of nationhood, it also shaped incorporation policies through the Federal Republic's institutions. The Basic Law paradoxically empowered noncitizens through equal protections, yet the federal structure of Germany created disparities in each *länder*'s enactment of social and economic programs for Germany's growing population of guest workers. Legislative passivity in the Bundestag only reinforced these disparities.[20] As a consequence, Germany's citizenship politics are characterized by an absence of policy centralization, administrative decree rather than legislation, and policy innovation in the judiciary rather than the executive.[21]

Against this institutional backdrop, politicians in the Federal Republic considered the issue of enfranchising resident aliens. Although the federal commissioner on immigration issues raised the possibility of the franchise for aliens as early as 1979, the executive branch remained passive on the issue, while "activist courts have expansively interpreted and defended the rights of foreigners."[22] In 1989, the disparities in local practices clashed with judicial activism over the issue of voting rights for resident aliens. For nearly a decade, various *länder* in the Federal Republic considered enfranchising at least some of their resident aliens. Influenced by the Netherlands' and Sweden's experiences with noncitizen voting rights, the state of Hamburg took the first preliminary steps in 1989, deciding to allow non-German EC citizens who had resided in the state for eight years to vote in "relatively unimportant" neighborhood council elections.[23] That same year Schleswig-Holstein enacted provisions for noncitizens to vote in local elections, though as in Hamburg the franchise extended only to citizens of specific nationalities.[24] Soysal reports that the government of West Berlin also adopted voting rights for resident aliens in 1990.[25] These modest innovations are noteworthy in two respects: First, like the Dutch initiatives in Rotterdam and Amsterdam, sub-national governments rather than the national executive propagated these voting rights. Second, the initiatives in Schleswig-Holstein and Hamburg were considerably more restrictive than the Dutch parliament's initiative to allow resident aliens to vote in local elections. The two German *länder* not only limited voting to local elections (the only elections over which the states arguably had legal domain), they also coupled this geographic restriction with the requirement that the resident alien satisfy a nationality criterion. Turkish or Polish resident aliens, therefore, had no prospects for voting in these *länder*. In this sense, even these limited voting rights reflected a logic that the political community is constituted along ethnic, linguistic, or national lines rather than on criteria of locality, residency, economic status, or community.

However, even these relative modest voting rights initiatives met with controversy and political resistance in the Federal Republic. Rath reports that, in contrast with the Netherlands' experience, political parties in the Federal Republic divided on the initiatives in Schleswig-Holstein and Hamburg: Social Democrats and Greens supported the enfranchisement of resident aliens, while the Kohl Government and the CDU/CSU "denounce[d] the immigrant franchise passionately."[26] These divides perhaps reflected public opinion in the Federal Republic: Rath found that only one-third of Germans favored the enfranchisement of noncitizens. Another difference from the Dutch experience (but similar to Belgium's experience) is that immigrants' groups in Germany actively campaigned for the franchise. The issue of resident alien voting rights in the Federal Republic consequently was more politically contentious than in the Netherlands, and it lacked the elite consensus and leadership at the national level that characterized the Dutch case. Rather, as the discriminatory nature of the rights in Schleswig-Holstein and Hamburg illustrate, Germany's experiment reflected both persistent ethno-cultural conceptions of the political community and the variation incubated by a federal system with weak or perhaps disinterested executive leadership at the national level. One can attribute both the emphasis on nationality and the weak federal structure as a consequence of Germany's historical experiences before and after the Second World War.

The enfranchisement of resident aliens in Schleswig-Holstein and Hamburg never led to a non-German casting a ballot. Soon after the states adopted these measures, opponents filed court challenges that quickly found their way to the Federal Constitutional Court. Joppke notes that "The German debate over alien suffrage was a foundational debate over the meaning of membership and citizenship in the nation-state."[27] In October 1990, the Court took up this debate. Ruling that the enfranchisement of resident aliens violated the Basic Law, it threw out the *länders'* laws. Neuman describes the Court's rationale as grounded in an understanding of citizenship as an ethnic and social construct rather than as a political community. The Court ruled that voting rights for resident aliens violated the Basic Law because the law grants the franchise to the *German* nation as a *collective* right, rather than as an individual right.[28] The emphasis on both adjectives is important: The opinion implies that the right to vote adheres to a pre-political community, rather than to individuals as citizens or as political subjects of the state's sovereign authority.

The Federal Constitutional Court's decision is ironic in a couple of respects. First, as Joppke notes, the judiciary had served as the leading institutional advocate for the social and economic rights of aliens in Germany, and had progressively extended rights to these groups in a manner that the Federal Republic's elected officials did not.[29] Yet judicial activism cuts both ways: While the courts willingly found social and economic protections for resident aliens in their reading of German law, the courts constructed political rights in a different way. Judicial activism need not be a progressive or liberalizing force, and may vary among issue areas. Because the vote speaks to membership in the polity in a way that economic and social rights do not, it is no surprise that the constitutional court found the alien franchise to violate a widely held conception of the German nation as an ethno-linguistic community that itself antedates the German state.[30] The second irony is that the Court's decision in 1989 to hear arguments over the enfranchisement of resident aliens occurred on the eve of the Berlin Wall's fall; the Court delivered its verdict a week before the Federal Republic consolidated with East Germany. The postwar division of Germany that perpetuated the notion of a German diaspora thus ended even as the Court reaffirmed the German nation as an ethnic construct. Hence, historical differentialist conceptions of the nation collided with the inclusive issue of noncitizen voting rights in ironic ways:

> In major intersections around [recently reunified] Berlin the dominant conservative CDU has put up large placards with two dialogue-balloons: "I'm against voting rights for foreigners." "So am I. Only a CDU majority will put a stop to it." Winning issue or not, it seems an odd source of imagery to appeal to people who recently won back their own voting rights under such duress.[31]

Belgium

Unlike Germany's abortive consideration of noncitizen voting rights, Belgians engaged in a debate over the enfranchisement of aliens for more than three decades. Rath notes that the earliest attempts to enfranchise resident aliens date to around 1970, with nearly a dozen bills introduced in Parliament in the 1970s and 1980s.[32] Unlike the Dutch experience, furthermore, immigrants' associations themselves, rather than political elites, have been the main proponents of voting rights for noncitizens. Political parties in Belgium have divided, furthermore, along both ideological and linguistic lines. In the absence of the elite consensus that typified the Dutch initiative, furthermore, partisan competition in Belgium became important with extremist parties from both ends of the spectrum opposing enfranchisement. Therefore, the patterns of contestation as well as the recurrent debate distinguish Belgium's experiment with noncitizen voting rights. Only recently have Belgians finally agreed to grant aliens with five years' residency the right to vote in local elections.[33]

The Belgian experience unsurprisingly reflects the politics of consociational democracy and linguistic communities. The division of Belgium in Francophone and Dutch-speaking populations (plus a substantial German-speaking population) reflects both the relative brevity of Belgium's statehood and its longer cultural associations with France and the Netherlands. Though this history did not necessarily imply linguistic and cultural segmentation, the linguistic divisions coincided with social and economic divisions, with Francophones enjoying both greater wealth and greater political power than Flemings did.[34] Belgium's early political history, therefore, is one of socioeconomic and political divisions as well as linguistic ones. These fault lines run deep in nearly all contemporary politics in Belgium: Not only does the state's consociational structure represent the tension between group identities and statehood, but also public discourse in Belgium over many issues often focuses on the implications of policy for the delicate balance between Belgium's linguistic communities. Furthermore, the state's political evolution has recurrently codified the identities of distinctive linguistic communities. The constitutional reform of 1993 identified, for example, French-speaking, German-speaking, and Dutch-speaking communities as fundamental cultural groups within the nation. These divisions found profound expression during the electoral crisis of 2007, when some Belgian politicians called for the dissolution of Belgium into sovereign Flemish and Francophone states.[35]

Belgium citizenship policy thus embodies a conception of nationality that differs from both the ethno-linguistic conception of Germany and the communal-liberal model of the Netherlands. It is a curious hybrid, rather, of the French liberal-republican ideal and the Dutch emphasis on community rights.[36] Because integration policy is a local and regional prerogative in Belgium, furthermore, these competing ideas create important differences in incorporation policies at the local level. Flemish political parties and policies support migrants' organizations as the means for incorporation, while Francophone parties generally propose problem-oriented policies rather than group-specific initiatives. Therefore, the rights and benefits that immigrants receive depend upon regional and partisan differences, factors that the consociational institutions and norms of political life reinforce. In this sense, the state's institutions organize these contrasting conceptions of individual rights and membership into discrete parts of the political community. One might even argue there are two distinct models for immigrant incorporation.

The role of the state in ordering multiculturalism in Belgium means that questions about the rights of immigrants invariably become intertwined with broader public debate over the rights of linguistic communities. The multicultural conception of rights ironically serves to delimit the economic, social, and particularly political opportunities for immigrants. Dutch-speaking Belgians not only emphasize the community-rights model typical of the Netherlands but also view such community rights as a necessary protection of their own political prerogatives in light of the historical dominance of Francophones in political and economic life. Flemish parties strongly oppose initiatives that explicitly or implicitly challenge this community-rights model. In this sense, the recurrent debate and political conflict over voting rights for resident aliens illustrates how profoundly the issue touches upon the broader balance of political power in Belgium.

Partisan competition also played an important role in Belgium's contestation over enfranchisement. While the debate touched on foundational debates about the relationship between Belgium's linguistic communities, Jacobs finds that parties reacted tactically as well.[37] For much of the three decades of Belgium's debate, opposition to the enfranchisement of aliens crossed the linguistic divide. Both Flemish and Francophone moderate parties of the right opposed enfranchisement in part because they feared a backlash among voters, but also to keep extremist xenophobic elements of both parties within the fold. When Belgium granted voting rights to EU nationals in 1999, however, Francophone parties changed their positions while Flemish parties remained opposed to enfranchisement. Right-center Francophones (particularly the VLD party) gradually came to support enfranchisement, in part to appeal to the growing ethnic Turkish population around Brussels that otherwise tends to be socially conservative. This tactical shift by right-center Francophones created new opportunities for immigrant groups and leftist parties to advance the cause of immigrant voting.

The Dutch-speaking community nevertheless resisted enfranchisement on the ground that it will strengthen Francophone parties at the polls, an intuition that the Francophone parties supporting legislation apparently also shared.[38] Rath asserts that attempts to enfranchise resident aliens in Belgium regularly failed due to "the fear that the ethnic vote might disturb the equilibrium between the Flemish- and French-speaking communities."[39] Jacobs argues that the implications of the alien franchise are profound for Belgian politics:

Flemish resistance to the enfranchisement of foreigners boils down to defending the power and positions of the Dutch-speaking. Enfranchisement is said to disrupt the existing system of checks and balances between Flemish and Francophones, which ultimately is the basis for the federal structure of the country.[40]

In this respect, the franchise for noncitizens touches on both constitutional issues and norms of consociational democracy. If individuals may join the political community irrespective of their community identity, then one must question whether or not the constitutional construction of Belgium as three distinctive cultural communities would survive. This was the crux of the issue. Belgium's decades-long debate over whether or not to enfranchise resident aliens thus reflects both this constitutional debate and the differences between Flemish and Francophone conceptions of individual rights.

So why did Belgium finally enfranchise resident aliens in February 2004? Clearly, the change in position of rightist Francophone parties gave rise to a broader coalition in support of enfranchisement. This tactical change by Francophones occurred, however, about the same time as Belgium enfranchised EU nationals to conform to the Treaty of Amsterdam. Because Belgium had already enabled EU nationals to vote in local elections, the enfranchisement of non-EU resident aliens was a relatively modest extension of the franchise. In this respect, international factors interacted with partisan competition in Belgium to create a new opportunity for enfranchisement. Another reason may be the examples set by other nearby states that had enfranchised noncitizens. Proponents of enfranchisement in Belgium cited the success of similar measures in the Netherlands, Ireland, Sweden, and Finland.[41] In these respects, Belgium's enfranchisement of resident aliens may reflect some of the international factors that transnationalist scholars emphasize. It remains to be seen, however, whether or not Belgium's enfranchisement will undermine Fleming rights and upset the delicate consociational balance. While Belgium has successfully enfranchised its resident aliens after three decades, it has yet to resolve the implications of this policy for Belgium's consociational norms.

Conclusion

One irony of Belgium's experience is immediately apparent. Whereas the liberal-communitarian model in the Netherlands encouraged elites to enfranchise noncitizens, in Belgium the importance of community rights stalled enfranchisement for decades. This fact illustrates that one cannot separate conceptions of nationality or citizenship from their historical and contemporary context: In Belgium and the Netherlands similar conceptions of rights produced widely different outcomes. To explain such variation, one must understand the unique configurations of both historical and contemporary social and political features in each state. While each state's history of political development has produced unique Dutch, German, and Belgian (or perhaps Fleming and Francophone) conceptions of membership in the polity, it is political parties, immigrant groups, citizens, and elites who contest these conceptions within the confines of contemporary institutions. In this respect, historically conditioned definitions of citizenship are an important feature of modern citizenship politics, but they are not determinative.

One important difference between Belgium, the Netherlands, and Germany is the role played by political elites. In the Netherlands, elites led the push to enfranchise resident aliens, and crafted a careful consensus based on the compromise that resident aliens would vote only in local elections. In Germany and Belgium, by contrast, elites played less of a role. Proposals in both Germany and Belgium reflected the initiatives of immigrants' groups themselves and left-leaning political parties. In Germany, local governments enfranchised aliens before elites at the national level had constructed a consensus (or perhaps because they had failed to do so). The role of the German *länder* illustrates a second important difference between the three cases: The issue of enfranchisement often arises at the level of local politics before it becomes a salient issue for national debate.[42] In the Netherlands as in Germany, localities enfranchised resident aliens before the national government did. In Belgium, the national initiative to enfranchise floundered for years because linguistic communities viewed it as an infringement on their local rights of self-governance.

The most important difference between the three cases appears to be, however, distinctive and historically conditioned conceptions of the political community. In Germany, the polity is an ethno-linguistic and pre-political community, a reflection not only of Germany's late unification as a nation-state but also its postwar division. In the Netherlands, the polity reflects Protestant norms of pluralism and tolerance and the state's colonial heritage. Belgium's political community reflects its consociational lineage: It is not one but several linguistic polities, each of which enjoys constitutional status as a fundament of the state. In Germany and Belgium, furthermore, debate over voting rights for noncitizens were debates about foundational and constitutional conceptions of the political community in a way they never were in the Dutch debate. In each of the three cases, citizens and political elites debated voting rights for noncitizens through the prism of these understandings. Germany's abortive experiment with noncitizen voting rights failed because the Federal Constitutional Court interpreted the franchise as a collective rather than an individual right. Belgium's initiatives stalled because they directly challenged the constitutional definition of Belgium as a community of distinctive cultural and linguistic groups. The Netherlands enacted voting rights with little conflict, by contrast, because its communitarian conception of the polity flexibly allowed for pluralism. In each case, then, the terms of debate reflected histories of unique political and social development. These histories continue to condition the experiences and rights of immigrants in Belgium, the Netherlands, and Germany today.

These case histories illustrate how some of the important factors identified in the statistical analyses played out in three states. Cultural understandings embodied in the jus soli variable conditioned the voting rights debates in all three. In none of these cases did political parties exhibit a clear left–right difference. Rather, as was clear in the Belgian and German cases, political parties reacted tactically to opportunities for electoral gain, often with local party leaders disagreeing with national party leaders.[43] In Germany, the federal courts foreclosed opportunities for immigrants, as the statistical analysis indicated activist judiciaries tend to do. The qualitative research thus illustrates some of the factors that the study's quantitative analysis has uncovered.

7

Theoretical Implications

The experiences of the Netherlands, Belgium, and Germany illustrate the importance of domestic factors in shaping the political opportunities of resident aliens. They also illustrate some shortcomings of nationalist explanations. Though nationalist factors perform well in the statistical analyses, activist judiciaries and political parties that control governments may affect the voting rights of aliens in ways that scholars have failed to explain. Conversely, though transnationalist factors do not perform well in the statistical analysis, the measure of neighborhood effects suggests that, as some scholars argue, transnational factors nevertheless may be important even though the causal mechanisms may not be apparent. This chapter turns to these theoretical implications and suggests next steps for researchers. It addresses the implications of this study's statistical findings for the debate between the nationalist and transnationalist theses, and concludes with a discussion of how this research might change our understanding of citizenship and state sovereignty.

The theoretical implications necessarily are limited to the twenty-five democracies this study examines. There are good reasons to look at these particular democratic states: They are those with the longest experiences of democratic practice and host many of the world's migrants. Indeed, of the world's immigrants in the year 2000, 45 percent reside in the states this study examines.[1] Therefore, even limited conclusions have considerable practical importance. Nevertheless, the experiences of transitional democracies—their receptivity to international organizations, their political parties and judiciaries, and so on—may differ considerably from the population this study examines. Also, transnational factors may have a greater impact on these newer

127

democracies than on established democracies. For this reason, to the degree one generalizes the findings of this study to other democratic states one must do so speculatively. Perhaps the most important next step for researchers, then, is to test the degree to which this study's findings hold for other democratic states.

The Influence of History: Citizenship, Nationhood, and Rights

The democratic societies in this study choose to enfranchise their aliens, or choose not to, in large part based upon the legal doctrines that guide their citizenship policies. To the degree these doctrines reflect shared conceptions of the meaning of "citizenship" and the "nation," these nationality laws are the products of centuries of national political development. This study uses Brubaker's distinction between democracies with citizenship policies based upon the doctrine of jus soli and those with laws based upon jus sanguinis principles.[2] This distinction explains much of the observed variance among the democracies in this study. Those democratic states that offer birthright citizenship to the children of aliens are more likely to have some form of voting rights for their resident aliens. These rights do not appear, furthermore, to be a substitute for citizenship. Jus sanguinis states, with their higher barriers to naturalization, do not seem to use voting rights as an alternative strategy to incorporate their aliens. Somewhat ironically, then, those democratic states in which aliens find it easier to naturalize are likely to be the same states that provide a broader range of political rights to aliens who choose not to naturalize. In this sense, jus soli states are likely to give aliens more options to join their political communities, including the option to vote without taking citizenship. By contrast, jus sanguinis not only have higher barriers to naturalization but also are less likely to adopt institutional alternatives to naturalization such as voting rights for resident aliens. This suggests that, rather than these democracies converging around a common set of norms and practices for the incorporation of aliens, they will likely continue to exhibit considerable variation in the political rights they give to their resident aliens.

As Brubaker has noted, the shared conceptions of nationhood on which states have constructed their polities are both historically contingent and highly resistant to change. Brubaker captured this path dependence and its contemporary consequences memorably in his differentiation between France and Germany:

> In the French tradition, the nation has been conceived in relation to the institutional and territorial frame of the state. Revolutionary and Republican definitions of nationhood and citizenship—unitarist, universalist, and secular—reinforced what was already in the ancien régime an essentially political understanding of nationhood. ... If the French understanding of nationhood has been state-centered and assimilationist, the German understanding has been *Volk*-centered and differentialist. Since national feeling developed before the nation-state, the German idea of the nation was not originally political, nor was it linked to the abstract idea of citizenship. This prepolitical German nation, this nation in search of a state, was conceived not as the bearer of universal political values, but as an organic cultural, linguistic, or racial community—as an irreducibly particular *Volksgemeinschaft*.[3]

These historical differences gave rise to French understandings of the "nation" that are historically inclusive and multinational, and to German understandings that historically have been ethnically and linguistically differentialist. In this way, Brubaker ties the contemporary experience of migrants in France and Germany to the path of political development of the respective states. This study finds considerable support for the path dependence that Brubaker and others emphasize. Although a democratic society may conceive of the polity as either multinational in character (as in the United Kingdom) or as ethnically homogenous (as in Japan), these conceptions seem to be robust and resistant to change. Democratic states that historically have been assimilationist have become more so as they have broadened their political rights to individuals on the boundaries of the polity. States that historically have been differentialist, by contrast, are likely to remain so today even in the face of expanding global human rights.

This has both important theoretical and practical implications. Theoretically, to the degree the spread of voting rights for resident aliens continues, it is likely to occur mostly in jus soli democracies such as the United States. There is evidence to suggest that, at least in the United States, support for giving resident aliens the right to vote is growing.[4] Rather than using voting rights as an alternative to incorporation, jus sanguinis states are unlikely to adopt such practices.[5] In this sense, one will likely see continued differences among democracies in the political rights they offer to their aliens. This expectation is contrary the "convergence" hypothesis of the transnationalist school: Democracies are unlikely to converge around a common set of rights and practices for their resident aliens. This observation is relevant to policy-makers and advocates for the rights of immigrants. In jus sanguinis states, advocates of such rights likely will face shared understandings of the political community that are highly elaborated, resistant to change, and unreceptive to demands for the inclusion of aliens. Policy-makers and advocates of voting rights for aliens likely will enjoy their greatest successes only when they carefully consider how such proposals conform to a democratic society's historical experiences and shared conceptions of nationhood. Truly universal voting rights—not only for *all* residents in a democratic society, but also particularly for *all* residents in *every* democratic society—are unlikely.

State Institutions and Voting Rights for Aliens

Scholars who study state-level factors are right to call attention to the importance of political parties and judiciaries, but this study challenges the expectations they have put forth. It challenges these researchers, furthermore, to consider the interaction of these institutions with electoral rules. The partisan composition of a democratic state's government may not affect the prospect for that state granting its aliens the right to vote. Contrary to Hammar's and Howard's explanations, this study finds no meaningful differences between governments composed of parties of the left and right-leaning governments.[6] It is nevertheless useful to consider why governments composed parties of the left might be no more likely to enfranchise aliens than rightist parties. There are several possible explanations. Foremost is the Janus-faced nature of parties of the left. While Hammar may be correct that resident aliens tend to vote for parties of the left, his analysis ignores the inherent tensions between immigrants and labor. Parties of the left may gain when they enfranchise aliens, but they also may face the prospect of losing the support of their core constituency of organized labor. Migrants compete with unions for jobs. Organized labor naturally has good reasons to oppose any measures, including the right to vote, that make it more attractive for migrants to settle in a democratic society. This uncertainty that parties of the left face may be exacerbated in multiparty systems, furthermore, where the competition among leftist parties is greater. Labor groups may choose to vote, for example, for the Communist Party instead of the Social Democrats. Indeed, this is what happened in France in 1981. After the Parti Socialiste had promised to enact voting rights for France's resident aliens, upon taking power the government discovered considerable opposition within its own ranks to the proposal. The government not only quickly reversed its position, but also went so far as to destroy the pamphlets that it had printed to explain the plan to the French nation.[7] Particularly in proportional representation systems, then, governments composed of parties of the left may face considerable electoral uncertainty when considering whether to give aliens the right to vote. Ironically, parties of the right likely face less electoral uncertainty, since their constituents are unlikely to defect to parties of the left. Perhaps it is no surprise, then, that in 2003 Gianfranco Fini, Italy's deputy prime minister under Silvio Berlusconi and leader of the conservative National Alliance party, proposed that Italy's resident aliens be allowed to vote in local elections.[8]

Likewise, Hammar's observation that leftist parties gain from enfranchising resident aliens belies the degree of competition among political parties for the votes of immigrants. As Belgium's experience shows, rightist parties do not willingly concede this constituency to left-leaning parties. It was a rightist party in Belgium that finally enabled the Belgian government to enfranchise resident aliens. The Francophone rightist VLD party abandoned its opposition to enfranchisement in part to appeal to the socially conservative Turkish population in the VLD's strongholds around Brussels. Thus, partisan competition for immigrant votes in Belgium created a new opportunity that, in the absence of competition from rightist parties, previously did not exist. This dynamic was evident in France's most recent presidential election, when in 2005 then Interior Minister Nicolas Sarkozy appeared "to have struck a chord with his controversial call for long-term foreign residents to have the right to vote in municipal elections."[9] Partisan competition for immigrant votes may create opportunities for new political rights for resident aliens.

Another reason there are no obvious differences in political parties may be the influence of diasporas in parties of the right. Unlike Hammar's supposition about resident aliens, émigrés who cast absentee ballots tend to vote for causes and parties across the political spectrum.[10] It is possible that governments are enacting voting rights for resident aliens not out of a sense of obligation or benevolence, but as a quid pro quo for other democracies that adopt similar provisions for their émigrés. This appears to be one reason why South Korea enfranchised resident aliens in 2006.[11] A number of democracies in this study have explicit reciprocal agreements that recognize the right to vote for each other's émigrés. Spain and Portugal have such an agreement, as do the United Kingdom and the Republic of Ireland. This study shows, furthermore, that the voting rights practices of a democracy's neighboring countries significantly predict its own practices. Together these findings suggest that governments may be enacting reciprocity arrangements to protect the interests of their émigrés. Reciprocity agreements therefore may be a means for governments to gain favor with an important constituency: their émigrés. While governments of any composition are likely to benefit from these reciprocal agreements, it may be that governments composed of right-leaning parties are more likely to negotiate these reciprocity agreements for two reasons. First, as noted above, on issues of citizenship politics right-leaning governments may be freer from the constituency conflicts that typify parties of the left. Second, to the degree that émigrés vote for right-leaning parties, governments composed of rightist parties may stand more to gain at the polls.[12]

A final possibility is that governments are responding to factors other than pure electoral calculus, such as pressures from grassroots transnational lobbying. The significance of neighborhood effects in both models suggests this is a possibility. The nature of this study's design and the data it uses prevents it from assessing the merits of this argument. Due to the paucity of reliable measures of transnationalism, the analysis relies on an admittedly crude measure that does not indicate how these transnational processes influence the policy decisions of democratic governments. Nevertheless, it appears that governments are behaving in ways that scholars from the nationalist thesis have failed to explain. It is also apparent that scholars from the nationalist thesis have failed to consider the role of electoral systems on their partisan arguments. If parties of the left face considerable electoral uncertainty when they adopt such voting rights measures, then they are likely to feel those pressures more acutely in proportional representation systems. These speculations and the absence of statistically significant partisan effects suggest that researchers need to investigate more explicitly the relationship of partisan factors and electoral systems.

The nationalist thesis also fails to explain the surprising role of national judiciaries in the political rights for resident aliens. Nationalist scholarship shows that, in the past, judiciaries rather than legislatures have extended civil rights and social protections to migrants. This study finds some evidence, however, that states with activist judiciaries are less likely to offer their resident aliens the right to vote. There may be two reasons for this. First, although activist judiciaries may have been progressive in the expansion of the civil and economic rights of aliens, there is no theoretical reason to expect

them to be progressive in the area of political rights. Courts may just
as often be activist in a conservative fashion: They may support laws
or enact rulings that reinforce fundamentally ethnic, linguistic, and
differentialist aspects of citizenship politics that serve to exclude resident aliens from the body of citizenship rights. As chapter 6 shows, an
illustrative example is the Federal Republic of Germany, where in
1990 the Federal Constitutional Court ruled that the voting rights
initiatives violated the Basic Law because the right to vote is a collective one belonging to the German nation, not an individual right.[13]
Austria's court similarly struck down Vienna's enfranchisement initiative.[14] These are examples of democratic states with strong and active
judicial review in which the courts upheld conceptions of the political
community that exclude resident aliens. While courts in assimilationist societies may be inclusive in their consideration of voting rights
provisions, those in differentialist democratic societies are likely to be
conservative and exclusionary.

A second reason for the surprising findings about the role of judiciaries is that, unlike in the areas of civil and economic rights, courts
may defer to legislatures on questions of the political rights of resident aliens. The case of Japan illustrates this point. In 1990, a group
of eleven Korean nationals who resided in Japan sued for the right to
vote in parliamentary elections.[15] When the Japanese supreme court
considered the case in 1995, it ruled that Japanese law neither entitled
foreign nationals to the right to vote nor precluded them from
voting. It also held that the Diet has the constitutional authority to
enact such rights for resident aliens if it so chooses. Although the
Diet has subsequently tabled two such measures, the court's ruling
illustrates how judiciaries may defer to legislatures on matters of the
political rights of migrants. Hur's summary of Japan's experience
illustrates how the interaction of conservative governments and deferential courts may delimit the substantive impact of de jure rights:

> Although constitutional provisions exist that confer equal treatment and
> respect for individual rights to all persons in Japan, these guarantees
> exist in the abstract—in the reality of legal and administrative practice,
> they have provided far fewer protections for individual rights, particu-
> larly for ethnic minorities. The scope of constitutional rights has been
> circumscribed by a conservative central government and a judiciary def-
> erential to executive and legislative branches of government.[16]

These examples highlight how political scientists need to explore further when courts will seek to include aliens rather than exclude them,
or when courts will choose to defer to legislatures.

While scholars are correct to emphasize the importance of the state's political institutions, this study shows how the nationalist thesis has misstated the impact of these factors. In the enactment of voting rights for resident aliens, both political parties and national courts appear to behave in ways researchers have yet to explain. Scholars must refocus on the roles of judiciaries and parties within government. This study has also highlighted the significance of electoral systems, which researchers have not fully considered. The interaction of partisan factors with electoral systems is a particularly important area for future research. In proportional representation systems, parties of the left may face greater electoral uncertainty and increasing competition from centrist or even rightist parties for the support of immigrant populations.[17] These are hypotheses and expectations that researchers can test.

Systemic Factors: Traces of Transnationalism

Transnationalist factors do not perform as well in the statistical models in this study. That a democracy's commitment to human rights does not predict whether or not it chooses to enfranchise its aliens is a surprising and important nonfinding, particularly since transnationalist researchers including Soysal and Sassen have argued that migrants and NGOs alike increasingly assert the claims of noncitizens in the language of global human rights.[18] There are two possible explanations for this nonfinding. The first is the population the analysis uses to test nationalist and transnationalist explanations. All twenty-five of the democracies in the study exhibit considerable commitment to human rights; likewise, their human rights practices contribute to the measures of democracy used as selection criteria for the study's population. In this sense, there is little variation in the commitment of the subject states to human rights (it is uniformly high) even as there is considerable variation in their voting rights practices.

Nevertheless, it is important to note a theoretical deficiency of the human rights argument. Although transnationalists may be correct that migrants increasingly assert claims for civil, social, and political rights in the vernacular of human rights, they have not demonstrated how states translate these abstract claims into tangible policies or practices. Indeed, although norms of human rights may demand states provide resident aliens a broad range of social and civil protections, they do not make similar demands for political rights. In the area of the political rights of noncitizens, human rights norms differ considerably from other norms such as the prohibition of governmental corruption or of the torture of prisoners. Though there remains some disagreement among states and non-state actors about certain activities (for example, is the death penalty a human rights violation?) generally broad agreement remains about what constitutes a violation of the prohibition against torture. By contrast, in the area of the political rights of migrants, there is little agreement among states and international NGOs as to what body of political rights democratic states should provide to resident aliens—let alone what policies constitute violations of these human rights. The transnationalist argument about the influence of human rights thus overstates the degree to which such ideas really are "norms." Although they may legitimate the participation in domestic politics of international governmental organizations or nongovernmental actors like Helsinki Watch, these norms fail to specify what states must and must not do.[19] In this sense, the transnationalist argument makes a better case for the constitutive nature of these norms—that is, the norms define certain actors as legitimate participants in policy decisions—than it does for their regulative effects—what state behaviors are expected or discouraged.

This argument highlights a second insufficiency of the transnationalist emphasis on global human rights. As Sikkink, Klotz, Wang and Rosenau and others have shown, international norms have the greatest regulative effect when they have an international or nongovernmental organization that champions them.[20] These organizations often specify modes of conduct that constitute compliance with the norms. Wang and Rosenau show, for example, how Transparency International's "islands of integrity" model provides specific steps for states to demonstrate their compliance with anticorruption norms.[21] Similarly, Klotz shows how TransAfrica, an international NGO, worked with the Organization for African Unity to reconstruc certain state and corporate policies toward South Africa as violations of human rights norms.[22] Unlike in these examples, however, in the area of the political rights of resident aliens there are neither clearly defined standard of violation and compliance, nor are there organizations that champion a given model of rights for states to adopt. Although international and nongovernmental organizations often monitor the citizenship practices of states (particularly emerging democracies), these organizations have yet to formulate a specific template of political rights for resident aliens.[23] The transnationalist argument therefore overstates the importance of human rights norms to the political rights of migrants. These norms are neither sufficiently well developed so that actors have shared understandings of what constitutes compliance and violation, nor do they have organizational champions that encourage and facilitate the development of such common understandings.

The transnationalist thesis thus suffers from an overstatement of the role of systemic factors on the voting rights of resident aliens. This study shows, nevertheless, that one of the systemic factors high-lighted by transnationalist scholarship may have some impact on the practices of democratic states. Neighborhood effects do matter: States bordered by democracies that enfranchise their aliens are more likely to do so themselves. What explains this trace of transnational-ism? There are several possible explanations. One is that resident aliens are working with their home governments to obtain the right to vote in their countries of residence—a form of "transnationalism from above" in Guarnizo's memorable phrase.[24] Since resident aliens more often arrive from states nearby than from those far away, they may well be working with home governments to facilitate reciprocal arrangements between democracies. Such reciprocal agreements may explain the significance of the spatial correlation observed by transna-tionalist researchers. A second plausible explanation is a demonstra-tion effect: Democracies that enfranchise their aliens demonstrate to their neighbors the beneficial effects of these practices—either to society as a whole, or in terms of electoral gain for specific parties. A study that specifically models the diffusion of this practice could test whether or not such demonstration effects explain this finding of sig-nificant border effects.

This study deliberately uses a TSCS design to test the systemic and transnational claims of transnationalist researchers. If their sys-temic claims were valid, one would observe similar effects across a broad population of democracies. Yet this study has found little sup-port for such systemic factors other than neighborhood effects. To the degree these neighborhood effects capture transnational processes, they may be important evidence of nascent transnationalist processes. Transnationalist researchers must now identify both research designs and measures that will allow us to trace these processes with greater theoretical productivity and confidence.

Next Steps

Many of the inadequacies of the extant research arise from its failure to test explanations across a broader population of democracies. As this study has shown, a larger test of competing nationalist and transnationalist hypotheses produces a number of surprising findings that neither thesis explains well. This is not to denigrate the case research that is the foundation of the literature on citizenship politics. Indeed, it is this body of research that has highlighted the importance of a democracy's history and its unique understandings of citizenship and nationhood. How migrants in a given democracy experience these understandings is particularly important, furthermore, for both policy-makers and for those who advocate greater rights for immigrants. Case research will continue to be important both theoretically and practically.

However, the existing nationalist and transnationalist literatures give an insufficient understanding for how and why democracies extend political rights to their noncitizens. Unlike in the domain of social or civil rights, activist judiciaries tend to exclude migrants from political rights rather than to incorporate them. Similarly, there are no discernable differences between left- and right-leaning governments. Neither the existing nationalist nor the transnationalist literature expected these findings.

These theoretical implications suggest important next steps for scholars of citizenship policies. A principle finding of this study is the importance of historical and path-dependent factors to the politics of citizenship in any democracy. These are factors best explored through case research, as illustrated in chapter 6. Democratic states and societies—even historically nondemocratic ones[25]—share understandings of the meaning of citizenship, the nation, and the political community that reflect their unique historical experiences. These shared understandings are deep-seeded and resistant to the transnational and international pressures commonly attributed to globalization. Therefore, citizenship scholars must continue to give due theoretical and empirical attention to the path dependencies that affect how citizens and migrants alike constitute their political communities and receive rights from the state.

Although political institutions nevertheless are important, citizenship scholars must revisit their commonly held expectations. Another important area of research is the relationship of political parties, electoral systems, diasporas, and the rights of migrants. Future case research must explore not only the influence of partisan affiliations but also the electoral calculus and pressures from diasporas that political parties face. Finally, future research needs to explicate the mechanisms through which transnational pressures affect state practices. A shortcoming of this study is its inability to specify how transnational pressures or international NGOs exercise influence over state practices toward their resident aliens. This study has argued, furthermore, that there are few if any organizations that champion the rights of resident aliens. If this is correct, it is all the more a mystery why democracies that enfranchise their aliens tend to cluster together. How do migrants organize themselves transnationally? What support have home states offered? While the existing research provides general answers to these questions, few have examined specifically whether or how migrants organize to claim the right to vote. Similarly, there is a dearth of research about the role of international NGOs in the advocacy of political rights for immigrants. Researchers need to trace the processes that provide an echo of transnationalism in democratic societies today.

8

———

Sovereignty and the Nation

> Sovereignty is an anachronistic concept originating in bygone times when society consisted of rulers and subjects, not citizens. It became the cornerstone of international relations with the Treaty of Westphalia in 1648. During the French Revolution, the king was overthrown and the people assumed sovereignty. But a nationalist concept of sovereignty soon superseded the dynastic version.... True sovereignty belongs to the people, who in turn delegate it to their governments.
>
> —George Soros, "The People's Sovereignty," 2004

George Soros's conception of popular sovereignty is commonplace today, so much so that his words hardly are objectionable. Whether it is the nominal commitment of even the most despotic governments to the welfare of the "people" or Fukuyama's end-of-history thesis, it is obvious that, as Soros observes, sovereignty today is a different institution than it was in 1648, in 1789, or even in 1945.[1] Yet while there may be a broad—even global—understanding that sovereignty resides with the people, the question of who precisely the "people" are remains an object of considerable political contestation. This is true not only in emerging democracies but also in those democratic societies with the longest histories of representative government. This contestation is particularly evident in the policies democratic states adopt toward those individuals in a society who reside on the periphery of the polity. These individuals are productive members of a democratic community, have resided in their communities for years or even decades, pay taxes, and shoulder other burdens that states expect of their citizens. Yet because these individuals are not citizens, in many democratic societies they remain outside the community of individuals who participate in the decision-making of

139

their governments. Soros's conception of popular sovereignty thus belies just how problematic any conception of "the people" really is.

In a juridical sense, a primary function of the modern, centralized nation-state is to define and enumerate those individuals who are objects of the state's authority. For this reason, contestation over the boundaries of the polity is as old as the modern nation-state itself. In the turmoil after the overthrow of the French monarchy, for example, republican leaders gave considerable thought to the role of noncitizens in the democratic French state, including such radical ideas as a provision in the constitution of 1793 that allowed some foreigners to participate in elections.[2] Yet the twentieth century gave new impetus to contestation within democratic societies about the meaning of the "people" and the "nation," for several reasons. For one, the growth in the number of democracies means that emerging democratic societies must consider anew precisely who belongs to the polity. Transitional democracies have done so with varying results. Several former Soviet republics have pursued divergent policies toward their Russian-speaking minorities, for example: Russian speakers have voted in Estonian elections but do not even have the right to choose a place of residence in Latvia, let alone the right to participate in politics.[3] Another reason for contestation over the boundaries of the polity is the explosive growth of international migration in the twentieth century—both at the century's outset and at its conclusion. These flows have provided democratic states with a large and growing population of permanent residents who are neither citizens nor strangers. The incorporation of these aliens into democratic societies has been and remains among the most important public policy issues for democratic states.

It is little surprise, then, that political scientists have studied the state's treatment of aliens as a means to examine the changing relationship between the state and the polity. Scholars have documented that the rights of citizens and those of aliens increasingly have become blurred. During the latter half of the twentieth century, as the number of resident aliens has grown, democratic states have broadened the civil and economic rights that these individuals enjoy, so much so that some researchers argue the differences in the rights of citizens and aliens are more symbolic than substantive. Yet democratic societies have only recently granted extensive political rights to their aliens; some have done so reluctantly, and most have done so incompletely. Perhaps this is because democratic societies view the act of casting a ballot as the apotheosis of participation in the political life of one's community. The right to vote speaks to the meaning of citizenship and the "nation" in a way that other rights—such as the right to receive unemployment benefits or the protection against unreasonable detention—do not. For this reason, it is little surprise that democratic states historically have been unwilling to allow noncitizens to vote.

It is therefore striking that in forty-five democratic states citizenship is no longer a qualification for the franchise. Though some have argued these rights are more procedural than substantive, the enfranchisement of aliens has considerable consequences both within and between states.[4] In Israel, for example, the Likud party reversed itself in 2003 and advocated for the first time the creation of an independent Palestinian state. Part of the explanation for this reversal is that Israeli leaders are concerned that the growing number of Palestinians residing within Israel's borders may demand the right to vote in Israeli elections, with obvious implications for an ethnically constituted state.[5] Estonia's Russian-speaking population of noncitizens cast almost 12 percent of the ballots in the 1999 election.[6] Obviously, the right of aliens to vote can have important practical consequences in democracies. Therefore, it is all the more astonishing that democratic societies have adopted the practice of noncitizen voting, and that it has spread during the last four decades.

This fact alone suggests that democratic societies have reconceived the nature and boundaries of their political communities. It is little surprise, perhaps, that some political scientists have argued that democratic societies today embody a Kantian cosmopolitanism that disentangles the state from the nation. Democracies are becoming, they argue, "postnational." The practical and theoretical implications of this argument are considerable. For policy-makers, this suggests the state has new obligations to its resident aliens, a population against which it has historically discriminated in the allocation of rights. When enforced by the international community and NGOs, these new obligations may have both considerable costs and benefits to democratic societies. To political scientists, the transnationalist thesis suggests the institutions of state sovereignty and citizenship are changing, so much so that they have renewed theoretical import. If sovereignty is an anachronism, as Soros and some researchers assert, then the organization of the international system (and the study thereof) around the principle of sovereignty also is a relic of the past. This has important implications for the discipline of political science.

For all these reasons, it is important to test competing arguments across a broad population of democratic states. This study shows, however, that transnationalist arguments are insufficient. To the degree democratic societies are becoming more inclusionary, it reflects not the growth of the international human rights regime or global civil society, but rather a society's shared understandings of the meaning of "citizenship" and "nation." Though both concepts are central to the exercise of democracy, democratic societies conceive of these ideas differently: As yet there is no shared understanding among democratic societies as to the meaning of these concepts. This is why the Federal Constitutional Court in Germany ruled that "elections in which foreigners can vote cannot convey democratic legitimacy" even as neighboring states, including Denmark and the Netherlands, willingly let resident aliens vote.[7] Individuals contest the legitimacy of voting rights for resident aliens within the confines of these common understandings about membership in the polity. These understandings reflect a democracy's history of national development. They are highly elaborated understandings, furthermore, that resist the globalizing pressures of the international human rights regime and the proliferation of international nongovernmental organizations. While these NGOs are new and assertive players in the politics of citizenship in democratic states, their participation is largely circumscribed by a society's shared historical conception of nationhood. New voters must coexist with old nations.

Citizens and aliens alike contest these shared understandings and attendant rights, furthermore, within the state's political institutions. Though this study shows some evidence of transnationalism, it is apparent that democratic states refract the systemic pressures cited by transnationalists through their political parties, electoral systems, and judiciaries. To the degree that shared global understandings of human rights are important, then, it is only as those rights are contested within the institutions of the state.

Democratic states seem to have enfranchised aliens, then, not because they are becoming "postnational" but rather because historically they have been assimilationist. Democratic states that traditionally have been inclusive are likely becoming more so, even as democracies that have legacies of nationalistic differentialism probably will remain exclusionary. While the state's courts and political parties remain the institutional locus of contestation over membership in the polity, each institution affirms preexisting conceptions of nationality. This is why Germany's experience with voting rights reflects the ethno-linguistic conception of German nationality, Britain's voting rights practices mirror the construction of a multinational Commonwealth citizenship, and Switzerland's practices exhibit the variation typical of federalism.

This study's findings have important practical implications as well. For newly established or transitional democratic states, the findings illustrate how problematic the constitution of a political community is. Though the experiences of post-Soviet republics in central Europe exemplify these problems, they also are apparent in democratic states with active separatist movements such as Mexico and Canada. Likewise, there are a growing number of "failed" states, to which the international community collectively has responded with "nation-building" military operations. This study's findings suggest the problematic nature of such nation-building policies. While public officials commonly refer to these missions as *nation*-building exercises, they in fact are *state*-building (or state-rebuilding) missions. The international community will not succeed at building an Afghan, Liberian, or Iraqi nation; though it may develop the necessary state institutions, the constitution of a Liberian or Iraqi nation (or alternatives) is a societal process that will reflect each society's unique legacies and experiences. Since the "nation" itself is a shared understanding, international institutions can do little to shape the construction of such shared conceptions—it is as much a bottom-up process as it is a top-down one. If international human rights regimes and global civil society have little impact in the world's most democratic societies, furthermore, how can political leaders expect them to constitute a nation in states with poorly developed civil societies and little history of democratic practice?

Ironically, then, state sovereignty remains paramount to the constitution of a democratic political community even as international leaders proclaim that state sovereignty is changing. One such leader is former United Nations Secretary General Kofi Annan. Echoing transnationalist thinkers, Annan wrote in 1999:

> State sovereignty, in its most basic sense, is being redefined—not least by the forces of globalisation and international co-operation. States are now widely understood to be instruments at the service of their peoples, and not vice versa. At the same time individual sovereignty...has been enhanced by a renewed and spreading consciousness of individual rights.[8]

While Annan is correct that democratic states are instruments of their "peoples," they nevertheless are the instruments through which the "people" define membership in their community. Though the "spreading consciousness of individual rights" may empower aliens and citizens alike to contest the state's exclusion of individuals from a body of rights, democratic states remain the principal agents of inclusion and exclusion. Michael Walzer has called the exclusion of aliens by citizens "the most common form of tyranny in human history."[9] To constitute a democratic political community, however, this tyranny likely will remain a feature of citizenship politics for the foreseeable future.

Appendix A

Problems with Demographic Data on Resident Aliens

Demographic factors may have considerable impact on whether or not, and how, democratic states offer their resident aliens the right to vote. Several researchers have noted that the political geography of the settlement of migrants may expand or foreclose the rights and opportunities migrants enjoy.[1] Similarly, some have argued that the ethnic similarity or differences between host societies and their migrant population may explain variations between democratic states as well as within democratic states over time. Both these arguments suggest that this study should include demographic measures to account for the political geography of migrant settlement and the in-group/out-group politics of migration. The available demographic data is unreliable, however, particularly for a TSCS study. While researchers may reliably measure the demography within a given democratic state over a short period of observation, it is difficult to do so for a population of democracies over a span of four decades. This is because there is no standard practice among democracies for the measurement and reporting of populations of migrants generally, and resident aliens in particular.

Some states enumerate "resident aliens" as those individuals residing within the country who are foreign citizens. Because this excludes foreign-born naturalized citizens, measurement only of foreign citizens arguably overlooks the importance of chain migration to the patterns in which migrants settle in a given host state. Seventeen of the study's twenty-five states enumerate their populations of migrants according to the criterion of the individual's citizenship. These are Austria, Belgium, Denmark, Finland, France, Germany, Greece, Italy, Japan, Netherlands, Norway, Portugal, Spain, Sweden, Switzerland, the United Kingdom, and Uruguay.

Of the other eight states in the study, five enumerate and report their populations according to the individual's place of birth (these are Australia, Canada, Ireland, New Zealand, and the United States). This measure includes all foreign citizens as well as naturalized citizens who were born in a different country. Thus, the measure of foreign-born individuals is more inclusive than the measure of foreign citizens. While this measure captures a number of plural nationals and perhaps better characterizes patterns of migration, as noted above only five states in the study report this data. Even though some foreign-born residents choose to naturalize in a given state, they nevertheless may continue to reside among resident aliens. Since a feature of chain migration is that newly arrived aliens tend to reside with other resident aliens, foreign-born naturalized citizens and resident aliens together will attract migrants. Hence, the individual's place of birth—along with his ethnic, linguistic, or religious heritage—may influence the settlement pattern of migrants irrespective of his or her citizenship status. Thus, the measurement of resident aliens by their citizenship alone will underestimate these effects.

In principle, one can correct for the difference between the number of foreign citizens and foreign-born individuals by adding the number of naturalized citizens to the number of foreign citizens resident within a country (or, alternatively, subtracting the number of naturalized citizens from the number of foreign-born individuals). However, this technique does not guarantee a valid or reliable count. For example, in jus sanguinis states this potentially would overcount the number of foreign-born individuals, since some naturalized citizens are nevertheless native-born persons. Clearly, it is difficult to equate place of birth and citizenship status between jus sanguinis and jus soli states.

Two other states—Hungary and Israel—enumerate their populations according to ethnic or ethno-religious criteria. Hungary's census data does not enumerate based on the place of the individual's birth or on his or her citizenship. Instead, Hungary census data reports its population according to "nationality." Given Hungary's history, it is perhaps unsurprising that census and statistical figures report residents as Hungarian, Slovak, Romanian, Croatian, Serbian, Slovenian, German, Gypsy, or other.[2] Unfortunately, this data does not delineate foreign citizens from Hungarian citizens; many if not most of the Slovak and Romanian nationals counted by the census undoubtedly have Hungarian citizenship. Israel presents a similarly difficult case. For two reasons it is likely a large number of Israeli citizens were born overseas. The first is obviously Israel's brief existence and the large number of settlers since Israel's establishment. The second is the Law of Return; because Jews qualify for automatic citizenship, a number of individuals who immigrate to Israel become citizens without first establishing residency, as many states require.[3] Perhaps for these reasons, Israel census figures report minority differences along an ethno-religious distinction—"Jews" and "Nonjews." With the Law of Return, all enumerated Jews are Israeli citizens or are eligible for immediate naturalization. The problem occurs, however, when one looks at the category of "Nonjews." This is an unreliable datum because the category includes both a number of native-born individuals who lack Israeli citizenship, and a number of Israeli Arabs who have citizenship (and some of them may have been born "overseas" in territories occupied by Israel during the various Mideast wars).

These observations indicate two other potential problems with data on resident aliens. The first is that state practices for the identification and enumeration of foreign-born residents have changed over time. Few of the states in the study report data of any type on migrants prior to 1960, no doubt due to the relatively low levels of immigration before then. A second problem is that state practices for enumerating resident aliens correlate highly with national conceptions of citizenship. For Israel and Hungary, this problem is obvious: Each enumerates elements of its population based on an ethnic or religious criterion. But this correlation extends to other states in the study as well. For example, jus sanguinis states such as Austria or Germany count children of foreign-born parents as foreign citizens even though they are born on Austrian or German soil. In other words, whereas a child born to resident aliens in a jus soli state reduces the percentage of aliens residing within a state, in a jus sanguinis state a child of resident aliens increases the percentage of resident aliens. An alternative measure, the number of newly arrived immigrants in a given year, might circumvent the problem of collinearity between national understandings of citizenship and the enumeration of resident aliens. Nevertheless, such a measure is equally questionable since it does not measure the number of resident aliens and hence is not a valid measure.

A Note about Sources for Demographic Data

Statistical annals published by the subject state's governments are the best source for data on each state's population of foreign citizens or foreign-born individuals. Several states (Australia, Belgium, Canada, Ireland, Italy, Japan, the Netherlands, New Zealand, Spain, Sweden, and the United Kingdom) supplement data from hardcopy sources with data published by the national statistical bureaus on the Internet. The bibliography lists sources for the twenty-five democracies in the study according to the publishing state and government agency.

Appendix B

Codebook

Dependent Variables: Measures and Sources

I measure the dependent variable according to three criteria: (a) whether a subnational government grants the franchise to resident aliens, or the national government does; (b) whether the voting rights are for local elections only or for national elections; and (c) whether or not a resident alien must satisfy a nationality requirement to qualify for the franchise. With these criteria, I code the dependent variable for the population of the study as follows:

0: No rights (Australia after 1984; Austria before 1993; Belgium before 1993; Costa Rica; Denmark before 1977; Finland before 1981; France before 1993; Germany before 1993 except for 1989–1990; Greece before 1993 ; Ireland before 1962; Italy before 1993; Japan; the Netherlands before 1979; Norway before 1978; Spain before 1985; Sweden before 1976; the United Kingdom before 1949; and the United States before 1968).

1: Rights granted only by subnational governments (Canada from 1975 to the present; West Germany in 1989; the Netherlands from 1979 to 1981; Switzerland from 1960 to the present; and the United States from 1968 to the present).

2: Local rights, discriminatory (Denmark from 1977 to 1980; Finland from 1981 to 1990; Israel from 1960 to the present; Norway from 1978 to 1981; and all EU member states after 1993).

3: National rights, discriminatory (Australia from 1960 to 1984; Canada from 1960 to 1974; Ireland from 1985 to the present; New Zealand from 1960 to 1974; Portugal; the United Kingdom).

4: Local rights, nondiscriminatory (Denmark after 1980; Finland after 1990; Hungary, Ireland 1963 to 1984; the Netherlands after 1981; Norway after 1981; Spain after 1985; Sweden after 1976).

5: National rights, nondiscriminatory (New Zealand after 1975; Uruguay).

For sources for the coding of each democracy, see chapter 2.

Identifiers, Independent and Control Variables

The following variables either identify each observation in the dataset or are independent or control variables in the study's models. The name within parentheses is the shorthand name for the variable in the Stata dataset.

Year (YEAR): Calendar year (range: 1960 to 2004).

Country Code (CCODE2): The standard country code from the Correlates of War dataset, corrected so that West Germany (CCODE = 255) and Germany (CCODE = 260) are estimated as a single panel (standardized to 260).[1]

Country name (COUNTRY): Name of the democracy.

Birthright Citizenship (JUS): Binary: whether (1) or not (0) the subject state offers birthright citizenship to children born within its borders to parents who are not citizens.[2]

Judicial Review (JREV): Lijphart's index of judicial review, coded from 0 (no judicial review) to 3 (strongest, most active judicial review).[3]

Social Security Transfers (SSXilag1): Amount of the state's per annum welfare spending, as a percentage of GDP, lagged one year.[4]

Partisan composition of government (PARTY): Difference between the percentage of cabinet seats held by parties of the left and the percentage of seats held by parties of the right.[5]

Commitment to International Human Rights (HR): Measured as a state's accession (+1), accession and ratification (+2), or inaction (+0) on three international human rights instruments: the International Covenant on Civil and Political Rights (ICCPR), the International Covenant on Economic, Social, and Cultural Rights

(ICESR), and a regional human rights accord. The relevant regional accords are the Inter-American Convention on Human Rights and the European Convention on Human Rights. No such regional accords exist for Asia or for the South Pacific during the time period of this study.[6]

Density of INGOs (NGO): The natural log of the number of international nongovernmental organizations with at least one member in the democracy, per one million residents. Data is from the Union of International Associations.[7] This measure counts organizations categorized by the UIA as types A, B, C, and D. The UIA did not collect data on organization types E, F, and G prior to 1984.

Border Effects (BORDER): The average score on the dependent variable of the states that border the observed democracy.

European Union Membership (EU): 1 if the state is a member of the European Union, 0 otherwise.

Commonwealth Membership (COMMON): 1 if the state is a member of the Commonwealth, 0 otherwise.

Proportional Representation electoral system (PR): 1 if the state has a proportional representation electoral system, 0 otherwise.[8]

History of representative rule (REPHIST): 1 if the state has a strong history of representative rule, 0 otherwise. The source for data on European states is Rokkan.[9] For other states, I coded the observations according to my understanding of Rokkan's measure, using the POLITY variable as a measure of continuous representative practice.[10]

State formation history (FORMHIST): 1 if the state seceded from another to become independent, 0 if it was a "center-formed" state. Again, I use Rokkan's classification of the European democracies, supplemented by my own coding for those democracies not included in Rokkan's analysis.[11]

Time (TIME): a counter variable centered on the year 1982. For observations before 1982, I coded the years as negative years. For example, an observation from 1960 is coded as –22; one from 1972 is a –10; and so forth. Years after 1982 are positive years (1990 = +8, 2004 = +22).

Appendix C

Descriptive Statistics and Correlation Matrix

Of the seventy-eight pairwise correlations of the study's independent and control variables, only one rises to the conventional threshold of $r = .70$ to raise a concern about multicollinearity. The PR variables correlates with the COMMON variable at $r = .79$. I omitted the PR variable and re-estimated the ordered probit model, and found the COMMON variable significant ($b = 0.563$, *s.e.* $= 0.270$, $p = 0.037$). I then re-estimated the model with the PR variable while omitting the COMMON variable. The PR variable did not become significant, though the EU control variable did ($b = -0.740$, *s.e.* $= 0.375$, $p = 0.048$). In both re-estimations, none of the variables of theoretic interests changed signs or became significant. I conclude that despite their high correlation, both the COMMON and PR control variables should remain in the model as omitted variable bias is statistically less desirable than inefficiency caused by multicollinearity. See Table C.3 for the full table of correlations.

Table C.1. Descriptive Statistics

Variable	Sample Period	States	N	Mean	St. Dev.	Min	Max
Voting rights score	1960–2004	25	1,013	1.69	1.69	0	5
Birthright citizenship	1960–2004	25	1,021	0.38	0.49	0	1
Strength of judicial review	1960–2004	25	1,021	2.14	0.99	1	4
Social security expenditures	1960–2004	25	986	15.14	6.68	2.3	34.7
Partisan control of government	1960–2004	25	1,002	-0.06	0.72	-1	1
Commitment to human rights	1960–2004	25	1,021	3.22	2.23	0	6
Density of NGOs	1960–2004	25	1,009	4.58	1.19	1.22	6.47
Mean DV score of bordering states	1960–2004	25	1,016	0.86	1.17	0	4
EU member	1960–2004	25	1,021	0.40	0.49	0	1
Proportional representation	1960–2004	25	1,021	0.81	0.39	0	1
History of representative institutions	1960–2004	25	1,021	0.53	0.50	0	1
Center–formed state	1960–2004	25	1,021	0.45	0.50	0	1
Commonwealth member	1960–2004	25	1,021	0.18	0.38	0	1
Time	1960–2004	25	1,021	1.15	12.89	-22	22

Table C.2. Data Coverage, by Country

Country	Years for which data is available	Number of observations
Australia	1960–2004	45
Austria	1960–2004	45
Belgium	1960–2004	45
Canada	1960–2004	45
Costa Rica	1976–2004	29
Denmark	1960–2004	45
Finland	1960–2004	45
France	1960–2004	45
Germany	1960–2004	45
Greece	1977 2004	28
Hungary	1991–2004	14
Ireland	1960–2004	45
Israel	1965–2004	40
Italy	1960–2004	45
Japan	1960–2004	45
Netherlands	1960–2004	45
New Zealand	1960–2004	45
Norway	1960–2004	45
Portugal	1977–2004	28
Spain	1983–2004	22
Sweden	1960–2004	45
Switzerland	1960–2004	45
United Kingdom	1960–2004	45
United States	1960–2004	45
Uruguay	1991–2000	10
Total:		981

Table C.3. Correlation Matrix for the Study's Variables

	1	2	3	4	5	6	7
1. Birthright citizenship	1.0000						
2. Strength of judicial review	−0.6823	1.0000					
3. Social security expenditures	0.2164	−0.2200	1.0000				
4. Partisan control of government	0.3106	−0.0937	−0.3914	1.0000			
5. Commitment to human rights	0.0495	−0.3082	−0.0058	−0.0879	1.0000		
6. Density of NGOs	−0.2965	0.2637	0.0790	−0.2721	−0.2151	1.0000	
7. Mean DV score of bordering states	0.0452	0.0834	−0.0289	−0.1913	−0.3864	0.0427	1.0000
8. EU memberhip	−0.0795	0.2745	−0.3718	0.2407	−0.5361	0.0990	0.1183
9. Commonwealth membership	−0.2333	0.4059	−0.3698	0.3332	−0.0254	−0.4871	−0.0991
10. Proportional representation	−0.0848	0.3382	−0.3966	0.3879	−0.0793	−0.6802	0.2061
11. History of representative institutions	−0.0690	0.3070	0.0860	0.1438	−0.0168	−0.3037	0.2233
12. Center-formed state	0.1502	0.2750	−0.0253	0.1530	−0.0795	−0.1192	−0.1377
13. Time	0.0916	0.0125	−0.5183	0.4678	−0.1644	−0.5005	−0.0949

	8	9	10	11	12	13
8. EU membership	1.0000					
9. Commonwealth membership	0.0941	1.0000				
10. Proportional representation	0.1858	0.7927	1.0000			
11. History of representative institutions	0.2148	0.4343	0.5761	1.0000		
12. Center-formed state	−0.1444	0.2880	0.1142	0.0708	1.0000	
13. Time	0.0768	0.6381	0.5496	0.0104	0.0999	1.0000

Notes

1. The Democratic Dilemma of Migration

1. Hong and Haldane 1993, B1.

2. Hammar 1990.

3. Hayduk 2006.

4. Salzmann 1999, 42.

5. Bauböck 1994, vii.

6. Koopmans and Statham 1999, 652–96; Galloway 2000, 82–118; Neuman 2002, 514–17.

7. Sassen 1996, 63.

8. Shanahan 1999, 68.

9. Marshall 1964.

10. Klausen 1995; Joppke 1999.

11. Aylsworth 1931, 114–16; Raskin 1993, 1391–1470.

12. Raskin 1993, 1395.

13. Prak 1999.

14. Sontag 1992, B1.

15. Tomforde 1990.

16. Joppke 1999, 198.

17. This argument seems to arise regularly in other states as well. Philip Dewinter, the leader of the Vlaams Blok party in Belgium, stated in 2004 that Belgium's proposal to enfranchise aliens sent "a permanent message to foreigners that Belgium is a land of milk and honey, where they have rights but no duties." See Vandyck 2004, 6.

18. Rousseau 1997, 50–51.

19. Shanahan 1999, 81.

20. Neuman 1992, 267.

21. Hugo 2003.

22. Dahrendorf 1963.

23. Schmitter 1980, 180–81.

24. Miller 1982; International Migration Review 1985, 400–414.

25. Yet even the small number may have a significant impact on a nation's policies. In Estonia, for instance, resident aliens cast nearly 12 percent of the vote in the October 1999 local elections. "Preliminary voting in local elections ends with good turnout," BBC Summary of World Broadcasts. ETA news agency 1999.

2. The Voting Rights of Resident Aliens

1. Again it is worth quoting Raskin: "While my Canadian and Brazilian neighbors and I may have different interests or approaches on international issues like acid rain or regional trade, we presumably have identical interests in efficient garbage collection, good public schools, speedy road repair, and so on." Raskin 1993, 1452.

2. Bauböck 2005, 684. Bauböck's tally relies upon Blais et al. 2001; Earnest 2004; and Waldrauch 2005.

3. Bauböck 2005, 685.

4. Jordan 1993 mentions Argentina as a state that allows all resident aliens to vote, for example, though I have found no other sources to confirm this.

5. Meran 2003; Waldrauch 2005, 11.

6. Examples from the United States demonstrate this point. Of the six towns in Maryland that allow resident aliens to vote in all municipal elections, for example, by far the largest is Takoma Park, with a population of 17,299 total residents according to the 2000 census.

7. A number of researchers have noted that resident aliens can vote in "school board elections" in Chicago as well; see Raskin 1993, 1429 and 1455; and Harper-Ho 2000, 283 and 313. However, Kathleen Coll, a social anthropologist at Harvard University, argues this is incorrect. She notes that the mayor of Chicago appoints the Board of Education. Resident aliens do participate in the election of members to local school councils, which are "powerless groups headed by the principal and mandated by education reform legislation to approve budgets, etc. that include parents in a school plus teachers and supposedly also other community members." Coll 2003. Nevertheless, these are not elections for public office, as Raskin and Harper-

Ho suggest. See also §105 Illinois Code 5/34–2.1 (2003), particularly subsection (ii)(c).

8. Tomforde 1990, Neuman 1992.

9. An important exception is Blais et al. 2001.

10. Beiming and Thorson 2003.

11. Earnest 2007; Shaw 2007a.

12. Neuman 1992; Soysal 1994, 128.

13. Neuman 1992.

14. "Zürich: Ausländer sollen abstimmen dürfen" 2006.

15. Waldrauch 2005, 11.

16. Agence France Press 2002; Deutsche Presse-Agentur 2002.

17. Waldrauch 2005, 11.

18. Soysal 1994, 128; Galloway 2001, 192. It is worth noting the discriminatory nature of these rights. See the following section that identifies other regimes that discriminate based on the resident alien's nationality.

19. Raskin 1993, 1429; Harper-Ho 2000, 319, fn. 3 and 4. Raskin and Harper-Ho are incorrect in asserting that resident aliens can vote in school board elections in Chicago. See note 7.

20. Chung 1996, 176.

21. These are Chevy Chase sections 3 and 5, Martin's Additions, Somerset, and Barnesville. See Raskin 1993, 1462.

22. Raskin 1993.

23. Harper-Ho 2000, 312–13.

24. Gowen 2002; "Noncitizens Should Get Vote, Too, Mayor Says" 2002.

25. "Noncitizens Seek Ballot Box Access" 2003, DZ07.

26. "Gonzalez Calls for Non-Citizen Voting in School Board Elections" 2003; Hayduk and Wucker 2003; Hayduk 2006.

27. Raskin 1993, 1425–30; Harper-Ho 2000, 291–298.

28. Aylsworth 1931.

29. One possible explanation for Jura's enfranchisement, if not Neuchâtel's, is that Jura is the newest canton in the Swiss federation. It was established in 1978, a time when several European states had started to enfranchise resident aliens.

30. The three other Swiss cantons that considered but failed to pass alien voting measures are Aargau, St. Gallen, and Solothrun.

31. Katz 2000, 174. Colonial relationships created other unexpected voting rights as well. Under the Fourth Republic (from 1946 to 1948), "residents of the French *Territoires d'Outre Mer* [French West Indies] and *Territoires sous Tutelle* [French Polynesia] were allowed to elect representatives to the French parliament." Katz 2000, 174. In other words, aliens residing in French possessions overseas elected representatives to Parliament. In essence, they had resident-alien voting rights without migrating to France, highlighting an implicit—but neither necessary nor sufficient—relationship between migration and resident-alien voting rights.

32. Laitin 1998.

33. Soysal 1994, 127; Rath 1990, 136; and Blais et al. 2001. Galloway 2001 argues by contrast that although Nova Scotia and Saskatchewan allow British subjects to vote in provincial elections, these rights are "anomalous" and should be considered a "legal anachronism."

34. Flanz 2003, vol. XV.

35. Katz 2000.

36. Laitin 1998. The ETA news agency reported that 194,525 resident aliens were eligible to vote in the 1999 elections. In the October 1999 local elections, resident aliens cast 11.7 percent of the total votes; "Preliminary voting in local elections ends with good turnout," 1999.

37. Perhaps these rights have less to do with colonial relationships per se than they have to do with the state's formation. Much like Estonia, Iceland, and Finland also are secessionist states that originally made the franchise available to nationals from the parent state. Since then, however, Finland has broadened the franchise to all resident aliens, while Iceland has rescinded its voting rights (but grandfathered those who already had the right to vote).

38. Aleinikoff and Klusmeyer 2002, 49.

39. Aleinikoff and Klusmeyer 2002, 51.

40. Martiniello 2000.

41. Soysal 1994; Rath 1990, 136–39; Aleinikoff and Klusmeyer 2002, 48.

42. Blais et al. 2001; Electoral Process Information Collection 2002.

43. Soysal 1994, 127–28; Rath 1990, 139.

44. Slattery 1999.

45. Soysal 1994.

46. It is interesting to note that alien suffrage in the Netherlands first emerged in municipalities, suggesting a "bottom-up" evolution of rights that evokes comparison to the current rights in municipalities in the United States and Switzerland. Rath 1990, 139.

47. Nagy 1995, 125.

48. Dong-shin 2006; Tong-hyung 2006.

49. Rokkan 1999.

50. Raskin 1993, 1459.

51. Flanz 2003, vol. VIII.

52. United States Library of Congress, 2004.

53. These examples suggest a possible relationship between the Commonwealth—or at least the United Kingdom's colonial legacy—and certain forms of resident-alien franchise rights. Although common political rights were a goal of the Commonwealth, they are an unrealized one. Some Commonwealth states extend voting rights to all immigrants, while other member states restricted rights to Commonwealth citizens or offered none at all. Given the variation in rights among the thirty-eight democracies that are members of the Commonwealth (not to mention the inclusion of twenty nondemocracies in the Commonwealth), the relationship between alien voting rights and the Commonwealth seems problematic at best.

54. Soysal 1994, 128; Katz 2000.

55. Soysal 1994.

56. Blais et al. 2001.

57. Flanz 2003, vol. IV.

58. Katz 2000.

59. To obtain permanent residency status in South Korea, a resident alien must not only live in the country for three or more years but also have invested $500,000 or more and employed three or more people. Tong-hyung 2006.

60. United Nations Population Division 2006.

61. Of the states discussed in this chapter, between 2000 and 2005 eight (Barbados, Belize, Bolivia, Colombia, Estonia, Hungary, Latvia, and Uruguay) had negative net migration rates per 1,000 citizens. Three others (Chile, Japan, and Venezuela) had a net migration rate per 1,000 citizens of less than 1. Of the twenty-one states with positive net migration, it is noteworthy that migration rate alone does not appear to predict whether or not a state will extend voting rights to resident aliens. While notable negative

cases like the Federal Republic of Germany (2.7 migrants per 1,000 citizens) and the United States (4 per 1,000) have relatively high net migration rates, some of the states offering the franchise to resident aliens have higher rates: Canada is 6.7 per 1,000 and Ireland is 9.8 per 1,000. Other notable negative observations have relatively *low* migration rates, furthermore: Japan is 0.4 per 1,000 and France is 1.002 per 1,000 (all figures are from United Nations Population Division 2006). Of course, net migration rates might be significant in a comprehensive model, or alternative measures of migration such as absolute levels might be more reliable. However, the prima facie impression is that migration rates alone are not sufficient to explain the variation among states offering resident aliens the right to vote.

62. See Flanz 2003, vol. IV.

63. See Flanz 2003, vol. VII.

64. European Union 1997.

65. European Union 1997.

66. See Aleinikoff and Klusmeyer 2002, 51.

67. Shaw 2002.

68. Council of Europe 2007.

69. Shaw 2002, 14–15.

70. Raskin 1993, 1458.

71. Universal Declaration of Human Rights 1948. This language creates another ambiguity, however. When it asserts the right of the individual to take part in the government of his or her "country," does this refer to his or her country of citizenship, or his or her country of residence?

72. Raskin 1993, 1458.

73. International Covenant on Civil and Political Rights 1966.

74. Rath 1990, 130.

75. Aleinikoff and Klusmeyer 2002, 51.

76. Kashiwazaki 2000, 457–58.

77. "European Local Authorities Congress' Chamber Passes Recommendations to Latvia," 1998; "MPs reject right of noncitizens to vote in local elections" 2000; "Human rights body presses for noncitizens' right to vote" 2000.

78. Rath 1990, 128. These are Aargau, Bern, Geneva, St. Gallen, Solothurn, Vaud, and Zurich.

79. Chung 1996; Harper-Ho 2000.

80. Schleswig-Holstein, the third *länder* to adopt voting rights for its resident aliens, is less urbanized than either West Berlin or Hamburg. It is interesting to note, however, that Schleswig-Holstein includes the entire German border with Denmark, another state that enfranchises resident aliens.

81. Money 1999.

82. Kondo 2001, 239.

83. Raskin 1993; Harper-Ho 2000.

84. Aylsworth 1931.

85. Held et al. 1999, 283–326.

86. This begs the question as to whether or not resident aliens actually have a right to vote. It is interesting to note that at least in American constitutional jurisprudence, there is no "right" to vote. So the interesting case of resident alien voters highlights two important questions: To what degree is the franchise a fundamental right in the various nation-states mentioned in this study? And to the degree it is a right, have states literally created "second-class citizens" in resident alien voters, whose franchise rights the state may arbitrarily abridge? While the case of the United Kingdom seems to affirm the vote-as-a-privilege argument, Iceland's and Australia's implementation of grandfather clauses for previously enfranchised resident aliens suggest that, at a minimum, states are reluctant to abridge voting privileges.

87. Raskin 1993, 1394.

88. Raskin 1993, Harper-Ho 2000.

89. Neuman 2000.

90. Neuman 1992, 283–87. This argument is similar to Rogers Brubaker's explanation (1992) of the differences in the naturalization rates of France and Germany. Brubaker argues the greater naturalization rates in France reflect the different "cultural definitions of citizenship" embedded in the competing legal traditions of jus soli in France (citizenship by birth) and jus sanguinis in Germany (citizenship by decent or ancestry).

91. Neuman 1992, 291.

92. Harper-Ho 2000, 282–83.

93. Raskin 1993, 1415–16.

94. Neuman 1992, 264.

95. The migration data for each of these states cast doubt upon Neuman's argument, however.

96. Neuman 1992, 261.

97. Raskin 1993, 1394.

98. Raskin 1993, 1456.

99. Raskin 1993, 1393.

100. Raskin 1993, 1458.

101. Earnest 2007; Shaw 2007a.

102. Shaw 2002; Shaw 2003; and Shaw 2007a.

103. As King, Keohane, and Verba (1994) note, researchers cannot use case studies to test more hypotheses than the number of cases, since this would result in negative degrees of freedom and standard errors that are too large to find significant effects.

104. Coppedge 1999, 465.

105. Weldon 2006 is one of the few examples of a large cross-sectional study of citizenship politics.

3. Nationalism and Transnationalism

1. Galloway 2001.

2. Koopmans and Statham 1999.

3. See inter alia Aleinikoff 2000 and 2001; Aleinikoff and Klusmeyer 2002; Gerstle and Mollenkopf 2001; and Kondo 2001.

4. Neuman 2002.

5. Marshall 1964; Rokkan 1999; Rokkan and Lipset 1967; Freeman 1995; Money 1999; and Brubaker 1992.

6. Rokkan 1999; Rokkan and Lipset 1967.

7. Freeman 1995; Money 1999.

8. Joppke 1999 and 2001; Aleinikoff 2001.

9. Klausen 1995.

10. Brubaker 1992.

11. Hammar 1990.

12. Barrington 2000.

13. Martiniello 2000, 354.

14. Castles and Davidson 2000, ix.

15. Carter 2001, 2. See also Falk 1995; Held 1996; and the essays in Hutchings and Dannreuther 1999. For a critique of the cosmopolitan thesis, see Bauböck 1994.

16. Soysal 1994.

17. See also Hammar 1990, particularly chapter 8; and Sassen 1996, chapter 3.

18. Hammar 1990; Layton-Henry 1990 and 1992.

19. Hammar adopted the term "denizen" from medieval English law, under which a denizen was a legal foreign resident in the kingdom but was not a subject of the monarchy.

20. Indeed, the very totemic nature of some "nationalist" practices may reflect the underlying influence of transnationalist forces. Castles and Davidson 2000.

21. Bauböck 1994.

22. Feldblum 2000.

23. Bauböck 2000; and Kashiwazaki 2000, 451.

24. Sassen 1996.

25. Kashiwazaki 2000; Hur 2002.

26. Barrington 2000; Kashiwazaki 2000.

27. Sassen 1996, 97.

28. Aleinikoff 2000.

29. Castles and Davidson 2000, 94; Carter 2001, 113; Soysal 1994, 113–27; Aleinikoff and Klusmeyer 2002, 45.

30. Rokkan 1999; Marshall 1964.

31. Rokkan 1999, 252–53.

32. Barrington 2000.

33. Laitin 1998.

34. Kashiwazaki 2000.

35. Aleinikoff and Klusmeyer 2002; Castles and Davidson 2000.

36. A striking recent example is Germany's decision in 2000 to adopt jus soli rules for naturalization despite a historically grounded emphasis on jus sanguinis practices. See Taspinar 2003, 77.

37. See Schmitter 1980; Brubaker 1992; Neuman 1992; Chung 1997; Laitin 1998; Joppke 1999; Koopmans and Statham 1999; Prak 1999; Shanahan 1999; Aleinikoff 2000; Barrington 2000; Galloway 2000 and 2001;

Kashiwazaki 2000; Martiniello 2000; Ramirez 2000; Shachar 2000; DeSipio 2001; and Guarnizo 2001.

38. Studies that look only at domestic factors include Hammar 1990; Harper-Ho 2000; Shachar 2000; and Dalton 2002. Studies that examine only systemic factors include Sassen 1996; Carter 2001; and Guarnizo 2001.

39. Martiniello 2000, 354.

40. Brubaker 1992.

41. Barrington 2000.

42. Hammar 1990.

43. Aleinikoff and Klusmeyer 2002, 47.

44. Aleinikoff and Klusmeyer 2002, 47.

45. Aleinikoff 2001.

46. Joppke 1999; Marshall 1964.

47. Klausen 1995.

48. Hammar 1990.

49. Howard 2006, 449.

50. Joppke 2003, 431–32.

51. I am grateful to Mark J. Miller for calling my attention to this episode.

52. Guarnizo 2001.

53. Gerstle and Mollenkopf 2001, 17.

54. For example, see Davis 2003.

55. DeSipio 2001, 77–78.

56. Kashiwazaki 2000, 458.

57. Soysal 1997, 520.

58. Similarly Turkish resident aliens in Germany have shied away from naturalizing in their country of residence; "Turks Reluctant to Take German Citizenship," January 1, 2000, *New York Times*, A13. The story of Mexico's dual citizenship policy is a fascinating example of transnational politics. Mexico adopted the measure largely in response to California's Proposition 187, which threatened to curtail the few social and economic rights that Mexican immigrants enjoyed in that state. The Mexican government sought to encourage its émigré community to naturalize both in order to protect its rights and to broaden its political influence in California and U.S. politics. However, for both cultural and legal reasons, Mexicans in the United States

historically have been reluctant to naturalize. The result was the 1997 legislation that enabled Mexicans who naturalize to maintain their "nationality" though not their "citizenship" and to enable these Mexicans to reactivate their citizenship and its attendant legal rights upon return to Mexico. The interdependent dynamics are obvious; illiberal policies in the United States caused Mexico to liberalize its policy, which caused an attendant increase in naturalization in the United States. See Ramirez 2000; Guarnizo 2001.

59. Hirschman 1970.

60. Guarnizo 2001. American political candidates increasingly engage in their own transnational campaigning. CBS News reported in September 2007 that presidential candidates from both the Republican and Democratic parties had visited London seeking financial support and votes from the American expatriate community there. See "Presidential candidates seeking funding from Americans living outside the US," September 23, 2007.

61. See Appendix A.

62. Barrington 2000.

63. International organizations that are a colonial legacy may also influence the state's policies and practices toward resident aliens: The United Kingdom's enfranchisement of Commonwealth subjects is one example. Another is the emerging rights of Korean, Okinawese, and Taiwanese resident aliens in Japan. Kashiwazaki 2000, 465.

64. Sassen 1996.

65. Ayers 2004; Racusin 2006.

66. Soysal 1994.

67. Martiniello 2000. A number of researchers have argued that symbolic rights, such as allowing resident aliens to vote in works' councils or, as in Chicago, school council elections, only demobilize and marginalize resident aliens rather than integrate them. See International Migration Review 1985, 405.

68. Aleinikoff and Klusmeyer 2002, 50.

69. Hammar 1990; Soysal 1994; Aleinikoff 2000; Feldblum 2000; and Kashiwazaki 2000.

4. Study Population, Measures, and Estimation Strategy

1. Rokkan 1999, 251.

2. Gastil 1990; Freedom House 2002. For usage see inter alia Burkhart and Beck-Lewis 1994; Helliwell 1994; and Quinn and Woolley 2001. Both

the political rights and civil liberties indices are scored on a scale of 1 to 7, with one indicating the greatest degree of political rights or civil liberties.

3. Norris 1997.

4. Marshall and Jaggers 2000.

5. The POLITY variable represents the summation of variables that measure overall democracy and autocracy in a given state, and varies from +10 (most democratic) to –10 (most autocratic).

6. The Polity IV dataset includes a dummy variable (D3) to denote the year in which a change in regime occurs for a given state. Hence, my measure combines ten consecutive observations of the POLITY variable with the D3 variable.

7. Lijphart 1999, chapter 4.

8. Diamond 2000.

9. Norris 1997.

10. United Nations Population Division 2002.

11. Ibid.

12. Joppke 2003.

13. Hence, these three cases, along with Australia, Austria, and Canada, offer important cases where the value of the dependent variable changes over time.

14. For purposes of coding each observation longitudinally, a state will be coded 0 for each time period before it considered, adopted, or rejected voting rights for resident aliens.

15, In essence, this binary dependent variable recodes the ordinal dependent variable of the original model so that $Pr(y_{i,t} = 2$ or 3 or 4 or 5) becomes $Pr(y_{i,t} = 1)$ in the binary model. To avoid unit of analysis problems, I exclude from $Pr(y_{i,t} = 1)$ those observations in which the rights are granted by a local government but the national government does not grant a voting right. This technique thus counts the United States, Switzerland, and Canada (after 1975) as negative observations even though in each state there are local or regional governments that offer voting rights to resident aliens.

16. Hammar 1990; Brubaker 1992; Neuman 1992; and Barrington 2000.

17. Adams 1993.

18. Adams 1993; Kondo 2001; and Weil 2001.

19. Nagy 2001.

20. See Flanz 2003. The provision in Costa Rica's constitution is Title II, Article 13(3) of the Constitution of 8 November 1949; Uruguay's provision is Section III, Chapter 1, Article 74 of the Constitution of 8 December 1966.

21. Brubaker 1992.

22. Aleinikoff and Klusmeyer 2002.

23. Lijphart 1999.

24. Howard 2001, 104 quoting Elster 1992.

25. Utter and Lundsgaard 1993.

26. Skaar 2002, chapter 6.

27. Klausen 1995.

28. Huber, Ragin, and Stephens 1997.

29. Ibid.

30. International Labour Office 1984, 1992, 1993, and 2000.

31. Organisation for Economic Co-operation and Development 2005; International Monetary Fund 2003 through 2006; and European Commission 2007.

32. I use the "ipolate" command for Stata version 8.2 to interpolate between missing data points within each panel. There are 742 total observations before interpolation, an average of 29.68 observations per panel. After interpolation, there are 986 total observations of the SSX variable, or a mean of 39.44 observations per panel.

33. Blais, Blake, and Dion 1993, 49–50.

34. Armingeon et al. 2006.

35. Beck et al. 2001.

36. Woldendorp, Keman, and Budge 1998. Blais, Blake, and Dion (BBD) use a continuous scale ranging from –1 to 1, with a lower score indicating a left-leaning government. Woldendorp, Keman, and Budge (WKB) use an interval scale ranging from 1 to 5, with a lower score indicating a left-leaning government. To convert WKB values to the BBD scale, I divide the WKB partisan variable by two to convert the range from 4 to 2, then I subtract 1.5 to normalize the range from –1 to 1. For the 629 shared observations of the WKB and the ABM datasets, this technique yields a correlation of 0.8477.

37. U.S. Central Intelligence Agency, 2001 through 2004; Israel 2007.

38. Guarnizo 2001.

39. See also DeSipio 2001, 77–78.

40. See Appendix A.

41. Black 2002; O'Neil 2002; and Van Hear 2002.

42. International Monetary Fund 1947–2001.

43. In 1995, for example, the IMF began to report to report capital transfers by migrants as distinct from remittances. Prior to 1995, the IMF data combines capital transfers and workers' remittances as a single figure. See International Monetary Fund 1993, and International Monetary Fund 1995, ix–x.

44. Beck 2001, 280–81.

45. Beck proposed such spatial measures as a means for controlling for confounding geographic factors in time-series cross-section studies—for example, to control for trade effects in comparative studies of macroeconomic performance. Hence, Beck treated spatial correlations as a contaminating factor for which one must control. In this study, however, the transnationalism hypothesis is precisely that spatial correlations should be significant. It is of explicit theoretical interest. I thus use the measure as an explanatory variable, even though Beck proposed it simply as a control variable.

46. Soysal 1994, 147–147 and 184–85. For a dissenting analysis of the ICCPR, see Keith 1999.

47. Sassen 1996.

48. Sikkink 1993, 416.

49. Simmons 2002.

50. Anheier 2001.

51. Anheier and Stares 2002; Union of International Organizations 1967 through 2005. For ease of comparison across time, I look only at organizations coded by UIA as types A, B, C, and D. The UIA did not collect data on organization types E, F, and G prior to 1984.

52. As with the study's social security data, I use Stata version 8.2's "ipolate" command to impute values for missing measures of NGOs between 1960 and 1966, 1966 and 1977, 1977 and 1981, and 1981 and 1984. Before interpolation, there are 381 total observations, or a mean of 15.24 observations per state. After interpolation, there are 1,033 observations, an average of 41.32 observations per state.

53. See Appendix C for summary statistics and the pairwise correlations of all variables.

54. Blais et al. 2001; Bauböck 2005.

55. Shanahan 1999.

56. Howard 2006, 447.

57. Lijphart 1995; and Beck et al. 2001.

58. Rokkan 1999.

59. Rokkan 1999, 249.

60. Howard 2006, 447.

61. In some cases, it is difficult to code whether or not a state seceded from another. Switzerland is an illustrative example. Neuchâtel, a canton that allows resident aliens to vote in its regional elections, joined the Confederation Helvetica in 1814 "subject to the overlordship of the King of Prussia who was elected sovereign in 1707–08.... The King of Prussia, resident in Berlin, was far removed from Neuchâtel. He was content, year by year, to receive his share of the taxes levied within the canton, and to leave high-policy decisions to Bern or the Swiss confederation under whose protection the Principality had been placed at the request of the king himself." Luck 1985, p. 390. Like numerous European principalities, Neuchâtel had historic ties to several dynasties, including the Hohenzollerns and the House of Orleans in France. For seven years it was a Napoleonic principality. The only other Swiss state to allow resident aliens to vote, Jura, once was the smallest (least populous) *département* of Napoleonic France. See Luck 1985, 736–37. Jura itself seceded in 1978 from the canton of Bern. Though the study codes Switzerland as a center-formed state, one might argue that the secessionist dynamics of its cantons may be relevant to their enfranchisement of resident aliens.

62. See Table C.2 in Appendix C for years of coverage by country.

63. Huber, Ragin, and Stephens 1997.

64. Beck and Katz 1995; Beck, Katz, and Tucker 1998; and Beck 2001.

65. Beck 2001. The "specification" of the model refers to the modeler's assumptions about its functional form and his or her choice of variables for inclusion in the model. "Estimation" refers to the modeler's choice of statistical function to perform on the model to test for the significance of the model's parameters.

66. For example, see Simmons 2002.

67. See inter alia Bowman 1996; Goldstein and Pevehouse 1997; Partell 1997; Yoon 1997; Drury 1998; Lowery and Gray 1998; and Soss, Schram, Vartarian, and O'Brien 2001.

68. Benoit 1996; Oneal, Oneal, Maoz, and Russett 1996; Oneal and Ray 1997; and Senese 1997.

69. Beck and Katz 1995.

70. Ibid.

71. Beck and Katz 1995, 2. Formally, panel heteroscedasticity is defined as the $E(\varepsilon_{i,t}) = \sigma_i^2$, or that the expectation for the variance of the error term for a given panel i at time t is not zero. See Beck and Katz 1995, 645 f/n 6 for formal definitions of panel assumptions for TSCS models.

72. This is formally defined as $Cov(\varepsilon_{i,t}, \varepsilon_{j,t}) = \sigma_{i,j}$ or that the covariance of the error terms of two panels at time t is not zero.

73. Beck 2001.

74. In effect, my measure of transnationalism controls for contemporaneous correlation by using a function on the spatially lagged dependent variable to model geographic dependence. This is a variant of spatial lag models. See Martin and Oeppen 1975, O'Loughlin et al. 1998, and Shin and Ward 1999.

75. Serial correlation is formally defined as $\varepsilon_{i,t} = \rho_i \varepsilon_{i,t-1} + \upsilon_{i,t}$, where ρ is the autocorrelation parameter and υ is the true homoscedastic error term.

76. Beck and Katz 1995, 639–42.

77. For example, see the democratic peace work of Russett 1990 and 1993; Maoz and Russett 1992; and Maoz and Russett 1993. See also Oneal et al. 1996 and Beck, Katz, and Tucker's 1998 discussion thereof.

78. Beck and Katz 1995, 638–42.

79. Green, Kim, and Yoon 2001.

80. Green, Kim, and Yoon 2001, 445. See also Teo 2002.

81. Teo 2002 argues that fixed-effects models of longitudinally invariant data can create selection bias, since concordant observations are "dropped" prior to estimating the regression. The remaining observations may not constitute a random sample. Green, Kim, and Yoon disagree; 2001, 455.

82. Green, Kim, and Yoon 2001, 455.

83. Beck and Katz 1995.

84. Beck 2001, 287, f/n 10.

85. See Farber and Gowa 1997 for an example with a binary dependent variable.

86. Robust standard errors typically are the Huber/White/sandwich estimator of variance, which will produce valid standard errors even if the modeler does not properly specify the within-group correlation structure. The Huber/White/sandwich estimator does require, however, that the model correctly specify the mean. See Huber 1967, White 1980, Rogers 1993, and Williams 2000.

87. Simmons 2002, 17.

88. Beck 2001.

89. Beck 2001, 281.

90. King, Tomz, and Wittenberg 2000.

5. Statistical Findings

1. Brubaker 1992; Aleinikoff and Klusmeyer 2002.

2. Klausen 1995.

3. Hammar 1990.

4. Joppke 2003; Howard 2006.

5. Earnest 2006.

6. Indeed, if one re-estimates the model using data only up until 2003, the partisan variable is significant and negatively signed, a finding consistent with the 2006 study.

7. For a good discussion, see Shaw 2003.

8. Martiniello 2000, 352–55; see also Shaw 2003.

9. Carter 2001, 119.

10. Aleinikoff and Klusmeyer 2002.

11. King, Tomz, and Wittenberg 2000. I use Tomz, Wittenberg, and King's 2003 CLARIFY modules in Stata version 8.2.

12. Notationally, one can represent the possibility of some form of voting rights as $\Pr(y_{i,t} \neq 0)$, or alternatively $\Pr(y_{i,t} = 1U2U3U4U5)$. Likewise, the probability of nondiscriminatory voting rights is $\Pr(y_{i,t} = 4U5)$.

13. For purposes of comparison and for validation of the findings, the study also conducted a PCSE regression analysis on the model. While such analysis is inappropriate for ordered dependent variables, Beck 2001, 273 notes that researchers using ordered variables with seven points commonly treat them as continuous and can estimated such variables with PCSE techniques. The dependent variable for this study has only six points, making tenuous any inferences from PCSE estimation. When using PCSE estimation I assume that there is panel-specific first-order autoregression. The PCSE analysis found the following nationalist and transnational factors significant: birthright citizenship (b = 0.705, $s.e.$ = 0.203); Density of NGOs (0.379, 0.084); and proximity to other states that enfranchise noncitizens (0.163, 0.046). The PCSE model also found several controls significant:

Membership in the British Commonwealth (1.214, 0.284); a history of representative institutions (0.699, 0.229); and the control for unexplained temporal variation (0.025, 0.007). The PCSE model thus seems to find more support for transnational arguments than the ordered probit model. This support is qualified, however, for two reasons. First, the control variable for time illustrates that there is an overall increase in voting rights over time that the PCSE model does not explain. Second, the reader is again advised to keep in mind Beck's caution that we know little about the consistency and unbiasedness of PCSE estimates when one uses an ordered dependent variable; the estimates presented in this note may be biased and/or inconsistent.

6. Case Studies

1. Martiniello 2000.

2. European Union 1992; European Union 1997.

3. Hammar 1990; Joppke 2003; and Howard 2006.

4. Stuurman 2004, 183.

5. Stuurman 2004.

6. Rokkan 1999.

7. Prak 1999.

8. North Holland had about 19 percent foreign citizens, while South Holland had about 14 percent. For the country as a whole, about 3 percent of the population was foreigners. Netherlands 1980.

9. The necessary constitutional reforms meant, however, that aliens did not vote in local elections until 1986.

10. Jacobs 1998, 351.

11. Jacobs 1998.

12. Rath 1990.

13. Brubaker 1992.

14. Neuman 1992.

15. Brubaker 1992.

16. See Joppke 2003 for a discussion of the politics of "de-" and "re-ethnicization" of citizenship laws.

17. Preuss 2004.

18. Rittsteig 1994.

19. Joppke 1999, 63.

20. Joppke 1999, 65–69.

21. Joppke 1999, chapter 3.

22. Joppke 1999, 69.

23. Joppke 1999, 194; Rath 1990, 132.

24. According to Rath, the rights extended only to resident aliens from Denmark, Norway, Sweden, the Netherlands, Switzerland, and Ireland. Rath 1990, 132.

25. Soysal 1994, 128.

26. Rath 1990, 133.

27. Joppke 1999, 195.

28. Neuman 1992, 283–87.

29. Joppke 1999, 69–75.

30. "In short, alien suffrage would take away the last major privilege of citizenship: the right to vote, and devalue the latter by leaving only duties, not rights as its distinguishing mark." Joppke 1999, 198. Note the similarity of Joppke's summary of the Federal Constitutional Court's decision and the position the editorial board of *The New York Times* takes in the epigraph on p. 1.

31. Schwartz 1990.

32. Rath 1990, 128–31.

33. Vandyck 2004.

34. Zolberg 1974.

35. Sciolino 2007.

36. Jacobs 2001.

37. Ibid.

38. Ibid., 117.

39. Rath 1990, 129.

40. Jacobs 2001, 118.

41. Vandyck 2004.

42. Earnest 2007.

43. Waldrauch 2005; Earnest 2007.

7. Theoretical Implications

1. This data was obtained from the United Nations Population Division's Population, Resources, Environment and Development (PRED) database; see United Nations 2007.

2. Brubaker 1992.

3. Ibid, 1.

4. See Hayduk and Wucker 2003; "Gonzalez Calls For Non-Citizen Voting in School Board Elections" 2003; "Noncitizens Seek Ballot Box Access" 2003, DZ07; "Noncitizens Should Get Vote, Too, Mayor Says; Latinos Fault Access to DC Services" 2002, B01; and Hayduk 2006.

5. Aleinikoff and Klusmeyer 2002, 47.

6. Hammar 1990; Howard 2006.

7. I am grateful to Mark J. Miller for illustrating the relevance of this episode to my argument.

8. "Former fascists seek respectability" 2003, 44.

9. Hollinger 2005.

10. Shain 1994–95. See also Honig 1997 and Tugend et al. 1997 about the role of the Jewish diaspora in Israeli electoral politics.

11. Hyun-joo 2006.

12. Tugend et al. 1997.

13. Neuman 1992.

14. Waldrauch 2005.

15. Kashiwazaki 2000, 457–58.

16. Hur 2002, 668.

17. It is worth noting that electoral uncertainty may be significant in plurality systems as well. In their analysis of how the Democratic and Republican Parties recruit immigrant voters in American cities, Andersen and Wintringham 2003 conclude that electoral uncertainty is a significant impediment to the expansion of the political incorporation of migrants.

18. Soysal 1994; Sassen 1996.

19. Barrington 2000.

20. Sikkink 1993; Klotz 1995; and Wang and Rosenau 2001.

21. Wang and Rosenau 2001.

22. Klotz 1995, 465–67.

23. For example, see Barrington 2000.

24. Guarnizo 2001; Smith and Guarnizo 1998.

25. Ndegwa 1997.

8. Sovereignty and the Nation

1. Fukuyama 1992.

2. Anderson 1908, 175.

3. Barrington 2000; see also Laitin 1998.

4. For a critique of these rights, see Martiniello 2000, 352–55.

5. Bennet 2003.

6. "Preliminary voting in local elections ends with good turnout" 1999.

7. Tomforde 1990.

8. Annan 1999, 49.

9. Walzer 1983, 62.

Appendix A. Problems with Demographic Data on Resident Aliens

1. Freeman 1995; Money 1999.

2. *Magyar statisztikai évkönyv* (*Statistical Yearbook of Hungary*), 1992 and 1997.

3. Shachar 2000; Weil 2001, 33; and Aleinikoff and Klusmeyer 2002, 98 f/n b.

Appendix B. Codebook

1. Correlates of War 2 Project, 2003.

2. Adams 1993; Flanz 2003; Kondo 2001; Nagy 2001; and Weil 2001.

3. Utter and Lundsgaard 1993; Lijphart 1999; Howard 2001; and Skaar 2002.

4. Huber, Ragin, and Stephens 1997; International Labour Office 1984, 1992, 1993, and 2000; Organisation for Economic Co-operation and

Development 2005; International Monetary Fund 2003 through 2006; and European Commission 2007.

5. Blais, Blake, and Dion 1993; Woldendorp, Keman, and Budge 1998; Beck, Clarke, Groff, Keefer, and Walsh 2001; and Armingeon, Beyeler, and Menegale 2002.

6. Source for the method of constructing this variable is Simmons 2002.

7. Union of International Associations, 1967 to 2005.

8. Data on electoral systems is from Lijphart 1995; and Beck, Clarke, Groff, Keefer, and Walsh 2001.

9. Rokkan 1999.

10. Marshall and Jaggers 2000.

11. Rokkan 1999.

References

"A Citizen's Right." *New York Times*. April 19, 2004.

"Belgium to allow non-Europeans to vote in local polls." Agence France Press (English version). February 20, 2004.

"European Local Authorities Congress' Chamber Passes Recommendations to Latvia." Baltic News Service. May 26, 1998.

"Former fascists seek respectability." *The Economist* 369, 8353. December 6-12, 2003. 44.

"Gonzalez Calls For Non-Citizen Voting in School Board Elections." *San Francisco Sentinel*. September 24, 2003.

"Human rights body presses for noncitizens' right to vote." BBC Summary of World Broadcasts. July 11, 2000. Interfax news agency, Moscow, in English 1743 GMT 6 July 2000.

"MPs reject right of noncitizens to vote in local elections." BBC Summary of World Broadcasts. January 31, 2000. BNS news agency, Tallinn, in English 1602 GMT 27 January 2000.

"Noncitizens Seek Ballot Box Access." *The Washington Post*. September 25, 2003. DZ07.

"Noncitizens Should Get Vote, Too, Mayor Says; Latinos Fault Access to DC Services." *The Washington Post*. October 1, 2002. B01.

"Preliminary voting in local elections ends with good turnout." October 16, 1999. BBC Summary of World Broadcasts. ETA news agency, Tallinn, in English 1208 GMT 14 October.

"Presidential candidates seeking funding from Americans living outside the US." *CBS Evening News*, 1800 EST 23 September 2007.

"Turks Reluctant to Take German Citizenship." *New York Times*. January 1, 2000. A13.

"Zürich: Ausländer sollen abstimmen dürfen." *20 Minuten*. June 1, 2006. http://www.20min.ch/news/zuerich/story/28708140.

Adams, Sarah. 1993. "The Basic Right of Citizenship: A Comparative Study." Washington, DC: Center for Immigration Studies. September. (http://www.cis.org/articles/1993/back793.html).

Agence France Press. 2002. "Vienna gives non-EU nationals right to vote in local elections." December 13. English language version.

Aleinikoff, T. Alexander. 2000. "Between Principles and Politics: U.S. Citizenship Policy." *From Migrants to Citizens: Membership in a Changing World*. T. Alexander Aleinikoff and Douglas Klusmeyer, eds. Washington, DC: Carnegie Endowment for International Peace.

———. 2001. "Policing Boundaries: Migration, Citizenship and the State." *E Pluribus Unum? Contemporary and Historical Perspectives on Immigrant Political Incorporation*. Gary Gerstle and John Mollenkopf, eds. New York: Russell Sage Foundation: 267–91.

Aleinikoff, T. Alexander, and Douglas Klusmeyer. 2002. *Citizenship Policies for an Age of Migration*. Washington, DC: Carnegie Endowment for International Peace.

Andersen, Kristi, and Jessica Wintringham. March 21, 2003. "Political Parties, NGOs, and Immigrant Incorporation: A Case Study." Paper Presented to the Workshop on Immigrant Incorporation. Syracuse, NY: Campbell Public Affairs Institute, Maxwell School of Citizenship and Public Affairs. http://www.maxwell.syr.edu/ campbell/Events/Anderson.pdf.

Anderson, Frank M. 1908. *The Constitutions and Other Select Documents Illustrative of the History of France 1789–1907* (2nd. ed.). Minneapolis: W. W. Wilson.

Anheier, Helmut. 2001. "Measuring Global Civil Society." *Global Civil Society 2001*. Helmut Anheier, Marlies Glasius, and Mary Kaldor, eds. New York: Oxford University Press. 221–30.

Anheier, Helmut, and Sally Stares. 2002. "Introducing the Global Civil Society Index." *Global Civil Society 2002*. Marlies Glasius, Mary Kaldor, and Helmut Anheier, eds. New York: Oxford University Press. 241–54.

Annan, Kofi. 1999. "Two concepts of sovereignty." *The Economist* 352, 8137: September 18. 49–50.

Armingeon, Klaus, Philip Leimgruber, Michelle Beyeler, and Sarah Menegale. 2006. Comparative Political Data Set 1960–2004. Berne: Institute of Political Science, University of Berne.

Australia. Bureau of Statistics. 1994 through 2000. "Australian Social Trends: Population—State Summary Tables." http://www.abs. gov.au.

———. Department of Immigration and Multicultural Affairs. Statistics Section. 2001. *Immigration: Federation to Century's End, 1901–2000*. Belconnen, ACT: Commonwealth of Australia.

Austria. Österreichisches Statistisches Zentralamt. 1992 and 2003. *Statistisches Jahrbuch für die Republik Österreich* (Statistical Yearbook for the Republic of Austria) (microfiche). Vienna: Das Zentralamt.

Ayers, Andrew B. 2004. "International Law as a Tool of Constitutional Interpretation in the Early Immigration Power Cases." *Georgetown Immigration Law Journal* 19 (Fall): 125–53.

Aylsworth, Leon E. 1931. "The Passing of Alien Suffrage." *American Political Science Review* XXV, 1. 114–16.

Barrington, Lowell. 2000. "Understanding Citizenship Policy in the Baltic States." *From Migrants to Citizens: Membership in a Changing World*. T. Alexander Aleinikoff and Douglas Klusmeyer, eds. Washington, DC: Carnegie Endowment for International Peace.

Bauböck, Rainer. 1994. *Transnational Citizenship: Membership and Rights in International Migration*. Aldershot: Edward Algar.

———. 2000. "Dual and Supranational Citizenship: Limits to Transnationalism: Introduction." *From Migrants to Citizens: Membership in a Changing World*. T. Alexander Aleinikoff and Douglas Klusmeyer, eds. Washington, DC: Carnegie Endowment for International Peace: 305–11.

———. 2005. "Expansive Citizenship—Voting beyond Territory and Membership." *PS: Political Science & Politics* 38, 4 (October): 683–87.

Beck, Nathaniel, and Jonathan N. Katz. 1995. "What To Do (And Not To Do) With Time-Series Cross-Section Data." *American Political Science Review* 89, 3 (September): 634–47.

Beck, Nathaniel, Jonathan N. Katz, and Richard Tucker. 1998. "Taking Time Seriously: Time-Series-Cross-Section Analysis with a Binary Dependent Variable." *American Journal of Political Science* 42, 4 (October): 1260–88.

Beck, Nathaniel. 2001. "Time-Series-Cross-Section Data: What Have We Learned in the Past Few Years?" *Annual Review of Political Science* 2001 (4): 271–93.

Beck, Thorsten, George Clarke, Alberto Groff, Philip Keefer, and Patrick Walsh. 2001. "New tools in comparative political economy: the Database of Political Institutions." *World Bank Economic Review* 15, 1 (September): 165–76.

Beiming, Ragne, and Claes Thorson. 2003. Personal communication with author. Washington, DC: June 5.

Belgium. Institut national de Statistique. 2003. "La population étrangere en Belgique par année, commune, nationalité, sexe et classes d'âge." http://ecodata.mineco.fgov.be/Fr/ begin_fr.htm.

Bennet, James. December 3, 2003. "Likud Debates a Palestinian State to Save Israel." *New York Times*, A1.

Benoit, Kenneth. 1996. "Democracies Really Are More Pacific (in General): Reexamining Regime Type and War Involvement." *Journal of Conflict Resolution* 40, 4 (December): 636–57.

Black, Richard. 2002. "Soaring Remittances Raise New Issues." Washington, DC: Migration Policy Institute. http://www.migrationinformation.org.

Blais, Andre, Donald Blake, and Stephane Dion. 1993. "Do Parties Make a Difference? Parties and the Size of Government in Liberal Democracies." *American Journal of Political Science* 37, 1 (February): 40–62.

Blais, Andre, Louis Massicotte, and Antoine Yoshinaka. 2001. "Deciding who has the right to vote: a comparative analysis of election laws." *Electoral Studies* 20, 1 (March): 41–62.

Bowman, Kirk S. 1996. "Taming the Tiger: Militarization and Democracy in Latin America." *Journal of Peace Research* 33, 3 (August): 289–308.

Brubaker, Rogers. 1992. *Citizenship and Nationhood in France and Germany*. Cambridge, MA: Harvard University Press.

Burkhart, Ross E., and Michael S. Beck-Lewis. 1994. "Comparative Democracy: the Economic Development Thesis." *American Political Science Review* 88, 4 (December): 903–10.

Canada. Statistics Canada. 2003. "Immigrant population by place of birth, provinces and territories." http://www.statcan.ca/english/Pgdb/popula.htm.

Carter, April. 2001. *The Political Theory of Global Citizenship*. London: Routledge.

Castles, Stephen, and Alastair Davidson. 2000. *Citizenship and Migration: Globalization and the Politics of Belonging*. New York: Routledge.

Chung, April. 1996. "Noncitizen Voting Rights and Alternatives: A Path Toward Greater Asian Pacific American and Latino Political Participation." *UCLA Asian Pacific American Law Journal* 4 (Fall): 163–85.

Coll, Kathleen. 2003. Personal e-mail to author. "Re: noncitizen voting." November 10.

Coppedge, Michael. 1999. "Thickening Thin Concepts and Theories: Combining Large N and Small in Comparative Politics." *Comparative Politics* 31, 4 (July).

Correlates of War Project 2. 2003. "State System Membership List, v2002.1." Correlates of War 2 website: http://cow2.la.psu.edu.

Council of Europe. 2007. Convention on the Participation of Foreigners in Public Life at the Local Level. CETS No. 144. http://www.conventions.coe.int/Treaty/Commun/ChercheSig.asp?NT=144 &CM=8&DF=9/25/2007&CL=ENG.

Dahrendorf, Rolf. 1963. "Recent Changes in the Class Structure of Western European Countries." *A New Europe?* S. Craubard, ed. Boston: Beacon Press.

Dalton, Russell J. 2002. *Citizen Politics: Public Opinion and Political Parties in Advanced Industrial Democracies*, 3rd. ed. New York: Chatham House.

Davis, Phillip. March 6, 2003. "Venezuelan community in Miami increases as wealthier Venezuelan refugees seek Florida residences." *All Things Considered*: 9:00 p.m. EST broadcast. Washington, DC: National Public Radio.

Denmark. Danmarks Statistik. 1970, 1975, 1980, 1984, 1985, 1995, and 1998. *Statistisk årbog* (Statistical yearbook) (microfiche). Copenhagen: Danmarks Statistik.

DeSipio, Louis. 2001. "Building America, One Person at a Time: Naturalization and the Political Behavior of the Naturalized in Contemporary American Politics." *E Pluribus Unum? Contemporary and Historical Perspectives on Immigrant Political Incorporation*. Gary Gerstle and John Mollenkopf, eds. New York: Russell Sage Foundation: 267–91.

Deutsche Presse-Agentur. February 19, 2001. "Mayor Haeupl threatens to quit if SP loses in Vienna elections." Deutsche Presse-Agentur (English language version).

Diamond, Larry. 2000. "A Report Card on Democracy." *Hoover Digest: Research and Opinion on Public Policy* 3 (Summer).

Dong-shin, Seo. March 27, 2006. "Foreigners to Cast Ballots." *Korea Times*.

Drury, A. Cooper. 1998. "Revisiting Economic Sanctions Revisited." *Journal of Peace Research* 35, 4 (July): 497–509.

Earnest, David C. 2004. Voting Rights for Resident Aliens: Nationalism, Postnationalism and Sovereignty in an Era of Mass Migration. Unpublished Dissertation. Washington, DC: The George Washington University.

———. 2006. "Neither Citizen nor Stranger: Why States Enfranchise Resident Aliens." *World Politics* 58, 2 (January): 242–75.

———. 2007. "From Alien to Elector: Citizenship and Belonging in the Global City." *Globalizations* 4, 2 (June): 137–55.

Election Process Information Collection. 2002. Election Process Information Collection website: http://www.epicproject.org.

Elster, John. 1992. "On Majoritarianism and Rights." *East European Constitutional Review* 1, 3 (Fall): 19.

European Commission. Eurostat. 2007. "Government finance statistics." Eurostat website: http://epp.eurostat.ec.europa.eu /portal/ page?_pageid=2373,47631312,2373_58674404&_dad=portal&_ schema=PORTAL#IV.3.

European Union. 1997. Consolidated Version of the Treaty Establishing the European Community, as Amended by the Treaty of Amsterdam. October 2, 1997. European Union Official Journal C340, October 11, 1997. 173–308.

Falk, Richard. 1995. *On Humane Governance*. Cambridge, UK: Polity Press.

Farber, Henry S., and Joanne Gowa. 1997. "Common Interests or Common Polities? Reinterpreting the Democratic Peace." *Journal of Politics* 59, 2 (May): 393–417.

Feldblum, Miriam. 2000. "Managing Membership: New Trends in Citizenship and Nationality Policy." *From Migrants to Citizens: Membership in a Changing World*. T. Alexander Aleinikoff and Douglas Klusmeyer, eds. Washington, DC: Carnegie Endowment for International Peace: 475–99.

Finland. Statistics Finland. 2002. "Population by Citizenship." http://www.stat.fi/index_en.html.

———. Tilastokeskus. 1970 and 1975. *Suomen Tilastollinen Vuosikirja* (Statistical Yearbook of Finland) (microfiche). Helsinki: Tilastokeskus (Central Statistical Office).

Flanz, Gisbert H. ed. 2003. *Constitutions of the Countries of the World*. Dobbs Ferry, NY: Oceana Publications.

Freedom House. 2002. *Freedom in the World 2001–2002*: The Annual Survey of Political Rights and Civil Liberties. New York: Freedom House.

Freeman, Gary P. 1995. "Modes of Immigration Politics in Liberal Democratic States." *International Migration Review* 29, 4 (Winter): 881–902.

Fukuyama, Francis. 1992. *The End of History and the Last Man*. New York: Free Press.

Galloway, Donald. 2000. "The Dilemmas of Canadian Citizenship Law." *From Migrants to Citizens: Membership in a Changing World*. T. Alexander Aleinikoff and Douglas Klusmeyer, eds. Washington, DC: Carnegie Endowment for International Peace. 82–118.

———. 2001. "Citizenship Rights and Non-citizens: a Canadian Perspective." *Citizenship in a Global World: Comparing Citizenship Rights for Aliens*. Atsushi Kondo, ed. New York: Palgrave. 176–95.

Gastil, Raymond D. 1990. "The Comparative Survey of Freedom: Experiences and Suggestions." *Studies in Comparative International Development* 25, 1 (Spring): 25–50.

Germany, Federal Republic. Federal Statistics Office. 1970–78, 1984–88, 1990, 1992–94, and 1996. *Statistiches Jahrbuch für die Bundesrepublik Deutschland* (Statistical Yearbook for the Federal Republic of Germany) (microfiche). Wiesbaden: Statistiches Bundesamt (Federal Statistics Office).

Gerstle, Gary, and John Mollenkopf, eds. 2001. "Introduction: The Political Incorporation of Migrants, Then and Now." *E Pluribus Unum? Contemporary and Historical Perspectives on Immigrant Political Incorporation*. New York: Russell Sage Foundation.

Goldstein, Joshua S., and Jon C. Pevehouse. 1997. "Reciprocity, Bullying, and International Cooperation: Time-series Analysis of the Bosnia Conflict." *American Political Science Review* 91, 3 (September): 515–29.

Gowen, Annie. September 18, 2002. "Rockville Mulls Giving Vote to Resident Aliens." *The Washington Post*. B04.

Greece. National Statistical Services. 1975, 1980, 1991, and 1997. *Statistical Yearbook of Greece* (microfiche). Athens: National Statistical Service of Greece.

Green, Donald P., Soo Yeon Kim, and David H. Yoon. 2001. "Dirty Pool." *International Organization* 55, 2 (Spring): 441–68.

Guarnizo, Luis Eduardo. 2001. "On the Political Participation of Transnational Migrants: Old Practices and New Trends. " *E Pluribus Unum? Contemporary and Historical Perspectives on Immigrant Political Incorporation*. Gary Gerstle and John Mollenkopf, eds. New York: Russell Sage Foundation: 213–63.

Hammar, Tomas. 1990. *Democracy and the Nation-State: Aliens, Denizens, and Citizenship in a World of International Migration*. Aldershot, UK: Avebury.

Harper-Ho, Virginia. 2000. "Voting rights for resident aliens: The History, the Law and Current Prospects for Change." *Journal of Law and Inequality* 18 (Summer): 271–322.

Hayduk, Ron, and Michele Wucker. September 22, 2003. "Let legal immigrants vote in city." *New York Daily News*.

Hayduk, Ron. 2006. *Democracy for All: Restoring Immigrant Voting Rights in the United States*. New York: Routledge.

Held, David. 1996. *Models of Democracy*. Cambridge, UK: Polity Press.

Held, David, Anthony McGrew, David Goldblatt, and Jonathan Perraton. 1999. *Global Transformations: Politics, Economics and Culture*. Stanford, CA: Stanford University Press.

Helliwell, John F. 1994. "Empirical Linkages between Democracy and Economic Growth." *British Journal of Political Science* 24, 2 (April): 225–48.

Hirschman, Albert O. 1970. *Exit, Voice and Loyalty: Responses to Decline in Firms, Organizations and States*. Cambridge, MA: Harvard University Press.

Hollinger, Peggy. October 31, 2005. "Sarkozy supports giving immigrants a vote in city polls." *Financial Times*, 6.

Hong, Peter Y., and David Haldane. September 23, 1996. "Local Armenians Cast Historic Ballots; Election: Expatriates Vote in Homeland's Presidential Race. But Opportunity May Be First and Last for Those Soon to Become U.S. Citizens." *Los Angeles Times*, B1.

Honig, Sarah. 1997. "Voting bill will never pass." *The Jerusalem Post*, January 24, 22.

Howard, A. E. Dick. 2001. "Judicial Independence in Post-Communist Central and Eastern Europe." *Judicial Independence in the Age of Democracy: Critical Perspectives from Around the World*. Peter H. Russell and David M. O'Brien, eds. Charlottesville: University of Virginia Press. 89–110.

Howard, Marc Morjé. 2006. "Comparative Citizenship: An Agenda for Cross-National Research." *Perspectives on Politics* 4, 3 (September): 443–55.

Huber, Evelyne, Charles Ragin, and John D. Stephens. 1997. Comparative Welfare States Data Set, Northwestern University and University of North Carolina. http://www.lis.ceps.lu/comp-wsp.htm.

Huber, Evelyne, and John D. Stephens. 2001. *Development and Crisis of the Welfare State: Parties and Policies in Global Markets*. Chicago: University of Chicago Press.

Huber, P. J. 1967. "The behavior of maximum likelihood estimates under nonstandard conditions." Proceedings of the Fifth Berkeley Symposium on Mathematical Statistics and Probability. Berkeley: University of California Press, vol. 1. 221–23.

Hugo, Graeme. 2003. "Circular Migration: Keeping Development Rolling?" Migration Information Source. June 1. http://www.migrationinformation.org.

Hungary. Central Statistical Office. 1993. *1992 Magyar statistztikai évkönyv* (1992 Statistical Yearbook of Hungary) (microfiche). Budapest: Központi Statisztikai Hivatal (Central Statistical Office).

Hur, Claire J. 2002. "Returnees from South America: Japan's Model for Legal Multiculturalism?" *Pacific Rim Law & Policy Journal* 11 (June): 643–86.

Hutchings, Kimberly, and Roland Dannreuther, eds. 1999. *Cosmopolitan Citizenship.* New York: St. Martin's Press.

Illinois State Code. 2003. §105 ILCS 5/34–2.1.

International Covenant on Civil and Political Rights. December 19, 1966. General Assembly Res. 2200, U.N. GAOR, 21st Sess., Supp. No. 16, at 55, U.N. Doc. A. 6316.

International Labour Office. 1984 through 2000. *World Labor Report.* Geneva: International Labour Office.

International Migration Review. 1985. "Introduction: Political Participation and Civil Rights of Immigrants A Research Agenda." *International Migration Review* 19, 3. Special Issue: Civil Rights and the Sociopolitical Participation of Migrants (Autumn): 400–414.

International Monetary Fund. 1947–2001. *Balance of Payments Statistics Yearbook.* Volumes 5–51. Washington, DC: International Monetary Fund.

———. 1993. *Balance of Payments Manual,* 5th ed. Washington, DC: International Monetary Fund.

———. 2003 through 2006. *Government Finance Statistics Yearbook.* Washington, DC: International Monetary Fund.

Ireland. Central Statistics Office. 1970/71, 1976, 1981, 1989, 1994, and 1997. *Statistical Abstract of Ireland* (microfiche). Dublin: Government Stationary Office.

Israel. Central Bureau of Statistics. 1970, 1975, 1980, 1985, 1990, 1995, and 1998. *Statistical Abstract of Israel* (various years) (microfiche). Jerusalem: Government Press.

———. Knesset. 2007. "All Governments of Israel." Knesset website: http://www.knesset.gov.il/govt/eng/GovtByNumber_eng.asp.

Italy. Instituto Nazionale Di Statistica. 1973, 1978, 1982, 1987, 1993, and 1998. *Annuario Stastico Italiano* (Italian Statistical Annual) (microfiche). Rome: Instituto Natzionale di Statistica.

———. Instituto Nazionale Di Statistica. 2000. "La popolazione straniera residente in Italia al 1° gennaio 2000." Instituto Nazionale Di Statistica website: http://www.istat.it/index.htm.

————. Instituto Nazionale Di Statistica. 2002. "Movimento migratorio della popolazione residente - Iscrizioni e cancellazioni anagrafiche - Anno 1999." Rome: Instituto Natzionale di Statistica.

Jacobs, Dirk. 1998. "Discourse, Politics and Policy: The Dutch Parliamentary Debate about Voting Rights for Foreign Residents." *International Migration Review* 32, 3 (Summer): 350–73.

————. 2001. "Immigrants in a Multicultural Sphere: The Case of Brussels." *Multicultural Policies and Modes of Citizenship in European Cities*. Alisdair Rogers and Jean Tille, eds. Aldershot, UK: Ashgate. 107–22.

Jaggers, Keith, and Ted Robert Gurr. 1995. "Tracking Democracy's Third Wave with the Polity III Data." *Journal of Peace Research* 32, 4 (November): 469–82.

Japan. Statistics Bureau. 1996 and 1999. *Japan Statistical Yearbook* (microfiche). Tokyo: Management and Coordination Agency.

————. Statistics Bureau. Ministry of Public Management, Home Affairs, Posts and Telecommunications. 2003. "1995 Population Census." Statistics Bureau website: http://www.stat.go.jp/english/data/kokusei/index.htm.

————. Statistics Bureau. Ministry of Public Management, Home Affairs, Posts and Telecommunications. 2003. "2000 Population Census." Statistics Bureau website: http://www.stat.go.jp/english/data/kokusei/index.htm.

Joppke, Christian. 1999. *Immigration and the Nation-State: United States, Germany, and Great Britain*. Oxford, UK: Oxford University Press.

————. 2001. "The evolution of alien rights in the United States, Germany, and the European Union." *Citizenship Today: Global Perspectives and Practices*. T. Alexander Aleinikoff and Douglas Klusmeyer, eds. Washington, DC: Carnegie Endowment for International Peace. 36–62.

————. 2003. "Citizenship between De- and Re-Ethnicization." *European Journal of Sociology* 44, 3 (December): 429–58.

Jordan, Howard. April 7, 1993. "Empowering Immigrants." *Newsday* (City Edition). 52.

Kashiwazaki, Chikako. 2000. "Citizenship in Japan: Legal Practice and Contemporary Development." *From Migrants to Citizens: Membership in a Changing World*. T. Alexander Aleinikoff and Douglas Klusmeyer, eds. Washington, DC: Carnegie Endowment for International Peace. 434–71.

Katz, Richard S. 2000. "Noncitizens and the Right to Vote." *International Encyclopedia of Elections*. Richard Rose, ed. Washington: CQ Press.

Keith, Linda Camp. 1999. "The United Nations International Covenant on Civil and Political Rights: Does It Make a Difference in Human Rights Behavior?" *Journal of Peace Research* 36, 1 (January): 95–118.

King, Gary. 1998. *Unifying Political Methodology: The Likelihood Theory of Statistical Inference*. Ann Arbor: University of Michigan Press.

King, Gary, Robert O. Keohane, and Sidney Verba. 1994. *Designing Social Inquiry: Scientific Inference in Qualitative Research*. Princeton, NJ: Princeton University Press.

King, Gary, Michael Tomz, and Jason Wittenberg. 2000. "Making the Most of Statistical Analysis: Improving Interpretation and Results." *American Journal of Political Science* 44, 2: 341–55.

Klausen, Jytte. 1995. "Social Rights Advocacy and State Building: T. H. Marshall in the Hands of Social Reformers." *World Politics* 47, 2 (January): 244–67.

Klotz, Audie. 1995. "Norms Reconstituting Interests: Global Racial Equality and U.S. Sanctions Against South Africa." *International Organization* 49, 3: 451–78.

Kondo, Atsushi. 2001. "Comparative Citizenship and Aliens' Rights." *Citizenship in a Global World: Comparing Citizenship Rights for Aliens*. Atsushi Kondo, ed. New York: Palgrave. 225–48.

Koopmans, Ruud, and Paul Statham. 1999. "Challenging the Liberal Nation-State? Postnationalism, Multiculturalism, and the Collective Claims Making of Migrants and Ethnic Minorities in Britain and Germany." *American Journal of Sociology* 105, 3 (November): 652–96.

Laitin, David. 1998. *Identity in Formation: The Russian-Speaking Populations in the Near Abroad*. Ithaca, NY, and London: Cornell University Press.

Layton-Henry, Zig, ed. 1990. *Political Rights of Migrant Workers in Western Europe*. London: Sage Publications.

Layton-Henry, Zig. 1992. *The Politics of Immigration: Immigration, 'Race' and 'Race' Relations in Post-war Britain*. Oxford, UK: Blackwell.

Leeds, Brett Ashley, and David R. Davis. 1999. "Beneath the Surface: Regime Type and International Interaction, 1953–78." *Journal of Peace Research* 36, 1 (January): 5–21.

Lijphart, Arend. 1995. *Electoral Systems and Party Systems: A Study of Twenty-Seven Democracies, 1945–1990*. New York: Oxford University Press.

———. 1999. *Patterns of Democracy: Government Forms and Performance in Thirty-Six Countries*. New Haven: Yale University Press.

Lowery, David, and Virginia Gray. 1998. "The Dominance of Institutions in Interest Representation: A Test of Seven Explanations." *American Journal of Political Science* 42, 1 (January): 231–55.

Luck, James Murray. 1985. *A History of Switzerland: The First 100,000 Years: Before the Beginnings to the Days of the Present*. Palo Alto, CA: Society for the Promotion of Science and Scholarship.

Maoz, Zeev, and Bruce Russett. 1992. "Alliance, Contiguity, Wealth, and Political Stability: Is the Lack of Conflict Among Democracies A Statistical Artifact?" *International Interactions* 17: 624–38.

———. 1993. "Normative and Structural Causes of the Democratic Peace, 1946–1986." *American Political Science Review* 87, 3 (September): 624–38.

Marshall, Monty G., and Keith Jaggers. 2000. *Polity IV Project: Political Regime Characteristics and Transitions, 1800–1999*. Dataset Users Manual. College Park: University of Maryland.

Marshall, T. H. 1964. *Class, Citizenship and Social Development: Essays*. Introduction by Seymour Martin Lipset. Garden City, NY: Doubleday.

Martin, R. L., and J. E. Oeppen. 1975. "The Identification of Regional Forecasting Models Using Space: Time Correlation Functions." *Transactions of the Institute of British Geographers* 66 (November): 95–118.

Martiniello, Marco. 2000. "Citizenship in the European Union." *From Migrants to Citizens: Membership in a Changing World*. T. Alexander Aleinikoff and Douglas Klusmeyer, eds. Washington, DC: Carnegie Endowment for International Peace. 342–85.

McKelvey, Richard D., and William Zavoina. 1975. "A Statistical Model for the Analysis of Ordinal Level Dependent Variables." *Journal of Mathematical Sociology* 4: 103–20.

Meran, Christoph. May 23, 2003. Personal e-mail to author. "WG: Your Letter to the Austrian Embassy."

Migration Policy Institute. June 1, 2003. "Remittance Data." Migration Information Source. Migration Policy Institute world wide website: http://www.migrationinformation.org.

Miller, Mark J. 1982. "The Political Impact of Foreign Labor: A Re-evaluation of the Western European Experience." *International Migration Review* 16, 1 (Spring): 27–60.

Money, Jeannette. 1999. *Fences and Neighbors: The Political Geography of Immigration Control.* Ithaca, NY: Cornell University Press.

Nagy, Gabor. 1995. "Citizenship in Hungary, From a Legislative Viewpoint." *Citizenship East and West.* Andre Liebich and Daniel Warner with Jasna Dragovic, eds. London: Kegan Paul International.

Ndegwa, Stephen N. 1997. "Citizenship and Ethnicity: An Examination of Two Transitional Moments in Kenyan Politics." *American Political Science Review* 91, 3 (September): 599–616.

Netherlands. Central Bureau of Statistics. 1972, 1975, 1977, and 1980. *Statistical Yearbook of the Netherlands* (various years: microfiche). The Hague: Staatsuitgeverij.

———. Statistics Netherlands. 2003. "Statline." Statistics Netherlands website: http://statline.cbs.nl/ .

Neuman, Gerald L. 1992. "'We Are the People': Alien Suffrage in German and American Perspective." *Michigan Journal of International Law* 13, 2 (Winter): 259–335.

———. 2002. "Citizenship Today: Global Perspectives and Practices." *American Journal of International Law* 96, 2 (April): 514–17.

New Zealand. Department of Statistics. 1970, 1975, 1980, 1985, 1990, and 1999. *New Zealand Official Yearbook* (microfiche). Wellington: A. R. Shearer, Government Printer.

———. Statistics New Zealand. 2003. "2001 Census: People Born Overseas." 2001 Census. Statistics New Zealand website: http://www.stats.govt.nz/ census.htm.

Norris, Pippa. 1997. "Designing Democracies: Institutional Arrangements and System Support." Paper presented to the John F. Kennedy School of Government Workshop on Confidence in Democratic Institutions: America in a Comparative Perspective. Washington, DC. August 25–27.

Norway. Norges offisielle statistikk. 1970, 1982, 1990, 1992 and 2000. *Statistical Yearbook of Norway* (various years: microfiche). Oslo/Kongsvinger: Statistisk sentralbyrå.

———. Statistics Norway. 2003. "StatBank Norway." Statistics Norway website: http://www3.ssb.no/statistikkbanken/.

O'Loughlin, John et. al. 1998. "The Diffusion of Democracy, 1946–1994." *Annals of the Association of American Geographers* 88, 4 (December): 545–74.

O'Neil, Kevin. 2002. "Remittances from the United States in Context." Washington, DC: Migration Policy Institute. MPI website: http://www.migrationinformation.org.

Oneal, John R., and James Lee Ray. 1997. "New Tests of the Democratic Peace: Controlling for Economic Interdependence, 1950–85." *Political Research Quarterly* 50, 4 (December): 751–75.

Oneal, John R., Frances H. Oneal, Zeev Maoz, and Bruce Russett. 1996. "The Liberal Peace: Interdependence, Democracy, and International Conflict, 1950–85." *Journal of Peace Research* 33, 1 (February): 11–28.

Organisation for Economic Co-operation and Development. 2005. *National Accounts of OECD Countries: Detailed Tables.* Vol. IIa: 1992–2003. Paris: OECD.

Partell, Peter J. 1997. "Executive Constraints and Success in International Crises." *Political Research Quarterly* 50, 3 (September): 503–28.

Portugal. Instituto Nacional De Estatística. 1976, 1982, 1986, 1991, 1995, and 2000. *Anuário Estatístico de Portugal* (Statistical Yearbook of Portugal) (various years: microfiche). Lisbon: Instituto Nacional De Estatística.

Prak, Maarten. 1999. "Burghers into Citizens: Urban and National Citizenship in the Netherlands during the Revolutionary Era (c. 1800)." *Extending Citizenship, Reconfiguring States.* Michael Hanagan and Charles Tilly, eds. New York: Rowman and Littlefield. 17–35.

Preuss, Ulrich K. 2004. "Citizenship and the German Nation." *Lineages of European Citizenship: Rights, Belonging and Participation in Eleven Nation-States.* Richard Bellamy and Dario Castiglione, eds. New York: Palgrave Macmillan. 22–45.

Quinn, Dennis P., and John T. Woolley. 2001. "Democracy and Economic Performance: The Preference for Stability." *American Political Science Review* 45, 3 (July): 634–57.

Racusin, Philip D. 2006. "Looking at the Constitution Through Rose-Colored Glasses: The Supreme Court's Use of Transnational Law in Constitutional Adjudication." *Houston Journal of International Law* 28 (Spring): 913–58.

Ramirez, Manuel Becerra. 2000. "Nationality in Mexico." *From Migrants to Citizens: Membership in a Changing World.* T. Alexander Aleinikoff and Douglas Klusmeyer, eds. Washington, DC: Carnegie Endowment for International Peace. 312–41.

Raskin, Jamin B. 1993. "Legal Aliens, Local Citizens: The Historical, Constitutional and Theoretical Meanings of Alien Suffrage." *University of Pennsylvania Law Review* 141 (April): 1391–1470.

Rath, Jan. 1990. "Voting Rights." *The Political Rights of Migrant Workers in Western Europe.* Zig Layton-Henry, ed. London; Newbury Park, CA: Sage Publications. 127–57.

Ray, Brian K. 1999. "Plural Geographies in Canadian Cities: Interpreting Immigrant Residential Spaces in Toronto and Montreal." *Canadian Journal of Regional Science/Revue canadienne des sciences régionales* XXII: 1, 2 (Spring/Summer): 65–86.

Rittsteig, Helmut. 1994. "Dual Citizenship: Legal and Political Aspects in the German Context." *From Aliens to Citizens: Redefining the Status of Immigrants in Europe.* Rainer Bauböck, ed. Aldershot, UK. 111–32.

Rogers, W. H. 1993. "Regression standard errors in clustered samples." *Stata Technical Bulletin* 13: 19–23. Reprinted in Stata Technical Bulletin Reprints, vol. 3, 88–94.

Rokkan, Stein, and Seymour Martin Lipset. 1967. *Party Systems and Voter Alignments: Cross-National Perspectives.* New York: Free Press.

Rokkan, Stein. 1970. "Nation-building, cleavage formation and the structuring of mass politics." *Citizens, Elections, Parties. Approaches to the Comparative Study of the Processes of Development.* Stein Rokkan, A. Campbell, P. Torsvik, and H. Valen, eds. Oslo: Universitetsforlaget.

———. 1999. "The Four Thresholds of Democracy." *State Formation, Nation-Building and Mass Politics in Europe: The Theory of Stein Rokkan.* Peter Flora, Stein Kunle, and Derek Unwin, eds. Oxford: Oxford University Press.

Rousseau, Jean-Jacques. 1997. *The Social Contract and other later political writings.* Cambridge Texts in the History of Political Thought. Edited and translated by Victor Gourevitch. Cambridge, UK: Cambridge University Press.

Russett, Bruce. 1990. "Economic Decline, Electoral Pressure, and the Initiation of International Conflict." *The Prisoners of War*, ed. by Charles Gochman and Ned Allen Sabrosky. Lexington, MA: Lexington Books.

———. 1993. *Grasping the Democratic Peace.* Princeton, NJ: Princeton University Press.

Salzmann, Ariel. 1999. "Citizens in Search of a State: The Limits of Political Participation in the Late Ottoman Empire." In

Extending Citizenship, Reconfiguring States. Michael Hanagan and Charles Tilly, eds. New York: Rowman and Littlefield. 37–66.

Sassen, Saskia. 1996. *Losing Control? Sovereignty in an Age of Globalization*. 1995 Columbia University Leonard Hastings Schoff Memorial Lectures. New York: Columbia University Press.

Schmitter, Barbara E. 1980. "Immigrants and Associations: The Role in the Socio-Political Process of Immigrant Worker Integration in West Germany and Switzerland." *International Migration Review* 14, 2 (Summer): 179–92.

Schwartz, Amy E. 1990. "History and Memory in Berlin." *The Washington Post*, November 11, B–7.

Sciolino, Elaine. September 21, 2007. "Belgians, Adrift and Split, Sense a Nation Fading." *The New York Times*. A4.

Senese, Paul D. 1997. "Between Dispute and War: The Effect of Joint Democracy on Interstate Conflict Resolution." *Journal of Politics* 59, 1 (February): 1–27.

Shachar, Ayelet. 2000. "Citizenship and Membership in the Israeli Polity." *From Migrants to Citizens: Membership in a Changing World*. T. Alexander Aleinikoff and Douglas Klusmeyer, eds. Washington: Carnegie Endowment for International Peace. 386–433.

Shain, Yossi. 1994–1995. "Ethnic Diasporas and U.S. Foreign Policy." *Political Science Quarterly* 109, 5 (Winter): 811–41.

Shanahan, Suzanne. 1999. "Scripted Debates: Twentieth-Century Immigration and Citizenship Policy in Great Britain, Ireland, and the United States." *Extending Citizenship, Reconfiguring States*. Michael Hanagan and Charles Tilly, eds. New York: Rowman and Littlefield. 67–96.

Shaw, Jo. 2002. "Sovereignty at the Boundaries of the Polity." Paper submitted to the European Consortium for Political Research Joint Sessions of Workshops. Turin, Italy: March 22–27.

———. 2003. "Alien Suffrage in the European Union." *The Good Society* 12, 2: 29–32.

———. 2007a. "Political rights and multilevel citizenship in Europe." Paper prepared for the European Union Studies Association, Tenth Biennial International Conference. Montreal: May 17–19.

———. 2007b. *The Transformation of Citizenship in the European Union: Electoral Rights and the Restructuring of Political Space*. Cambridge, UK: Cambridge University Press.

Shin, Michael, and Michael D. Ward. 1999. "Lost in Space: Political Geography and the Defense-Growth Trade-Off." *Journal of Conflict Resolution* 43, 6 (December): 793–817.

Sikkink, Kathryn. 1993. "Human Rights, Principled Issue-Networks, and Sovereignty in Latin America." *International Organization* 47, 3 (Summer): 411–41.

Simmons, Beth A. 2002. "Why Commit? Explaining State Acceptance of International Human Rights Obligations." Lecture to the Colloquium on Law, Economics and Politics. New York University School of Law. 24 September.

Skaar, Elin. 2002. "Judicial independence: A key to justice. An analysis of Latin America in the 1990s (Argentina, Chile, Uruguay)." Unpublished dissertation. University of California, Los Angeles. 466 pages.

Slattery, Luke. 1999. "British Subjects May Hold Key to Australian Vote." *The Scotsman*, October 22, 15.

Smith, Michael Peter, and Luis Guarnizo. 1998. *Transnationalism from Below*. New Brunswick, NJ: Transaction Publishers.

Sontag, Deborah. 1992. "Noncitizens and the Right to Vote: Advocates for Immigrants Explore Opening Up Balloting." *New York Times*, July 31, B1.

Soros, George. 2004. "The People's Sovereignty." *Foreign Policy* (January/February): 66–67.

Soss, Joe, Sanford F. Schram, Thomas P. Vartarian, and Erin O'Brien. 2001. "Setting the Terms of Relief: Explaining State Policy Choices in the Devolution Revolution." *American Journal of Political Science* 45, 2 (April): 378–95.

Soysal, Yasemin Nuhoglu. 1994. *Limits of Citizenship: Migrants and Postnational Membership in Europe*. Chicago and London: University of Chicago Press.

———. 1997. "Changing Parameters of Citizenship and Claims-Making: Organized Islam in European Spaces." *Theory and Society* 26, 4: Special Issue on Recasting Citizenship (August): 509–27.

Spain. Instituto Nacional De Estadistica. 2003. "Efectivo de extranjeros residentes en España clasificados por ccaa de residencia Decenio 1992–2001." Instituto Nacional De Estadistica website: http://www.ine.es/inebase/indexi.html.

———. 1970, 1977, 1983 and 1998. *Anuario Estadístico de España* (various years: microfiche). Madrid: Presidencia del Gobierno.

Stolke, Verena. 1997. "The 'Nature' of Nationality." *Citizenship and Exclusion*. Veit Bader, ed. New York: St. Martin's Press. 61–80.

Stuurman, Siep. 2004. "Citizenship and Cultural Difference in France and the Netherlands." *Lineages of European Citizenship: Rights, Belonging and Participation in Eleven Nation-States.* Richard Bellamy and Dario Castiglione, eds. New York: Palgrave Macmillan. 167–85.

Sweden. Statistiska centralbyrån. 2003. "Statistical Database." Statistics Sweden: http://www.scb.se/databaser/makro/start. asp?lang=2.

———. Utgiven av Statistiska centralbyrån. 1970. *Statistisk Årsbok för Sverige 1970* (Statistical Abstract of Sweden 1970; microfiche). Stockholm: Utgiven av Statistiska centralbyrån.

Switzerland. Bundesamt für Statistik. 1979, 1982, 1991, 1992, and 2000. *Statistisches Jarbuch der Schweiz/Annuaire statistique de la Suisse* (Statistical Yearbook of Switzerland) (microfiche). Berne and Neuchâtel: Bundesamt für Statistik.

———. Swiss Federal Statistics Office. 2003. "Key Data." Swiss Federal Statistics Office website: http://www.statistik.admin.ch.

Taspinar, Omer. 2003. "Europe's Muslim Street: Muslims confront the United States, in the place where their votes count most." *Foreign Policy* (March/April): 76–77.

Teo, Tze Kwang. 2002. "Fixed Effects versus Between- and Within-Cluster Effects Logit When Data Structures are TSCS." Nashville: Vanderbilt University.

The Election Process Information Collection. The United Nations Development Programme, the International Foundation for Electoral Systems, and the International Institute for Democracy and Electoral Assistance. EPIC website: www.epicproject.org.

The National Election Studies and the Comparative Study of Electoral Systems, Center for Political Studies, University of Michigan. NES website: www.umich.edu/~nes. Ann Arbor: University of Michigan, Center for Political Studies [producer and distributor], 1995–1998.

Tomforde, Anna. 1990. "Court bars Bonn's aliens from voting." *The Guardian* (London), November 1.

Tomz, Michael, Jason Wittenberg, and Gary King. January 5, 2003. CLARIFY: Software for Interpreting and Presenting Statistical Results. Version 2.1. Stanford University, University of Wisconsin, and Harvard University. http://gking.harvard.edu/.

Tong-hyung, Kim. 2006. "Foreigners Cynical About Voting Rights." *Korea Times*, June 7.

Tugend, Tom, Marilyn Henry, Douglas Davis, and Uriel Heilman. 1997. "Letting Them Have Their Say." *The Jerusalem Post*, January 31, 10.

Union of International Associations. 1967 through 2005. *Yearbook of International Organizations*. 11th through 39th editions. Brussels: Union of International Associations.

United Kingdom. Office for National Statistics. 1970, 1975, 1980, 1985, 1990, 1995, and 2000. *Annual Abstract of Statistics* (various editions: microfiche). London: The Stationery Office.

United Nations. 2002. Department of Economic Affairs and Social Affairs. Population Division. *International Migration Report 2002*. New York: United Nations.

———. 2006. Department of Economic Affairs and Social Affairs. Population Division. *International Migration*. New York: United Nations.

———. 2007. Department of Economic Affairs and Social Affairs. Population Division. "Population, Resources, Environment and Development: The 2005 Revision." http://unstats.un.org/pop/dVariables/DRetrieval.aspx.

United States. Bureau of the Census. 1999. "Nativity of the Population, for Regions, Divisions, and States: 1850 to 1990." U.S. Bureau of the Census website: http://www.census.gov/population/www/documentation/twps 0029/tab13.html.

———. Central Intelligence Agency. Directorate of Intelligence. 2001 through 2004. "Chiefs of Staff and Cabinet Members of Foreign Governments." U.S. Central Intelligence Agency webpage: https://www.cia.gov/library/publications/world-leaders–1/index.html.

———. Library of Congress. 2004. The Library of Congress Country Studies. Library of Congress website: lcweb2.loc.gov/frd/csquery.html.

Universal Declaration of Human Rights. December 10, 1948. General Assembly Res. 217A (III), U.N. Doc A. 810.

Uruguay. Direccion General de Estadística Y Censos. 1991 and 2000. *Anuario Estadístico* (microfiche). Montevideo: Instituto Nacional de Estadístico.

Utter, Robert F., and David C. Lundsgaard. 1993. "Judicial Review in the New Nations of Central and Eastern Europe: Some Thoughts from a Comparative Perspective." *Ohio State Law Journal* 54 (Summer): 559–606.

Van Hear, Nicholas. 2002. "Refugee Diasporas, Remittances, Development, and Conflict." Washington, DC: Migration Policy Institute. MPI website: http://www.migrationinformation.org.

Vandyck, Tom. 2004. "In Europe, a voting-rights debate." *Christian Science Monitor*, February 3, 6.

Waldrauch, Harald. June 2–5, 2005. "Electoral Rights for Foreign Nationals: A Comparative Overview." Paper Presented to the ESF/LESC–SCSS Exploratory Workshop: Citizens, Non-citizens and Voting Rights in Europe. School of Law, Old College, University of Edinburgh, UK.

Walzer, Michael. 1983. *Spheres of Justice: A Defense of Pluralism and Equality*. New York: Basic Books.

Wang, Hongying, and James N. Rosenau. 2001. "Transparency International and Corruption as an Issue of Global Governance." *Global Governance* 7, 1 (January–March): 25–49.

Watts, Martin. 1998. "Occupational Gender Segregation: Index Measurement and Econometric Modeling." *Demography* 35, 4 (November): 489–96.

Weil, Patrick. 2001. "Access to Citizenship: A Comparison of Twenty-Five Nationality Laws." *Citizenship Today: Global Perspectives and Practices*. T. Alexander Aleinikoff and Douglas Klusmeyer, eds. Washington: Carnegie Endowment for International Peace. 17–35.

Weldon, Steven A. 2006. "The Institutional Context of Tolerance for Ethnic Minorities: A Comparative, Multilevel Analysis of Western Europe." *American Journal of Political Science* 50, 2 (April): 331–49.

White, H. 1980. "A heteroskedasticity-consistent covariance matrix estimator and a direct test for heteroskedasticity." *Econometrica* 48: 817–30.

White, Michael J. 1983. "The Measurement of Spatial Segregation." *American Journal of Sociology* 88, 5 (March): 1008–18.

Williams, R. L. 2000. "A note on robust variance estimation for cluster-correlated data." *Biometrics* 56: 645–46.

Woldendorp, Jaap, Hans Keman, and Ian Budge. 1998. "Party Government in 20 Democracies: An Update (1990–1995)." *European Journal of Political Research* 33, 1: 125–64.

Yoon, Mi Yung. 1997. "Explaining U.S. Intervention in Third World Internal Wars, 1945–1989." *Journal of Conflict Resolution* 41, 4 (August): 580–602.

Zolberg, Aristide. 1974. "The Making of Flemings and Walloons: Belgium: 1830–1914." *Journal of Interdisciplinary History* 5, 2 (Autumn): 179–235.

Index

International Studies—Rudra Sil and Eileen M. Doherty (eds.)

International Relations—Still an American Social Science? Toward Diversity in International Thought—Robert M. A. Crawford and Darryl S. L. Jarvis (eds.)

Which Lessons Matter? American Foreign Policy Decision Making in the Middle East, 1979—1987—Christopher Hemmer (ed.)

Hierarchy Amidst Anarchy: Transaction Costs and Institutional Choice—Katja Weber

Counter-Hegemony and Foreign Policy: The Dialectics of Marginalized and Global Forces in Jamaica—Randolph B. Persaud

Global Limits: Immanuel Kant, International Relations, and Critique of World Politics—Mark F. N. Franke

Money and Power in Europe: The Political Economy of European Monetary Cooperation—Matthias Kaelberer

Why Movements Matter: The West German Peace Movement and U. S. Arms Control Policy—Steve Breyman

Agency and Ethics: The Politics of Military Intervention—Anthony F. Lang, Jr.

Life After the Soviet Union: The Newly Independent Republics of the Transcaucasus and Central Asia—Nozar Alaolmolki

Information Technologies and Global Politics: The Changing Scope of Power and Governance—James N. Rosenau and J. P. Singh (eds.)

Theories of International Cooperation and the Primacy of Anarchy: Explaining U. S. International Monetary Policy-Making After Bretton Woods—Jennifer Sterling-Folker

Technology, Democracy, and Development: International Conflict and Cooperation in the Information Age—Juliann Emmons Allison (ed.)

Systems of Violence: The Political Economy of War and Peace in Colombia—Nazih Richani

The Arab-Israeli Conflict Transformed: Fifty Years of Interstate and Ethnic Crises—Hemda Ben-Yehuda and Shmuel Sandler

Debating the Global Financial Architecture—Leslie Elliot Armijo

Political Space: Frontiers of Change and Governance in a Globalizing World—Yale Ferguson and R. J. Barry Jones (eds.)

Crisis Theory and World Order: Heideggerian Reflections—Norman K. Swazo